ISSUES IN

DISPENSATIONALISM

ISSUES IN

DISPENSATIONALISM

Wesley R. Willis
John R. Master
General Editors

Charles C. Ryrie
Consulting Editor

MOODY PRESS

CHICAGO

CONTENTS

ABOUT THE EDITORS

John R. Master, Th.M., Th.D., is professor of Bible and chairs the biblical studies division at Philadelphia College of Bible.

Charles C. Ryrie, Th.M, Th.D., Ph.D., is professor of systematic theology emeritus, Dallas Theological Seminary, and serves as adjunct professor of systematic theology at Philadelphia College of Bible. He is well known as the author of the The Ryrie Study Bible.

Wesley R. Willis, Th.M., Ed.D., is vice president for academic affairs and academic dean at Philadelphia College of Bible.

ABOUT THE CONTRIBUTORS

Charles H. Dyer, Th.M., Th.D, is professor of Bible exposition at Dallas Theological Seminary.

Thomas R. Edgar, Th.M., Th.D., is professor of New Testament literature and exegesis at Capital Bible Seminary.

Paul D. Feinberg, M.A., Th.D., serves as professor of biblical and systematic theology at Trinity Evangelical Divinity School.

Arnold G. Fruchtenbaum, Th.M., Ph.D., is director of Ariel Ministries.

Zane C. Hodges, Th.M., is copastor of Victor Street Bible Church, Dallas, Texas, as well as partner and editorial director at Redencion Viva Publishers in Dallas.

Thomas D. Ice, Th.M., is executive director of the Pre-trib Research Center, Washington, D.C.

Elliott E. Johnson, Th.M., Th.D., is professor of Bible exposition and acting chairman of the department of Bible exposition at Dallas Theological Seminary.

J. Randall Price, Th.M., Ph.D., is scholar-in-residence at Grace Bible Church, San Marcos, Texas, and president of World of the Bible Ministries.

Earl D. Radmacher, M.A., Th.D., serves as chancellor at Western Conservative Baptist Seminary.

John F. Walvoord, M.A., Th.D., is chancellor, minister-at-large, and professor of systematic theology emeritus, Dallas Theological Seminary.

AN INTRODUCTORY WORD

It was reported to me recently that someone said that dispensationalism is dying and there will be no dispensationalists left to attend the funeral.

Is it? Or is it already dead? Or alive and well?

Is it changing? Or being reincarnated in a different form?

Should we even care what is happening to dispensationalism?

In the past three years two books on this topic have been published by university presses. Christian publishers have issued three books (not counting this one) addressing the subject of dispensationalism. A corpse would not merit such attention, would it?

Why this book? It is not a primer on dispensationalism. Nor does it promote the kind of changes that some who call themselves dispensationalists are making today. It is not presented in the format of a debate. Rather it addresses a variety of topics that are particularly relevant in today's theological climate.

Not all of the contributors are from a past generation of dispensationalists. Some names are well known, others the reader may not readily recognize. But all are committed to normative dispensational teachings. Some chapters may interest certain readers more than others, but all make significant contributions to the subject.

Dispensationalism dying? Hardly—read on.

CHARLES C. RYRIE, Th.D., Ph.D.
Consulting Editor

PREFACE

At one time those who described themselves as "dispensationalists" generally agreed upon the meaning of the term *dispensationalism.* However, today there seem to be wide differences of opinion concerning key features of the system. Descriptions such as "revised dispensationalism," "essentialist dispensationalism," and "progressive dispensationalism" have been employed in an attempt to clarify and to distinguish nuances of dispensationalism. But many feel that these attempts actually have made the system more difficult to understand.

Our purpose in compiling this book is to provide a forum for those who view themselves as traditional dispensationalists. These persons embrace a system of interpretation that is generally compatible with the system affirmed by Charles C. Ryrie in *Dispensationalism Today* (Moody, 1965). The chapters in this book are not intended to be "benchmarks" or any sort of "litmus test" to judge the correctness of a given dispensational system. Rather, the ideas are presented to stimulate positive interaction and discussion within current dispensational dialogue.

The contributors to this volume are widely diverse in their ministries and represent a variety of constituencies. Some of the patriarchs of dispensationalism, as well as younger, less published individuals have been invited to participate so that we could include as much breadth and diversity as possible. Some of the contributors have approached their topics with a strong research orientation. Others have taken more of an exegetical approach, while some have addressed their topics theologically. As one can recognize by scanning the table of contents, individual chapters address a wide variety of subjects that are important to dispensationalism. Many of these are particularly relevant to the issues currently being discussed by dispensationalists.

Philadelphia College of Bible (PCB) is pleased to be able to provide the forum in which these issues can be considered. The consulting editor, Charles Ryrie, is a past president of PCB and currently is visiting professor of theology at PCB. John Master chairs its biblical education division and is professor of Bible. Wesley Willis is vice president for academic affairs and academic dean of PCB.

Philadelphia College of Bible is a regionally accredited college conferring an undergraduate degree in Bible upon all graduates, offering various church ministry programs. Students also may earn, in addition to their B.S. in Bible, degrees certified by national agencies for a variety of programs in education, music, music education, and social work. The college also has extension campuses in New Jersey and Wisconsin. Philadelphia College of Bible Graduate School offers a variety of accredited masters degrees. Currently, well over one thousand students are enrolled in PCB degree programs.

The editors are responsible for the choice of topics and for deciding whom to invite to contribute to the book. Individual authors are responsible only for the ideas included in their own chapters. They may or may not agree with ideas that are presented by other individuals in their chapters. We would like to thank all of the contributors who faithfully met their deadlines and cooperated graciously throughout the various stages of editing and proofing. We feel that they have offered informative presentations in a stimulating and comprehensible manner. The editors have worked diligently to assist in the flow and linguistic accuracy of the chapters. We have tried to insure that this important information is delivered with clarity and simplicity. We especially thank Elaine Willis who worked countless hours in reviewing, analyzing, questioning, editing, formatting, and enhancing the readability of these chapters. We all trust that you will find that this book makes a significant contribution to your understanding and application of the Word of God.

JOHN R. MASTER, Th.D., and
WESLEY R. WILLIS, Ed.D.
General Editors

ABBREVIATIONS

AUSS *Andrews University Seminary Studies*

CBQMS Catholic Biblical Quarterly—Monograph Series

EDNT *Exegetical Dictionary of the New Testament*

JETS *Journal of the Evangelical Theological Society*

LXX Septuagint (Greek translation of the Old Testament)

NICNT New International Commentary of the New Testament

NICOT New International Commentary of the Old Testament

TDNT *Theological Dictionary of the New Testament*

R ecent discussions in dispensationalism raise the
question, Is dispensationalism developing, or is it
changing? In order to answer this question, we must
compare the views of current dispensationalists with
those of the past. Only then is it possible to evaluate
whether current emphases are developments or
changes. We need to consider current views on the
essentials of dispensationalism, the Davidic covenant, distinctions between Israel and the church, and
the hermeneutics of new dispensationalists. If indeed
these represent changes, then we need to consider
what may be the ramifications for the future of dispensationalism and eschatology.

———————

1

UPDATE ON
DISPENSATIONALISM

Charles C. Ryrie

Consider the dictionary definition of two words.

The first is the word *develop,* which means "to set forth or make clear by degrees or in detail: expound."

The second is the word *change,* which "implies making either an essential difference often amounting to a loss of original identity or a substitution of one thing for another."

Hopefully, theology will *develop* in that sense of being made clearer. But theology may *change* either for the better or for the worse. If the substitution is more biblical, such change is desirable. If not, then it is not.

It goes without saying that any legitimate development (i.e., heightened clarity of exposition) and any legitimate change (i.e., substitution) should be based on careful exegesis and theological study. Still, exegesis and theology do not resolve all the interpretive questions in the Bible. But they certainly must be used in the attempt to do so. If on the basis of careful and earnest study an Arminian becomes a Calvinist, or vice versa, that is surely a change, not a development. If either the Calvinist or Arminian, studying and reflecting on Hebrews 6, for instance, comes to a clearer explanation of the passage that is compatible with his theological system, that is development.

Sometimes, however, the difference between development and change is not so readily apparent as with the Calvinism/Arminianism example. To make the difference clearer one must ask, "What are the

15

essentials of the matter under consideration?" For example, "Is the doctrine of limited redemption an essential to the Calvinistic system?" If so, when one moves from limited to unlimited redemption (i.e., from a so-called five-point to a four-point position), to a five-point Calvinist who considers that teaching to be an essential to the system, such a move is a change. An essential has been abandoned or denied, making the four-point Calvinist not a true or pure Calvinist. If a five-point Calvinist finds a clearer explanation for, say, 2 Peter 2:1 than he formerly had, that is a development enabling him more clearly to expound a verse that might be considered troublesome to his system.

Or take another example: "What is essential to premillennialism? Is a particular view on the time of the Rapture an essential?" If not, when one moves from a pretribulational rapture view to a posttribulational one, he has not "changed" premillennialism. He has only embraced a "development" in that system of eschatology. But if one believes that pretribulationism is an essential of consistent premillennialism, then to move to mid-, or partial-, or posttribulationism is a change, not a development. Though opinions may differ on what are the essentials (in whatever is under discussion), to set forth essentials is imperative; otherwise we would have no criteria by which to measure the difference between development and change.

To sum up: (1) development and change are not synonymous but have different meanings; and (2) in order to decide whether something is developing or changing one must consider what the essentials of the matter are.

This is the question: Is dispensationalism developing or changing? Today we are being told that dispensationalism is developing—that it is being given a clearer explanation—and that this development should be expected and welcomed since dispensationalism has always been developing since its original articulation. Has there been development in dispensationalism in the last 150 years? Certainly. The theological perspective has been more clearly articulated by a number of dispensationalists during that span of time. Has it changed? Or is it developing *and* changing? Those are different and important questions that bring into play the matter of essentials.

A LOOK AT THE PAST

Darby and Early Dispensationalism

Dispensationalism was first promoted through the study and teachings of John Nelson Darby (1800–1882). Whereas he had differences with his contemporaries, and although he did not fully develop all aspects of dispensational teachings, certain teachings were paramount and were expressed clearly.

One important element was an insistence on literal interpretation as opposed to a historicist one. This literal hermeneutic was deemed especially important to the correct understanding of Revelation, Daniel, and other Old Testament prophecies. In fact, it was this literal principle of interpretation of Isaiah 32 that convinced Darby of a change in dispensations and the setting up of a new one involving the reign of Christ.[1] To be sure, Darby and other Brethren saw Christ in the Psalms and the church in the Song of Songs (which some call allegorizing or spiritualizing). But he did not do this to the exclusion of the grammatical-historical meaning of such passages. It is one thing to give a passage only an illustrative or "spiritualized" interpretation, thus eliminating the literal, plain, and grammatical-historical meaning. It is quite a different thing to recognize the literal meaning and then, without eliminating or changing it, see illustrations of other truths in the passage. The hermeneutic of early dispensationalism was literalistic.

Darby's view of the church included several features. One was his view that the established church was in ruins and apostasy. Though he served for some years in Ireland as a minister of the Church of England, he eventually resigned his curacy. The straw that broke the camel's back was a decree from the Archbishop that included the inherent demand that all members swear allegiance to the king as head of the church. This, Darby felt, prevented a believer from discharging his individual responsibility before God. When in Dublin, even before his resignation, he fellowshiped with a group whose meetings were based on scriptural principles, exhibited a spiritual worship, and embraced saints of all communions.

As Darby's doctrine developed, the dichotomy between Israel and the church became paramount. He wrote of the unity of believers in the body of Christ who are joined to the Head by the Holy Spirit. He saw the messianic kingdom postponed during the time of the church, and he placed the rapture of the church before the seventieth week of Daniel's great prophecy.[2] No wonder Bass concludes, "Even a casual reading of Darby's prophetic interpretations reveals how deeply contemporary dispensationalism is rooted in them. This is not to say that they are identical in all details, or that there has been no further development since Darby's time. But the basic elements, and the hermeneutical pattern, of Darby's eschatology persist unchanged in contemporary dispensationalism."[3] Development, yes; change, no (this from a scholar who is not a dispensationalist).

Dispensationalism in America

1. The early Bible conferences. Early Bible conferences in this country included, but did not always emphasize, dispensational teaching. "The Believers' Meeting for Bible Study" began in Massachusetts in 1876 and continued in various places until 1900. From 1883 to 1897 conferences were held at Niagara-on-the-Lake in Ontario. The teaching opposed postmillennialism, annihilationism, and perfectionism. It promoted premillennialism, unity of the Body of Christ, and Bible study through Bible "readings." During this period two important prophecy conferences were also held—the first in New York City in 1878 and the second in Chicago in 1886.

What were the themes of these meetings? The Bible readings were based on what some speakers themselves described as a grammatical-historical method of interpretation. Though to promote dispensationalism was not the reason for calling these conferences (opposing postmillennialism and modernism was), eventually dispensational teaching emerged. An "any-moment" coming was linked to premillennialism. Distinctions between the dispensations of the church and the coming kingdom, between the church and Israel, between a new covenant for the church and one for Israel in the kingdom were made by the speakers. In the 1878 prophetic conference a speaker from England gave an entire address that was "explicitly dispensational," and in the 1886 conference another dispensational message was heard, including a dispensational scheme, emphasis on the literalness of the characteristics of the Millennium, the withdrawal by Jesus of the kingdom in the latter part of His earthly ministry, and the pretribulational rapture of the church.[4]

It is important to remember that these early conferences were called to oppose postmillennialism and to promote premillennialism. Today new dispensationalists seem to be holding up these conferences as an example of ecumenicity in order to justify their interest in finding a rapprochement between dispensationalism and covenant theology. The early conferences in America sought no rapprochement between themselves and postmillennialists (and annihilationists and perfectionists).

2. C. I. Scofield (1843–1921) and Lewis Sperry Chafer (1871–1952). A brief word about Scofield will suffice, and it centers on the Scofield Reference Bible (1909). Undoubtedly this work popularized dispensationalism as much as any other single entity. Literal interpretation and the distinction between Israel and the church (and other distinctions) are preeminent in its notes. He saw the church as related to a heavenly destiny, whereas Israel related to an earthly one. The first edition (1909) lists twelve distinguishing features of the Bible, the tenth of which is "the dispensations are distinguished." The second edition (1917) points to a new section entitled "A Panoramic View of the Bible," which was added to "show the unity of the Book" and which detailed seven marks of this unity. Only eternity will reveal how many were introduced to serious Bible study through this work.

The distinction between Israel and the church was certainly prominent in the theology of the notes of the Bible. The first chapter of C. I. Scofield's booklet *Rightly Dividing the Word of Truth* is entitled "The Jew, the Gentile, and the Church of God" in which some of the distinctions between Israel and the church are placed in side-by-side columns.[5] The principle of literal interpretation, though not spelled out formally, is evident in the notes.

Dallas Theological Seminary was founded in 1924, not primarily to promote dispensational premillennialism, but to train expositors of the Word. Of course, the theology was dispensational and premillennial as witnessed by the systematic theology of its founder, Lewis Sperry Chafer, and by the doctrinal statement of the Seminary. Scofield popularized; Chafer systematized. Both maintained the essentials of grammatical-historical interpretation, which produced a clear, detailed outline of future events and the distinction between Israel and the church.

Chafer's contributions were significant. He insisted that a systematic theology be unabridged, and his was. As a result, it dealt with all areas of theology in a balanced and complete way. Chafer was committed to a premillennial interpretation of the Bible. In evaluating Chafer's contribution, his successor, John F. Walvoord wrote that the doctrine of a future Millennium

> naturally stems from interpreting prophecy in the literal or normal sense. A corollary to premillennialism is the doctrine of dispensationalism. . . . The distinction between God's future program for Israel and His present program for the church is one of the essential ingredients in premillennialism. Consistent premillennialism also involves the belief that the rapture of the church is imminent, that it will occur before the tribulation. . . . The pretribulational rapture was usually accepted by those who interpreted the Scriptures literally and distinguished God's program for Israel from His program for the church.[6]

The baptizing ministry of the Holy Spirit uniting believers in the Body of Christ, an activity of the Spirit distinct to this dispensation, constitutes a major support for this distinction.

Though insisting on the distinction between Israel and the church, it is interesting to note that in his theology Chafer listed twenty-four contrasts between Israel and the church and thirteen similarities.[7] Furthermore, the doctrinal statement of Dallas Theological Seminary states that the church "is completely distinct from Israel" (Article XIII).

To sum up, in both Scofield and Chafer the essentials of plain interpretation, which leads to the premillennial picture of the future, and the teaching that the church "is completely distinct from Israel" can be seen through their writings.

3. Dispensationalism Today. In 1965 my book by this title was published. Its expressed purpose was to correct misconceptions and give a positive presentation concerning dispensationalism. Its unexpressed (until now) purpose was to defend the theological integrity of some of the stalwarts of dispensationalism, past and at that time, from misrepresentation and frivolous attacks. Some of those stalwarts were named in the bibliography and were divided into dispensationalists of former days and more recent ones, not to indicate anything more than a chronological distinction. Even if one disagrees with almost everything in the book, it is important to read the concluding chapter.

Among other things the book offers a concise definition of dispensationalism. It included three elements: (1) a clear distinction between Israel and the church; (2) consistent use of literal interpretation;[8] and (3) the underlying purpose of God being to show His own glory. More of this *sine qua non* later.

If *development* means to express something more clearly, this book attempted to do that. But it did not substitute any changes in the essentials of dispensationalism as taught previously.

A LOOK AT THE PRESENT

On the theological scene there has appeared today an aberration from what has been considered normative dispensational teaching. The label its proponents have given to it is "progressive dispensationalism."[9] The adjective "progressive" refers to a central tenet that the Abrahamic, Davidic, and new covenants are being progressively fulfilled today (as well as having fulfillments in the millennial kingdom). Since the word "progressive" may inevitably cast aspersions on previously taught dispensationalism, a better label may well be in order (such as "revised," "reconstructed," "new," or "kingdom" dispensationalism). The ideas are promoted as modifications and development within dispensationalism (although one promotional piece released by Zondervan uses the word *change*).

The Tenets of Progressive Dispensationalism

1. A strenuous rejection of the (and perhaps any) sine qua non. In "The Search for Definition" (also the subtitle of the book *Dispensationalism, Israel and the Church*), the authors not only fail in "the search" but also realize that in order to search they must knock down any *sine qua non.* The reason is simple: a *sine qua non,* whether it refers to the structural components or theological essence of dispensationalism, is too restrictive to allow for the kind of restructuring that progressive dispensationalism promotes. A *sine qua non* emphasizes "essentials" that if changed might indicate an abandonment of what has been previously known as dispensationalism.

In the new dispensationalism (1) the "clear distinction" between Israel and the church is replaced by "a distinction"; (2) the literal hermeneutic is replaced by something called a "complementary" hermeneutic; and (3) the overall doxological purpose is replaced by Christocentricity. We will discuss the implications of only the first two in this chapter.

2. The covenant with David. Until now the Davidic covenant was understood by dispensationalists as related only to Israel, with its ultimate fulfillment in the reign of Christ on David's throne in the Millennium. Progressive dispensationalism, however, teaches that the Lord Jesus is now reigning as David's king in heaven at the right hand of the Father in an "already" fulfillment aspect of the Davidic kingdom and that He will also reign on earth in the Millennium in the "not yet" aspect.[10] They also assert that at Christ's ascension He was inaugurated as Davidic king, that the right hand of the Father is the throne of David in heaven, and that the present church age is indistinct from the kingdom.

Kingdom, like the meaning of progressive dispensationalism, is not defined. There are various uses of *kingdom* in the Bible, and the failure to define these uses is a major deficiency in this new dispensationalism (see chapter 4). Furthermore, the already/not yet concept of realized eschatology appears to be quite similar to that taught by George E. Ladd, who was considered a covenant premillennialist. The progressives attempt to distance themselves from Ladd since they wish to be considered as still within the dispensationalist camp. Kenneth Barker in his chapter in Blaising and Bock's book[11] affirms more than once his agreement with Ladd, and Bruce Waltke in his response to the book calls its teaching realized eschatology.[12] Even Bock in a question-and-answer session at one of the Dispensational Study Group meetings acknowledged that Ladd "would not disagree with" the fundamental thrust of the structure of progressive dispensationalism.[13] This does not prove that either Ladd or the new dispensationalists are wrong; but it indicates that more than development has occurred.

3. The Israel/church distinction. We have seen that in the history of dispensational teaching the consistent distinction between Israel and the church has been an essential from the beginning. Now it is being blurred. To be sure, the new dispensationalism does not (yet) teach that the church is spiritual Israel today or that Israel has replaced the church, although David Turner calls "the 'new Israel,' the church."[14] Of course, there are similarities between Israel and the church (as Chafer, among others, recognized), but in the new dispensationalism the church is reduced to the present phase of the Davidic kingdom. New dispensationalists do not like the concept of the church as a parenthesis, failing to recognize that when older dispensationalists used that word they meant that the church was a parenthesis in God's program with Israel. But how do the progressives describe the church? It is no longer a mystery unrevealed in the Old Testament, for *mystery,* according to Robert Saucy, means something unrealized rather than unrevealed. Saucy also quotes with approval Karl Barth's description of the church as "a functional outpost of God's kingdom."[15] Bock calls the church a "sneak preview" of the kingdom.[16] Significantly, no discussion appears of the mystery (unrevealed) character of the church in Colossians 1:26 or of the baptizing ministry of the Holy Spirit as making the church, the Body of Christ, very distinct from Israel and unique to this dispensation. First Corinthians 12:13 has four entries in the Scripture index with no real discussion. Daniel 9:24–27 has only three entries and no real discussion, a significant omission especially if there is a gap (could that be called a parenthesis?) between the sixty-ninth and seventieth weeks of that prophecy (as premillennialists hold).

In reality Christ was identified as the Davidic king before His birth (Luke 1:31–33), but He will not be inaugurated as Davidic king until He returns. Logically, progressives ought to say that He was inaugurated not at His ascension but at His birth, rather than saying that the Gospels and Acts "are not clear" on this point.[17] But these points are clear: the Davidic kingdom for Israel was genuinely offered by our Lord at His first coming; that offer and His credentials were authenticated by signs and wonders; that offer was refused; the announcement of the church, not the inauguration of the kingdom, was made (Matt. 16:18); and Peter's references on the Day of Pentecost to our Lord's fulfilling Davidic promises were to prove that Jesus of Nazareth is both Lord (God) and Christ (Messiah), *not,* as some new dispensationalists teach, that He began His reign on David's throne (i.e., "the Father's right hand") in heaven (Acts 2:36). Exegetical evidence that the above statements are not so, but rather that Christ is now a "reigning Davidite sitting on David's throne,"[18] seems rather uncertain and unconvincing when Bock has to acknowledge that key texts only "allude" or are "not clear" or are a "pictorial description" (at least eight times in one chapter).[19]

Also one might ask, Why, if the Davidic kingdom has already been inaugurated, do we not see signs now (though Pentecostal dispensationalists do acknowledge them today)? Another question is, Why does the Davidic covenant as recorded in 2 Samuel 7 not include the ministry of the Spirit and salvation provisions?

A summary question: Are these teachings merely development or are they changes that involve major substitutions?

4. Hermeneutics and new dispensationalism. New dispensationalism insists that literal interpretation is not an essential element of dispensationalism. While not denying the grammatical-historical hermeneutic, this teaching introduces "complementary hermeneutics." This means that "the New Testament does introduce change [note that word] and advance; it does not merely repeat Old Testament revelation. In making complementary additions, however, it does not jettison old promises. The enhancement is not at the expense of the original promise."[20] The last two sentences keep progressive dispensationalists from becoming amillennialists (who do jettison OT promises), while the first sentence gives them hermeneutical basis for their already/not yet view of the kingdom. And if that view was held by nondispensational European theologians and non-dispensational American theologian George Ladd before progressive dispensationalism came on the theological scene, then is progressive dispensationalism really dispensational? Why not call it realized eschatology or covenant premillennialism?

PONDERING THE FUTURE

Obviously no one can predict what will develop or change in dispensationalism in the future, but one can ponder what these new teachings may lead to.

Acceptance and rapprochement

Newer dispensationalists seem to want to get the attention of covenant theologians and other scholars within the broadest scope of dispensationalism but not rank-and-file dispensationalists. They state that they wish to reach out to the whole Body of Christ, though in practice, so far at least, that reach has been primarily directed to covenant theologians. In turn, covenant theologians are taking note of this attempted rapprochement.

But basic differences remain. Can the reformed covenant of grace ever be satisfactorily assimilated into any dispensational system? Can the Millennium ever be deliteralized enough or placed far enough in the background to make the premillennial system tolerable to amillennialists (which almost all covenant people are)? Can the discontinuities in dispensationalism be overshadowed by the continuities enough to bring acceptability, or will the discontinuities (i.e., distinctives) fade into near oblivion? Will the discussion about hermeneutics ever arrive at the place where all can agree on a hermeneutic that can and will be consistently applied to Scripture and not be adjusted by the conclusions interpreters want to get from the Scriptures? Will God's special program for Israel be lost in the movement toward seeing only one people of God? Will the teaching of some (not all, by any means) amillennialists that Israel's yet unfulfilled promises will be fulfilled on the new earth be accepted by dispensationalists and nondispensationalists? If so, will there be the river of Egypt and the river Euphrates on the new earth, or will hermeneutics allow for reinterpreting that particular promise? If so, why will there be a need for the premillennialist's present-earth Millennium?

If rapprochement refers to a "state of having cordial relations," then I, for one (and there are many others) have always had such a relationship with believers I have known who have held to differing theological viewpoints (including covenant amillennialists, errantists, Pentecostals, Roman Catholics, Arminians, and Lordship salvationists). But if rapprochement means "conformity" or "accord" applied to theology, then there simply will not be rapprochement between various theological viewpoints as long as we are here on earth.

As for the present effort toward rapprochement between covenant theologians and modified dispensationalists, it seems that most of the "give" is from dispensationalists and not from covenant people. One covenant writer (though acknowledging that he does not speak for all) has concluded that "provided we are able to treat the question of Israel's relative distinctiveness in the Millennium as a minor problem [!], no substantial areas of disagreement remain."[21]

The Distinctiveness of the Church

It already has been observed that the church is less distinct in the new dispensationalism. The mystery character of the Body of Christ is being redefined. The important ramifications of the baptizing ministry of the Holy Spirit in relation to the Body of Christ in this dispensation are not prominent. The relation of the gap between the sixty-ninth and seventieth weeks of Daniel 9:24–27 to the distinctiveness of the church in the program of God is receiving little attention. Someone has suggested that in progressive dispensationalism the church is being neutered.

Eschatological Fallout

Less distinctiveness for the Body of Christ may lead to some changes in traditional dispensational premillennial eschatology.

1. The Rapture. One can well ponder what will happen to the pretribulational Rapture teaching in years to come. In *Dispensationalism, Israel and the Church* there is no discussion of the Rapture question. At one of the Dispensational Study Group meetings one dispensationalist wondered "if we will find more posttribulationalists as the Dispensational Study Group moves on." He himself had not moved to that position but was apparently concerned about this fallout from the teachings of progressive dispensationalism. Let us hope he is not a true prophet.

In 1952 former dispensationalist George E. Ladd published *Crucial Questions About the Kingdom of God,* which taught the already/not yet concept of the kingdom. In 1956 he published *The Blessed Hope,* in which he attacked pretribulationalism while still affirming his belief in the personal return of Christ to set up the millennial kingdom. In 1972 in his commentary on Revelation he taught that Revelation 20 was "a prophecy of the destiny of the church" and distanced himself from the view that sees the millennial kingdom primarily in terms of God's theocratic promises to Israel. He also doubted that the 1,000 years in Revelation 20 should be interpreted "with strict literalness."[22] Of course, one case does not a movement make, but this one case did happen (as have others).

2. The Millennium. Covenant premillennialists certainly have not abandoned the doctrine of a present-earth millennial kingdom, and one would not necessarily expect that progressive dispensationalism will lead to that. It is not inconceivable, however, that the Millennium and the eternal state could become so blurred or merged that the Millennium disappears and amillennialism takes over. Amillennialists do teach the already/not yet view of the kingdom in which the "not yet" aspect is the eternal state.[23] And there are those, of course, who have moved completely from dispensationalism to amillennialism.

But one may rightly ponder whether or not the "Jewishness" of the Millennium will be deemphasized. For example, when asked about differences in progressive dispensationalism, Bock reportedly said that it was "less land centered" and less "future centered."[24] Nevertheless, he does affirm the offering of Jewish sacrifices during the Millennium. In *Dispensationalism, Israel and the Church,* Carl Hoch says that ethnic Israel's privileges "were restricted to Israel before the death of Christ and the creation of the church,"[25] and Robert Saucy says that the inheritance that belongs to those who are believers in Christ may be viewed as "all the blessing pledged to Abraham and his descendants."[26] Logically, where does this leave the need for a Millennium (though Saucy clearly affirms his belief in the future Millennium)? All this does make one wonder and ponder.

A CONCLUDING WORD

Essentials such as consistent literal interpretation and a clear distinction between Israel and the church have been taught throughout the history of dispensationalism. The basic question remains: Is current dispensational teaching a development or have substitutions been made that must be regarded as change in the system? And whether one answers "development" or "change," it is imperative to examine carefully what is being said in order to judge how major or minor these developments or changes are. But above all, one must always and continually test developments and changes in the light of God's inerrant Word.

NOTES

1. For detailed quotes, see R. A. Huebner, *Precious Truths Revived and Defended Through J. N. Darby* (Morganville, N.J.: Present Truth, 1991), 1:17, 23, 25, 166. See also Ernest R. Sandeen, *The Roots of Fundamentalism* (Chicago: Univ. of Chicago Press, 1970), 107–12.

2. See Huebner, *Precious Truths,* 1:17, 19, 67, 79, 85; Sandeen, *The Roots of Fundamentalism,* 38; and Clarence B. Bass, *Backgrounds to Dispensationalism* (Grand Rapids: Eerdmans, 1960), 128–32.

3. Bass, *Backgrounds to Dispensationalism,* 128.

4. C. Norman Kraus, *Dispensationalism in America* (Richmond: John Knox, 1958), 71–100, esp. pp. 83, 85.

5. C. I. Scofield, *Rightly Dividing the Word of Truth* (Wilmington, Del.: Pettingill, 1935), 6–8.

6. John F. Walvoord, *A Torch of Great Significance* (Dallas: Dallas Theological Seminary, 1984), 5–6.

7. Lewis Sperry Chafer, *Systematic Theology* (Dallas: Dallas Seminary Press, 1948), IV:47–53.

8. Though "literal" is the word used in *Dispensationalism Today* (Chicago: Moody, 1965), I equate that with a grammatical-historical hermeneutic, a term I used (along with the phrase "historically conditioned") in *Biblical Theology of the New Testament* (Chicago: Moody, 1959), which was published six years earlier.

9. Craig A. Blaising and Darrell L. Bock, eds., *Dispensationalism, Israel and the Church: The Search for Definition* (Grand Rapids: Zondervan, 1992). Prior to the publication of this book, Robert Saucy wrote a number of essays along these same lines. Also beginning in 1986 public meetings of the Dispensational Study Group (where many of these issues have been discussed) were held in connection with the annual meetings of the Evangelical Theological Society.

10. Ibid., 381, 46.

11. Kenneth L. Barker, "The Scope and Center of Old and New Testament Theology and Hope," in *Dispensationalism,* Blaising and Bock, eds., 293–328.

12. Bruce K. Waltke, "A Response," in ibid., 347–59.

13. Darrell L. Bock, Taped proceedings of the question-and-answer session following Bock's presentation at the Evangelical Theological Society annual meeting, Kansas City, 1991.

14. David L. Turner, "The New Jerusalem in Revelation 21:1–22:5: Consummation of a Biblical Continuum," in *Dispensationalism,* Blaising and Bock, eds., 288.

15. Robert L. Saucy, "The Church as the Mystery of God," in ibid., 155.

16. Darrell L. Bock, "The Reign of the Lord Christ," in ibid., 53 (cf. p. 382).

17. Ibid., 55.

18. Ibid., 49.

19. Ibid., 37–67.

20. Craig A. Blaising and Darrell L. Bock, "Dispensationalism, Israel and the Church: Assessment and Dialogue," in *Dispensationalism,* Blaising and Bock, eds., 392–93.

21. Vern S. Poythress, *Understanding Dispensationalists* (Grand Rapids: Zondervan, 1987), 51.

22. George Eldon Ladd, *A Commentary on the Revelation of John* (Grand Rapids: Eerdmans, 1972), 261–62.

23. R. C. Sproul, "The Object of Contemporary Relevance," in *Power Religion: The Selling Out of the Evangelical Church?* Michael Scott Horton, ed. (Chicago: Moody, 1992), 317.

24. *Christianity Today,* 9 March 1992, 50.

25. Carl B. Hoch, Jr., "The New Man of Ephesians 2," in *Dispensationalism,* Blaising and Bock, eds., 125.

26. Robert L. Saucy, "The Church as the Mystery of God," in ibid., 134.

M uch of the discussion among dispensationalists focuses on hermeneutics, especially on the nature of literal interpretation. The generally accepted dispensational definition of literal interpretation, employed as a literary principle, differs from how it often is characterized by nondispensationalists. Some current writers from within the dispensational tradition have suggested replacing "literal interpretation" with a so-called "complementary hermeneutic," which seems to combine spiritualizing and literal methodology. It is important to our understanding and evaluation of the "complementary hermeneutic" that we examine how the New Testament interprets the Old Testament. We also need to understand how the biblical writers utilize symbolic speech in communicating concepts. And it is vitally important to consider the context in which the prophetic utterances occur as we attempt to interpret those prophecies.

2

DISPENSATIONAL HERMENEUTICS

Thomas D. Ice

C onsistently literal or plain interpretation is indicative of a dispensational approach to the interpretation of the Scriptures," declared Charles Ryrie in 1965. "And it is this very consistency —the strength of dispensational interpretation—that irks the nondispensationalist and becomes the object of his ridicule."[1] "Consistently literal interpretation" was listed by Ryrie as the second most important *sine qua non* of dispensationalism, which forms the foundation for the most important essential, "the distinction between Israel and the Church."[2] Earl Radmacher, in 1979, went so far as to say that literal interpretation "is the 'bottom-line' of dispensationalism."[3] While the ridicule of nondispensationalists has continued, there also appear to be signs of hermeneutical equivocation within the ranks of dispensationalism.

Within contemporary dispensationalism, some are moving away from the generally held hermeneutical statements of Ryrie and Radmacher. Craig Blaising concluded "that consistently literal exegesis is inadequate to describe the essential distinctive of dispensationalism. Development is taking place on how to characterize a proper hermeneutic for dispensationalists."[4] Blaising and his coauthor Darrell Bock assert that the grammatical-historical hermeneutic "is shared broadly in evangelicalism, so consequently present-day dispensationalists do not think of themselves as having an exclusive hermeneutic."[5]

Outside dispensational circles some would admit that dispensational hermeneutics "continues to exercise a widespread influence among evangelical Christians today."[6] However, many do continue to see the literal approach as an object of ridicule. Most likely, the loudest voice of dissent against the consistent literal hermeneutic of dispensationalism is from Christian Reconstructionists. Kenneth Gentry labels the dispensational claim to consistently literal interpretation as a "presumption" that "is unreasonable" and "an impossible ideal."[7]

A DEFINITION OF
LITERAL INTERPRETATION

Many times dispensationalists have explained what they mean when they speak of "literal interpretation." Ryrie begins his discussion of literal interpretation by referring to Bernard Ramm, who wrote the standard hermeneutics textbook of his day: "Dispensationalists claim that their principle of hermeneutics is that of literal interpretation. This means interpretation which gives to every word the same meaning it would have in normal usage, whether employed in writing, speaking or thinking.[8]

He then formulates an extensive definition:

> This is sometimes called the principle of grammatical-historical interpretation since the meaning of each word is determined by grammatical and historical considerations. The principle might also be called normal interpretation since the literal meaning of words is the normal approach to their understanding in all languages. It might also be designated plain interpretation so that no one receives the mistaken notion that the literal principle rules out figures of speech. Symbols, figures of speech and types are all interpreted plainly in this method and they are in no way contrary to literal interpretation. After all, the very existence of any meaning for a figure of speech depends on the reality of the literal meaning of the terms involved. Figures often make the meaning plainer, but it is the literal, normal, or plain meaning that they convey to the reader.[9]

Ryrie concludes his statement of the dispensational position by quoting E. R. Craven's oft cited summary of literalism:

> The *literalist* (so called) is not one who denies that *figurative* language, that *symbols*, are used in prophecy, nor does he deny that great *spiritual* truths are set forth therein; his position is, simply, that the prophecies are to be *normally* interpreted (i.e., according

to received laws of language) as any other utterances are interpreted—that which is manifestly figurative being so regarded.[10]

On the one hand, many current dispensationalists believe that Ryrie's statement is adequate and that literal interpretation still is (should be) a defining tenet of dispensationalism. Many believe that they have been able to satisfactorily interpret the details of Scripture and harmonize their exegetical conclusions into a theology that is the product of consistent literal interpretation. On the other hand, there are many, inside and outside of dispensationalism, who see problems with such an approach. We will now consider some objections.

USES OF LITERALISM

Vern Poythress spends two chapters interacting with Ryrie and other dispensational expressions of literal interpretation in *Understanding Dispensationalists*.[11] Poythress presents dispensationalists as using the word *literal* in such a fluid manner that it is often difficult to know exactly what is meant. "Perhaps the word," he suggests, "has already unconsciously been loaded with some of the assumptions belonging to the theological system."[12]

He says literal interpretation can be used in four ways. First is "first thought meaning," which is said to describe "the meaning for words in isolation."[13] The second kind he calls "flat interpretation," by which he means an *a priori* commitment to an idea of "literal *if possible.*"[14] Third, the one who uses grammatical-historical interpretation "reads passages as organic wholes and tries to understand what each passage expresses against the background of the original human author and the original situation."[15] His fourth type is "plain interpretation," where one "reads everything as if it were written directly to oneself, in one's own time and culture." This is opposed to grammatical-historical interpretation.[16] Poythress sees the dispensationalist use of literal interpretation as "a confusing term, capable of being used to beg many of the questions at stake in the interpretation of the Bible."[17]

Though it is true that dispensationalists have used *literal* in at least two ways, Poythress's charge that it has lead to confusion and not answered important questions is not justified. Apparently Ryrie's statement was clear enough for Poythress to work his way through it and break it up into classifications corresponding with his categories. Much of the verbiage used by dispensationalists (i.e., normal, plain, grammatical-historical) are attempts to spell out what is meant by *literal* in light of critical objections to such an approach.

Elliott Johnson has noted that much of the confusion over literal interpretation can be removed when one properly understands the two primary ways the term has been used down through church history: "(1) the clear, plain sense of a word or phrase as over against a figurative use, and (2) a system that views the text as providing the basis of the true interpretation."[18] Thus, dispensationalists, by and large, have used the term *literal* to refer to their system of interpretation (the consistent use of the grammatical-historical system), and once inside that system, *literal* refers to whether or not a specific word or phrase is used in its context in a figurative or literal sense. This helps us understand why Radmacher describes the system of literal interpretation (Johnson's no. 2) as "both plain-literal and figurative-literal"[19] (Johnson's no. 1).

Johnson's second use of *literal* (i.e., systematic literalism) is simply the grammatical-historical system consistently used. The grammatical-historical system was revived by the Reformers. It was set against the spiritual (spiritualized) or deeper meaning of the text that was the approach of the middle ages. The literal meaning was used simply as a springboard to a deeper ("spiritual") meaning, which was viewed as more desirable. A classic spiritualized interpretation would see the four rivers of Genesis 2—the Pishon, Havilah, Tigris, and Euphrates—as representing the body, soul, spirit, and mind. Coming from such a system, the Reformers saw the need to get back to the literal or textual meaning of the Bible. For instance, Martin Luther wanted to debate John Eck from the *text* of the Bible.

The *system* of literal interpretation is the grammatical-historical, or textual, approach to hermeneutics. Use of literalism in this sense could be called "macroliteralism." Within macroliteralism, the consistent use of the grammatical-historical system yields the interpretative conclusion, for example, that *Israel* always and only refers to national Israel. The church will not be substituted for Israel if the grammatical-historical system of interpretation is consistently used because there are no indicators in the text that such is the case. Therefore, one must bring an idea from outside the text by saying that the passage really means something that it does not actually say. This kind of replacement approach is a mild form of spiritualized, or allegorical, interpretation. So when speaking of those who do replace *Israel* with the church as not taking the Bible literally and spiritualizing the text, it is true, since such a belief is contrary to a macroliteral interpretation.

Consistently literal interpreters, within the framework of the grammatical-historical system, do discuss whether or not a word, phrase, or the literary genre of a biblical book is a figure of speech (connotative use of language) or is to be taken literally/plainly (denotative use of language). This is Johnson's first use of *literal,* which could be called "microliteralism." Ramm has said:

> The literal meaning of the figurative expression is the proper or natural meaning as understood by students of language. Whenever a figure is used its literal meaning is precisely that meaning determined by grammatical studies of figures. Hence, figurative interpretation does not pertain to the spiritual or mystical sense of Scripture, but to the literal sense.[20]

Thus, within microliteralism, there may be discussion by literalists as to whether or not a given word or phrase is being used as a figure of speech, based on the context of a given passage. Some passages are quite naturally clearer than others and a consensus among interpreters develops, whereas other passages may find literal interpreters divided as to whether or not they should be understood as figures of speech. This is more a problem of application than of method.

Reconstructionist Kenneth Gentry, in his attack on consistent literal interpretation, argues that "*consistent* literalism is unreasonable."[21] One of the ways he attempts to prove his point is by arguing that, since dispensationalists take some words and phrases as figures of speech, they are not consistently literal.[22] He asserts that "the dispensational claim to '*consistent* literalism' is frustrating due to its inconsistent employment."[23] Gentry seeks to discredit the dispensational hermeneutic by giving examples of dispensationalists who interpret certain passages as containing figures of speech, citing this as inconsistent with the system of literal interpretation. According to Gentry, the dispensationalist has to abandon literal interpretation when he realizes that Jesus refers figuratively to Himself as a door in John 10:9.[24] Gentry is not defining literal interpretation the way dispensationalists do. Therefore, his conclusions about literal interpretation are misguided because he commonly mixes the two senses described by Johnson. When speaking of the macroliteral, he uses an example from microliteralism, and vice versa, therefore appearing to have shown an inconsistency in literal interpretation. In reality, the examples cited fall within the framework of how dispensationalists have defined what they mean by literal interpretation.

IS LITERALISM PRIMARILY
A PHILOSOPHICAL CONCEPT?

Vern Poythress has charged that "classic dispensationalists have 'hedged' on the idea of fulfillment. They possess an idea of fulfillment and an idea of literalness that make it almost impossible *in principle* for the opponent to give a counterexample."[25] Gentry echoes Poythress when he says that aspects of dispensational interpretation are "a preconceived hermeneutic," and asks, "Why must we begin with the assumption of literalism?"[26] The implication is that, if it is an idea, then it did not develop from Scripture and is thus suspect.

Ryrie did state his hermeneutic as ideals, but that is because he is summarizing principles. These principles have been verified and developed, in the mind of the dispensationalist, through volumes of specific exegesis from the text of Scripture. It would be hard to prove that literal interpretation is merely a form of idealism forced upon the text because some have expressed principles of interpretation or tried to support the literal approach with a philosophical argument. How else can one present a summary of conclusions except as principles that include ideas?[27] Many dispensationalists believe that a philosophical rationale could be removed from the defense of literalism and the approach could still be developed and defended inductively from Scripture.

No doubt, the human thought process involves an interplay between ideas and data, so nothing is purely the product of sheer inductive observation. Presuppositions can be tested and verified or rejected through the hermeneutical spiral or circle. But to argue against literalism on the grounds that it is a form of idealism, masking the richness of God's Word, is misguided.

In a related issue, some say dispensationalists reflect a "common sense" or "plain sense" *a priori* philosophical influence from eighteenth or nineteenth century rationalism when employing the "literal if possible" principle.[28] David Cooper gives a classic statement of this hermeneutical principle in his "Golden Rule of Interpretation":

> When the plain sense of Scripture makes common sense, seek no other sense; therefore, take every word at its primary, ordinary, usual, literal meaning unless the facts of the immediate context, studied in the light of related passages and axiomatic and fundamental truths, indicate clearly otherwise.[29]

Cooper's "Golden Rule" should not necessarily be classified as one reflecting "Scottish Common Sense Realism" (as some have asserted) primarily because it is a literary not a philosophical statement. Cooper does not use the phrase "common sense," as critics suggest, by appealing to an abstract theory of common understanding latent in humanity. Instead, he defines it within a literary context. Common sense for Cooper is controlled by the context of Scripture, not some idea of common meaning residing in the reader of Scripture. Terms like "primary," "ordinary," "usual," and "literal" meaning are developed literarily from Scripture within Cooper's rule, as well as theologically (i.e., "axiomatic and fundamental truths"). The tactic of pouring a meaning not intended by its users into "common sense" falls by the wayside upon close examination. Cooper's rule is a helpful guide for discerning the Bible's use of literal or figurative language within the consistently literal system of interpretation.

Kenneth Gentry, who has charged dispensationalists with having a "preconceived hermeneutic" which builds upon "the assumption of literalism,"[30] could be accused of a similar fault. He says, "it should be the Christian's practice that: (1) the clearer statements interpret the less clear . . . and (2) our hermeneutic should not be *a priori*, but derived from Scripture itself, allowing Scripture to interpret Scripture."[31] While agreeing with these two canons of interpretation, the point to be made is that, if a "flaw of dispensationalism is its *a priori* 'literal' hermeneutic,"[32] how do Gentry's two points escape the same problem? What may be presumed to be a clear statement by one person may not be for another. If hermeneutics should not be *a priori*, how does one ever start the process of biblical investigation without at least assuming an approach that could then be verified? That is the approach commonly taken by literalists; they believe that their hermeneutic has been verified from the Scriptures themselves as a result of dealing with specific texts.[33]

COMPLEMENTARY HERMENEUTICS?

"Progressive Dispensationalism" is the self-proclaimed title of a new form of dispensationalism that has arisen within the last few years. This new dispensationalism denies that consistent literal interpretation is a defining essential. One of its formulators, Craig Blaising, has declared "that consistently literal exegesis is inadequate to describe the essential distinctive of dispensationalism."[34] It appears, however, after reading Blaising and Bock's book containing a statement of this new dispensationalism (*Dispensationalism, Israel and the Church*), even though subtitled *The Search for Definition,* that they do not even attempt to delineate essentials.

Blaising believes that earlier dispensationalists were ill-affected by Baconian inductivism, which produced unwarranted certainty about their theology. He believes that the Baconian propensity to produce a list of summary points flowing from inductive analysis accounts for Ryrie's *sine qua non* of dispensationalism (apparently instead of valid interaction with the biblical text.) Therefore, Blaising called Ryrie's formulation of dispensationalism "conceptual naïveté"[35] and labeled this phase "essentialist dispensationalism"[36] because of the three essentials. Instead of recognizing clear essentials, Blaising appears to think one can only say that there are patterns characteristic of the phases of the dispensational tradition.[37]

Blaising's "pattern approach" raises some important questions about his definition of dispensationalism. Mainly, if there are no essential guidelines, or proposed guidelines are vague and fluid, how does one determine who is a dispensationalist? It seems that with the pattern approach one simply observes the different forms dispensationalism has taken in the past, while at the same time allowing for virtually any new "developments," resulting in no meaningful definition.

It appears that by following the pattern approach anyone who claims to be a dispensationalist would have to be considered one. To conclude otherwise would reflect an "essentialist" standard such as Ryrie has suggested, which is to be rejected, according to Blaising. If one opts to use only past historic patterns, then they have not allowed for development, the very thing the new dispensationalism advocates. Perhaps this explains why Blaising and Bock only *describe* progressive dispensationalism in their concluding summary chapter, while avoiding a list of essentials.

Examination of the progressive dispensational approach helps to explain why its proponents would need to discredit a hermeneutical *sine qua non* in order to propose a looser system they call "complementary hermeneutics." Complementary hermeneutics involves "the New Testament . . . introduc[ing] change and advance; it does not merely repeat Old Testament revelation," according to Blaising and Bock. "In making complementary additions, however, it does not jettison old promises. The enhancement is not at the expense of the original promise."[38]

Complementary hermeneutics appears to involve an attempted synthesis of the spiritualizing and literal methods that have developed out of issues relating to the New Testament's use of the Old

Testament. "The issue is not a distinct hermeneutic but debate about how to apply the hermeneutic that we share. The question most simply put is, "How does 'new' revelation impact 'old' revelation and expression?"

This approach leads to a position that sees Christ currently reigning on David's throne. Traditionally, dispensationalists have made a distinction between Christ's present session at the right hand of the Father's throne versus His future, but not yet, millennial reign from Jerusalem on David's throne. A present spiritual reign, as put forth by Bock, has in the past been the position of amillennialists, postmillennialists, and a few nondispensationalist premillennialists, but not of dispensationalists.[39] Bock does not go so far as to replace Israel of the Old Testament with the church, since he retains a significant amount of literalism that can be seen in his commitment to a futurist eschatology. But this hermeneutic involves a spiritualized interpretation rejected by earlier dispensationalists, in spite of revisionist attempts by Blaising to characterize older dispensationalists like Darby and Scofield as occasional spiritualizers.[40]

Did Darby and Scofield use a spiritualized hermeneutic? It does not appear that they did in the sense being suggested by Poythress and Blaising. Poythress treats the dispensationalist's approach to typology as if it were part of their hermeneutical approach. Typology, for dispensationalists like Darby and Scofield, is used for theological illustrations only after all passages involved have first been interpreted literally. Then "patterns" are observed and comparisons made only for the purpose of illustrating (1 Cor. 10:6, 11). Thus, if the story of Joseph in Genesis were to be used typologically to correspond to aspects of the life of Christ or God's program for Israel, it would only be so used after the Genesis narrative had been interpreted literally. Typology would not be involved in interpreting the Genesis text.

However, typology is also a part of the hermeneutic of some nondispensational approaches to the Bible. This sometimes appears to be used as a form of spiritualization (i.e., the church replaces Israel). Indeed, Poythress realizes that he may be misrepresenting Scofield when he says, "Many present-day dispensationalists would see Scofield's examples of spiritualization as 'applications' rather than interpretations that give the actual meaning of the passage."[41] (Actually, they probably are closer to illustration than to application.) Therefore, Poythress, and then Blaising, confused Darby and Scofield's use of typology as a part of their hermeneutic—hence the misrepresentation that they used a form of spiritualized hermeneutic. Could it be that Blaising is using this misrepresentation as part of his historical polemic against Ryrie's belief that consistent literal interpretation is an essential feature of dispensationalism, and thus be suggesting that this is justification for the spiritualizing of the new dispensationalism? If Poythress's and Blaising's contention of spiritualization by older dispensationalists cannot be supported, then new dispensationalism's claim to be practicing a hermeneutic that has been used by previous phases of dispensationalism would not, in fact, have that historical antecedent in dispensationalism (see chapter 4).

HOW THE NEW TESTAMENT
USES THE OLD TESTAMENT

Development of "complementary hermeneutics" by new dispensationalists revolves around issues related to how New Testament writers handle the Old Testament. Blaising and Bock present three approaches to the question. They could be viewed as the traditional literal approach, the spiritual approach, and the new complementary approach.[42]

The complementary approach put forth by Blaising and Bock is claimed to be a synthesis combining the answer of older dispensationalism, which demonstrates a greater sensitivity to "the historical interpretation of the Old Testament," while adopting covenant theology's view that includes the "adding of new revelation."[43] Bock has suggested, in the process of interpreting Peter's use of Joel in Acts 2, that the "eschaton has begun; the movement toward the culmination of the eschaton has started, as have the benefits associated with the coming of the Day of the Lord."[44]

It appears that, in the minds of Blaising and Bock, their complementary hermeneutical synthesis lends support to their theological dualism of an "already/not yet" view of the Davidic kingdom rule. "Both dispensations [Church Age and Millennium] are also united as aspects of the messianic reign of Christ. . . . Both dispensations are seen in the New Testament as fulfillments of the Davidic covenant."[45] Bock sees "the presence of fulfillment" in Peter's use of Joel in Acts 2 and adds, "it is not a comparison."[46] However, Blaising and Bock appear to be in agreement with older dispensationalists who tend to see the Old Testament passages as left untouched by New Testament development: "The enhancement is not at the expense of the original promise."[47]

Ken Gentry, representing a traditional covenant approach, believes that *"the Christian exegete must allow the New Testament to interpret the Old Testament.* . . . This approach to biblical interpretation allows *the conclusive revelation of God in the New Testament* authoritatively to interpret incomplete revelation in the Old."[48] This would be a sound statement if Gentry meant that the Scripture was expanded down through history (progressive revelation) as more details and explanation are added in such a way as not to change the meaning of an original Old Testament passage through reinterpretation in the New Testament (i.e., the church replacing Israel in OT passages). But that is not what Gentry means. His approach is a so-called "grammatical-historical-*theological*" hermeneutic, whereby it is believed that the New Testament gives a theological basis for changing the original meaning of the Old Testament. Gentry believes that New Testament theology gives him the liberty to take Old Testament passages and apply them "spiritually" to the church. He asks, "Why cannot there be a *spiritual Israel?*"[49] From the perspective of covenant theology, it is sometimes taught that spiritualization of the Old Testament is needed to make it conform to the doctrine of the New Testament.

But must one adopt an element of spiritualization (i.e., the New Testament [re]interprets the Old Testament) into one's hermeneutic in order to properly understand how the New Testament uses the Old Testament? That seems to be unnecessary.

Arnold Fruchtenbaum claims that the New Testament writers (all were Jewish) quote the Old Testament in the common Jewish way in the first century. "They often gave a spiritual meaning or a new application to an Old Testament text without denying that what the original said literally did or will happen."[50] Fruchtenbaum cites four ways the New Testament quotes from the old and notes that Matthew 2 contains an example of all four uses (see chapter 4). "The first example is called *literal prophecy plus literal fulfillment*":[51]

> This example is found in Matthew 2:5–6, which quotes Micah 5:2. In the original context of Micah 5:2, the prophet is speaking prophetically and prophesying that whenever the Messiah is born, He will be born in Bethlehem of Judah. That is the literal meaning of Micah 5:2. When a literal prophecy is fulfilled in the New Testament, it is quoted as a literal fulfillment. Many prophecies fall into this category, such as Isaiah 7:14, 52:13–53:12, Zechariah 9:9, etc.[52]

The second classification is called *literal plus typical*:[53]

> This example is found in Matthew 2:15, which is a quotation of Hosea 11:1. However, the original context is not a prophecy, it is

an historical event. It is a reference to the Exodus when Israel, the national son of God, was brought out of Egypt. It is obvious that Hosea is thinking of literal Israel for in the following verses he points out how Israel quickly slipped into idolatry. The *literal* meaning in context of Hosea 11:1 is a reference to the Exodus. There is nothing in the New Testament that can change or reinterpret the meaning of Hosea 11:1, nor does the New Testament deny that the literal Exodus actually happened. However, Israel as the national son of God coming out of Egypt becomes a *type* of the individual Son of God, the Messiah coming out of Egypt. The passage is quoted, not as a fulfillment of prophecy, since Hosea 11:1 was not a prophecy to begin with, but as a type. Matthew does not deny, change, or reinterpret the original meaning. He understands it literally, but the literal Old Testament event becomes a type of a New Testament event. This is literal plus typical. Many of the citations in the Book of Hebrews of Exodus and Leviticus fall into this category.[54]

Fruchtenbaum calls the third approach *literal plus application:*[55]

This example is found in Matthew 2:17–18 which is a quotation of Jeremiah 31:15. In the original context, Jeremiah is speaking of an event soon to come as the Babylonian Captivity begins. As the Jewish young men were being taken into captivity, they went by the town of Ramah. Not too far from Ramah is where Rachel was buried and she was the symbol of Jewish motherhood. As the young men were marched toward Babylon, the Jewish mothers of Ramah came out weeping for sons they will never see again. Jeremiah pictured the scene as Rachel weeping for her children. This is the *literal* meaning of Jeremiah 31:15. The New Testament cannot change or reinterpret what this verse means in that context, nor does it try to do so. In this category, there is a New Testament event that has one point of similarity with the Old Testament event. The verse is quoted as an *application.* The one point of similarity between Ramah and Bethlehem is that once again Jewish mothers are weeping for sons that they will never see again and so the Old Testament passage is applied to the New Testament event. This is literal plus application. The original text may be history or prophecy. The Jeremiah quote is an example of history. An example of prophecy is in Acts 2:16–21 which quotes Joel 2:28–32. Virtually nothing that happened in Acts 2 is predicted in Joel 2. Joel was speaking of the outpouring of the Holy Spirit on the nation of Israel in the last days. However, there was one point of similarity, an outpouring of the Holy Spirit, resulting in unusual manifestations. Acts 2 does not change or reinterpret Joel 2, nor does it deny that Joel 2 will have a literal fulfillment when the Holy Spirit will be poured out on the whole nation of Israel. It is simply applying it to a New Testament event because of one point of similarity.[56]

Finally, the fourth is called *summation*:[57]

The example is found in Matthew 2:23. "... *that it might be ful-filled which was spoken by the prophets, that he should be called a Nazarene.*" However, no such statement is found anywhere in the Old Testament. Since Matthew used the plural *prophets*, one should be able to find at least two, yet there is not even one. The fourth category does not have an actual quotation as in the first three categories, but only a summary of what the prophets actually said. The plural use of *prophets* is a clue to this category. In the first century, *Nazarenes* were a people despised and rejected and the term was used to reproach and to shame (John 1:46). The prophets did teach that the Messiah would be a despised and re-jected individual (*e.g.* Isa 53:3) and this is summarized by the term, *Nazarene.* Another example of this category is Luke 18:31–33. Us-ing the plural for prophet again, Jesus states that the time for fulfill-ment has come and He states what is to be fulfilled: "the Messiah will go to Jerusalem, be turned over to the Gentiles; the Gentiles will mock Him, treat Him shamefully, spit on Him, scourge Him, and kill Him, but He will rise again the third day." Not one prophet ever said all this, but the prophets together did say all this. Hence, this is a summation.[58]

Fruchtenbaum believes that every quotation of the Old Testa-ment in the New will fit into one of these four categories. He notes that the "procedure is not simply 'to interpret the Old by the New' as Covenant Theology insists. . . . There is no need to conclude that the New Testament changes or reinterprets the Old Testament."[59] An approach such as this contributes to a consistently literal hermeneu-tic and demonstrates why many dispensationalists still believe that older approaches to interpretation are to be preferred. How the Old Testament is used in the New is no basis on which to abandon or modify a consistently literal hermeneutic.

FIGURES AND SYMBOLS

Critics of consistently literal interpretation sometimes contend that literalism is impossible because of the presence of figures of speech and symbols. An example is seen in a series of questions from the pen of Ken Gentry: "May not so rich a work as the Bible, dedicated to such a lofty and spiritual theme (the infinite God's re-demption of sinful man), written by many authors over 1,500 years employ a variety of literary genres? No symbols? No metaphors? No analogies?"[60]

Gentry goes on to admit that dispensationalists do recognize literary devices such as figures of speech. However, he then presents the consistently literal approach of many dispensationalists as unworkable.[61] By presenting the literal approach as not allowing for symbols, metaphors, and analogies, he misrepresents literal interpretation.

In light of Gentry's characterization, it is interesting to note that the most extensive work we have on figures of speech was done by the dispensational literalist, E. W. Bullinger in 1898. *Figures of Speech Used in the Bible: Explained and Illustrated* is said to have "never been duplicated or equaled in point of thoroughness and detail." "No one has done more to open the eyes of Bible students to this key than has Bullinger." It is said that Bullinger "catalogs and discusses no less than two hundred fifteen distinct figures . . . giving full explanation of its use in each instance."[62] Bullinger's work demonstrates that literalists have at least thought about the use of figures in a detailed and sophisticated way and do not consider such usage to conflict with literalism.

SENSE AND REFERENT

Recently I came home one hot afternoon from the office and sat down to eat dinner. Still perspiring, I began putting pepper on my vegetables. My mother-in-law asked, "Is it hot?" Thinking that she was referring to the climate, I gave an answer that did not make sense to her. She then pointed out that she was referring to the pepper, not the weather. Once I understood what she referred to, I was able to answer her question. Since the meaning of *hot* has a sense that can be used in various ways, it is important to clarify to which of those ways one has referred. So it is with symbols and figures.

A phrase like "white house" can relate to many different referents. One could be referring to the white house across the street from one's own house. Or one could be speaking of any house painted white in contrast to another color. One could have in mind the building in Washington, D.C., that serves as home and workplace of the president. Or one could be using "White House" as a figurative synonym for "office of the president of the United States." Building upon the basic sense of the phrase, context serves to specify possible meanings of a referent. "Sense and referent" are an important issue for biblical interpretation.[63]

Advocates of the preterist school of interpretation (who accept that most of John's Revelation and the Olivet Discourse were fulfilled in A.D. 70 in events relating to the destruction of Jerusalem[64]) give us a hermeneutical example relating to sense and referent.

In the Olivet Discourse, one of the most difficult sections for the preterist is Matthew 24:29–30. This passage speaks of the sun and moon being darkened, stars falling from the sky, the sign of the Son of Man appearing in the sky for all the world to see, and Christ "coming on the clouds of the sky with power and great glory" (v. 30). Preterists believe that these phrases do not describe a future coming of Christ; instead they believe that it refers to God's coming in judgment upon Israel in A.D. 70 through the agency of the Roman army's destruction of Jerusalem. "The sign that the Son of Man is in heaven was the smoking rubble of Jerusalem,"[65] declares Gentry. Gary DeMar agrees: "In speaking of the sun and moon going dark and stars falling (Matt. 24:29), Jesus is describing the nation of Israel under judgment."[66] Instead of seeing Matthew 24 as the judgment of God during the future seventieth week of Daniel, preterists see it as "a providential coming of Christ in *historical judgments upon men.*"[67] Gentry explains:

> In the Old Testament, clouds are frequently employed as symbols of divine wrath and judgment. Often God is seen surrounded with foreboding clouds which express His unapproachable holiness and righteousness. Thus, God is poetically portrayed in certain judgment scenes as *coming in the clouds* to wreak historical vengeance upon His enemies. For example: "The burden against Egypt. Behold, the Lord rides on a swift cloud, and will come into Egypt; the idols of Egypt will totter at His presence, and the heart of Egypt will melt in its midst" (Isa. 19:1). This occurred in the Old Testament era, when the Assyrian king Esarhaddon conquered Egypt in 671 B.C. Obviously it is not to be understood as a literal riding upon a cloud, any more so than Psalm 68:4: "Sing to God, sing praises to His name; Extol Him who rides on the clouds, By His name YAH, And rejoice before Him."
>
> The New Testament picks up this apocalyptic judgment imagery when it speaks of Christ's coming in clouds of judgment *during history.*[68]

Gentry cites the following passages as support of his thesis: 2 Samuel 22:8, 10; Psalms 18:7–15; 68:4, 33; 97:2–39 (sic; Ps. 97 only has 12 verses); 104:3; Isaiah 13:9; 26:21; 30:27; Joel 2:1, 2; Micah 1:3; Nahum 1:2ff; Zephaniah 1:14–15.[69]

Most likely all would agree in principle that just because various passages have a similar sense does not mean that they have the same referent. They may, but each specific instance must be verified by contextual usage. There is no question that a divine judgment sense is related by the clouds in the passages cited by Gentry. The picture of smoke, fire, clouds, and darkness gives a universal sense of the Lord's wrath. However, differences exist, which supports the view that there are at least two referents.

First, there are those passages related to the Lord's judgment of Israel's enemies on behalf of Israel. These are events that have either taken place in the past or are taking place at the time of writing, where the Lord is pictured as "riding" across the skies in a chariot of judgment (2 Sam. 22:8, 11; Pss. 18:7–15; 68:4, 33; "walks," Ps. 104:3). While the other passages cited by Gentry do have a judgment theme, they do not employ the "cloud" motif and/or a nonpreterist would locate their timing at the future Day of the Lord (Isa. 13:9; 26:21; 30:27; Joel 2:1, 2; Mic. 1:3; Nah. 1:2ff; Zeph. 1:14–15).

Second, Matthew 24:30 says that "all the tribes of the earth . . . will see the Son of Man coming on the clouds of the sky with power and great glory." Here we have a picture of Christ, not just riding across the sky, as in the cited Old Testament passages, but One who is "coming" from heaven to earth. The picture here is of a different event, even though elements are present that characterize all of God's judgment. It may be that the Lord is pictured as "riding" or "walking" among the clouds in smaller, local judgments. Then when the time comes for the grand finale, the Bible continues the judgment theme depiction, but this time He actually comes to the earth in a display of visible glory and power.

Third, the preterist sees Matthew 24 as a judgment upon Israel from the Lord, who is in the clouds, through the Roman army. A close examination of the passage reveals that in Matthew 24 the Lord returns to earth to rescue His people Israel (see 24:31); the judgment is not upon Israel but upon Gentile nations that are persecuting Israel. Just because a similar sense is painted in some passages, it does not follow that all passages with that general sense refer to the same event. The figures of speech must be controlled by their specific context.

We understand that Luke 21:20–24 records Christ's reference to the A.D. 70 destruction of Jerusalem because it says "when you see Jerusalem surrounded by armies, then recognize that her desolation is at hand" (21:20). And Jerusalem is said to be "trampled underfoot by the Gentiles until the times of the Gentiles be fulfilled" (21:24).

But then the language in Luke 21:25–28 (a section paralleling Matthew 24:30–34) changes to the language of God's intervention, which shifts from judgment upon Israel (as in A.D. 70 and Luke 21:20–24) to His judgment upon "the earth," where there is "dismay among nations" (*ethnon*, 21:25), and "the world" (*oikoumene*, 21:26) and to His *rescue* of Israel from her enemies (21:25–28). This is said to involve "signs in sun and moon and stars" (21:25).[70]

Finally, preterists such as Gentry do see some passages that have "cloud language" referring to the Second Coming (Acts 1:9–11; 1 Thess. 4:13–17).[71] Further, Gentry interprets 2 Thessalonians 1:7–10 as a reference to the Second Coming,[72] when it contains many elements of judgment, such as "the Lord Jesus shall be revealed from heaven with His mighty angels in flaming fire, dealing out retribution to those who do not know God" (1:7b–8a). It would seem that the grounds he uses to argue for a past fulfillment of Matthew 24:30 could be applied to these passages also. These observations demonstrate that it is important to recognize the distinctions between sense and referent. Failure to do so may lead one to draw faulty conclusions and to overlook basic literary principles.

CONCLUSION

We suggest that it is premature to abandon, as an essential of dispensationalism, the use of a consistently literal hermeneutic that avoids changing the originally understood meaning of an earlier text. Even though the grammatical-historical hermeneutic is used by all evangelicals, many believe that only dispensationalists attempt to apply it consistently from Genesis to Revelation. Nondispensational evangelicals tend to use a grammatical-historical-*theological* hermeneutic (a mild form of spiritualization, since they replace OT Israel with the church on what they believe are NT theological grounds). At this point dispensationalists simply believe that grammatical-historical interpretation should be consistently applied.

When it comes to the role of pre-understanding, why do the critics of the older dispensational hermeneutic not invest some time examining the impact that the antirational, mystical ethos of today's culture is having on their own hermeneutical pre-understanding? To put today's skepticism in the language of a popular TV commercial, "Why ask why?" implying that one cannot really know. Paul Karleen notes,

> Poythress never questions this presupposition [covenant theology's covenant of grace]. . . . He urges the dispensationalist over

and over to examine cherished assumptions. Yet he does not do the same. Is it the case that everything is open to negotiation for him but the covenant? In spite of his appeal to all of us to look at the Bible, tradition may condition his thinking far more than he suspects.[73]

Walter Kaiser has warned,

> The grammatical-historical method of exegesis has served us all very well. But in recent decades, the hue and cry has gone up from scholarship at large to allow the reader and the modern situation to have as much (or in some cases, more) to say about what a text means as has traditionally been given to the original speaker of the text. . . . Can we profit from the insights of modernity without being sucked into its vortex? This will be the question of the next years.[74]

Perhaps some of the critics of the consistently literal hermeneutic (as defined in this chapter) are bothered by the certainty they see among older dispensational brethren because of the impact upon their hermeneutical pre-understanding that our modern culture represents. Today's climate is one of self-centered relativism, with no epistemological orientation to a concept of absolute truth. This mind-set is destructive of certainty and creates in people an attitude of tentativeness. While all evangelicals believe in absolute truth, perhaps modernity has eroded a valid belief in certainty that God's children can understand His Word in a detailed way.

If pre-understanding impacts thought, which it does, then it may be possible that a rejection of a consistent, literal interpretation (accepted by Ryrie and others as a *sine qua non* of dispensationalism) is less a development of dispensationalism and more reflects the adoption of a hermeneutic widely accepted outside of dispensationalism.

NOTES

1. Charles C. Ryrie, *Dispensationalism Today* (Chicago: Moody, 1965), 46.
2. Ibid., 47.
3. Earl D. Radmacher, "The Current Status of Dispensationalism and Its Eschatology," in *Perspectives on Evangelical Theology,* Kenneth S. Kantzer and Stanley N. Gundry, eds. (Grand Rapids: Baker, 1979), 171.
4. Craig A. Blaising, "Development of Dispensationalism by Contemporary Dispensationalists, *Bibliotheca Sacra* 145, no. 579 (July-September 1988), 272.

5. Craig A. Blaising and Darrell L. Bock, "Dispensationalism, Israel and the Church: Assessment and Dialogue," in *Dispensationalism, Israel and the Church: The Search for Definition,* Craig A. Blaising and Darrell L. Bock, eds. (Grand Rapids: Zondervan, 1992), 380.

6. O. Palmer Robertson, "Hermeneutics of Continuity," in *Continuity and Discontinuity: Perspectives on the Relationship Between the Old and New Testaments,* John S. Feinberg, ed. (Westchester, Ill.: Crossway, 1988), 107.

7. Kenneth L. Gentry, Jr., *He Shall Have Dominion: A Postmillennial Eschatology* (Tyler, Tex.: Institute for Christian Economics, 1992), 148, 146.

8. Bernard Ramm, *Protestant Biblical Interpretation* (Boston: Wilde, 1956), 89–92.

9. Ryrie, *Dispensationalism Today,* 86–87.

10. E. R. Craven and J. P. Lange, ed., *Commentary on the Holy Scriptures: Revelation* (New York: Scribner, 1872), 98 (cited in Ryrie, *Dispensationalism Today,* 87).

11. Vern S. Poythress, *Understanding Dispensationalists* (Grand Rapids: Zondervan, 1987), 78–96.

12. Ibid., 78.

13. Ibid., 82–83.

14. Ibid., 83–84. Poythress (Review of Books, *Westminster Theological Journal* 55, no. 1 [Spring 1993], 165) dismisses Robert L. Thomas's *Revelation 1–7: An Exegetical Commentary* (Chicago: Moody, 1992) as one that "cannot be recommended" because "the over-all impact is dominated by the initial decision in favor of literalism." "This principle of 'literal if possible,'" contends Poythress, is nothing more than a "stringent idea of 'literalism,' wildly underestimating the pervasiveness of symbolism."

15. Poythress, *Understanding Dispensationalists,* 84–85.

16. Ibid., 85–86.

17. Ibid., 96.

18. Elliott E. Johnson, *Expository Hermeneutics: An Introduction* (Grand Rapids: Zondervan, 1990), 9.

19. Radmacher, "Current Status of Dispensationalism," 167.

20. Ramm, *Protestant Biblical Interpretation,* 141 (cited in Radmacher, "Current Status of Dispensationalism," 167).

21. Gentry, *He Shall Have Dominion,* 148.

22. For examples of his approach, see ibid., 153–58.

23. Gentry, *He shall Have Dominion,* 153.

24. Ibid., 148.

25. Poythress, *Understanding Dispensationalists,* 53.

26. Gentry, *He Shall Have Dominion,* 147.

27. For a recent presentation of a dispensational and literal hermeneutic, complete with hundreds of specific examples illustrating various principles of interpretation, see Roy B. Zuck, *Basic Bible Interpretation* (Wheaton, Ill.: Victor, 1991).

28. I have heard these charges in a number of personal conversations with those opposed to consistent literal interpretation.

29. David L. Cooper, *The World's Greatest Library Graphically Illustrated* (1942; Los Angeles: Biblical Research Society, 1970), 11.

30. Gentry, *He Shall Have Dominion,* 147.

31. Greg L. Bahnsen and Kenneth L. Gentry, Jr., *House Divided: The Break-Up of Dispensational Theology* (Tyler, Tex.: Institute for Christian Economics, 1989), 265.

32. Ibid., 44 n.

33. For an article-length discussion of how a literalist relates to the analogy of faith, see Elliott E. Johnson, "What I Mean By Historical-Grammatical Interpretation and How That Differs From Spiritual Interpretation," *Grace Theological Journal* 11, no. 2 (Fall 1990), 157–69.

34. Blaising, "Development of Dispensationalism," 272.

35. Craig A. Blaising, "Dispensationalism: The Search for Definition," in *Dispensationalism*, Blaising and Bock, eds., 29. See pp. 16–34 for Blaising's discussion of the Baconian impact upon dispensationalism.

36. Blaising and Bock, "Dispensationalism, Israel and the Church: Assessment and Dialogue," in ibid., 379.

37. Ibid. This conclusion also appeared to be supported in personal discussion with Blaising.

38. Ibid., 392–93.

39. For a presentation of Bock's position, see "The Reign of the Lord Christ" in ibid., 37–67. For interaction with Bock's view, see David A. Dean, *A Study of the Enthronement of Christ in Acts 2 and 3* (Th.M. thesis, Dallas Theological Seminary, May 1992). For a recent presentation of the traditional dispensational position of an exclusively future reign of Christ in the Millennium, see Renald E. Showers, *There Really Is a Difference! A Comparison of Covenant and Dispensational Theology* (Bellmawr, N.J.: Friends of Israel, 1990), 87–97. See also John F. Walvoord, *Major Bible Prophecies: 37 Crucial Prophecies That Affect You Today* (Grand Rapids: Zondervan, 1991), 96–109.

40. Blaising ("Dispensationalism: The Search for Definition," in *Dispensationalism*, Blaising and Bock, eds., 26) contends that "Darby and Scofield approved of spiritual or allegorical interpretation of the Old Testament." This is doubtful. Blaising may have picked up this idea from Poythress in *Understanding Dispensationalists*, 22–29.

41. Poythress, *Understanding Dispensationalists*, 24 n. 1.

42. Blaising and Bock, "Dispensationalism, Israel and the Church: Assessment and Dialogue," in *Dispensationalism*, Blaising and Bock, eds., 392–93.

43. Ibid., 393.

44. Darrell L. Bock, "The Reign of the Lord Christ," in ibid., 49.

45. Blaising and Bock, "Dispensationalism, Israel and the Church: Assessment and Dialogue," in ibid., 381. One cannot help but wonder how such statements can be considered compatible with several affirmations in the current Doctrinal Statement at Dallas Seminary. After listing three dispensations—Mosaic Law, the present dispensation of grace, and the future millennial kingdom—the Doctrinal Statement says, "We believe that these are distinct and are not to be intermingled or confused, as they are chronologically successive" (Article V The Dispensations). Then the Doctrinal Statement says that the church "is completely distinct from Israel" (Article XIII The Church, A Unity of Believers).

46. Bock, "The Reign of the Lord Christ," in ibid., 47.

47. Blaising and Bock, "Dispensationalism, Israel and the Church: Assessment and Dialogue," 393.

48. Gentry, *He Shall Have Dominion*, 156.

49. Ibid., 167. Gentry argues that Paul in Galatians 6:16 calls the church "spiritual Israel." Dispensationalists see Paul's statement "the Israel of God" as a reference to Jewish believers. For a rebuttal of Gentry's "spiritual Israel" view, see S. Lewis Johnson, Jr., "Paul and 'The Israel of God': An Exegetical and Eschatological Case-Study," in *Essays in Honor of J. Dwight Pentecost*, Stanley D. Toussaint & Charles H. Dyer, eds. (Chicago: Moody, 1986), 181–96.

50. Arnold G. Fruchtenbaum, *Israelology: The Missing Link in Systematic Theology*, rev. (Tustin, Calif.: Ariel Ministries, 1992), 842.

51. Fruchtenbaum picks up these classifications from David L. Cooper, *Messiah: His Historical Appearance* (Los Angeles: Biblical Research Society, 1958), 74.

52. Fruchtenbaum, *Israelology*, 843.

53. Cooper, *Messiah*, 175.

54. Fruchtenbaum, *Israelology*, 843–44.

55. Cooper, *Messiah*, 176.

56. Fruchtenbaum, *Israelology*, 844–45.

57. Cooper, *Messiah*, 177.

58. Fruchtenbaum, *Israelology*, 845.

59. Ibid, 845.

60. Gentry, *He Shall Have Dominion*, 147.

61. Ibid., 147–49.

62. Ethelbert W. Bullinger, *Figures of Speech Used in the Bible: Explained and Illustrated* (Grand Rapids: Baker, 1968), inside flap on dust jacket.

63. For a discussion on how "sense and reference" are involved in philosophy of language and its relation to hermeneutics, see John S. Feinberg, "Truth: Relationship of Theories of Truth to Hermeneutics," in *Hermeneutics, Inerrancy, and the Bible*, Earl D. Radmacher and Robert D. Preus, eds. (Grand Rapids: Zondervan, 1984), 28–30. See also Paul D. Feinberg, "Hermeneutics of Discontinuity," in *Continuity And Discontinuity: Perspectives on the Relationship Between the Old and New Testaments*, John S. Feinberg, ed. (Westchester, Ill.: Crossway, 1988), 117–20.

64. Preterist David Chilton (*Paradise Restored: An Eschatology of Dominion* [Tyler, Tex.: Reconstruction Press, 1985], 166) says, "The Book of Revelation is not about the Second Coming. It is about the destruction of Israel and Christ's victory over Rome. In fact, the word *coming* as used in the Book of Revelation *never refers to the Second Coming.*"

65. Gentry, *He Shall Have Dominion*, 274.

66. Gary DeMar, *Last Days Madness: The Folly of Trying to Predict When Christ Will Return* (Brentwood, Tenn.: Wolgemuth & Hyatt, 1991), 98.

67. Gentry, *He Shall Have Dominion*, 273.

68. Ibid., 273–74.

69. Ibid.

70. For more interaction with the preterist viewpoint, see H. Wayne House and Thomas Ice, *Dominion Theology: Blessing or Curse? An Analysis of Christian Reconstructionism* (Portland: Multnomah, 1988), 285–334.

71. Gentry, *He Shall Have Dominion*, 275–76, 279.

72. Ibid., 253–54, 386, 418.

73. Paul S. Karleen, "Understanding Covenant Theologians: A Study in Presuppositions" *Grace Theological Journal* 10, no. 2 (Fall 1989), 134.

74. Walter C. Kaiser, Jr., "An Epangelical Response," in *Dispensationalism*, Blaising and Bock, eds., 376.

Before one can determine when a prophecy is fulfilled, first one must know exactly what is being predicted. The meaning of the prophecy must be determined within its original context. Then one must examine the New Testament to see if the prophecy corresponds to later events that actually transpired. Biblical fulfillment occurs when the meaning of a specific Old Testament prophecy finds its exact correspondence in a New Testament person, activity, or event. One cannot automatically use the word fulfill to determine prophetic fulfillment since the word can mean more than just "to fulfill a prophecy." Neither can one rely on analogous language to determine the fulfillment of an Old Testament prophecy. It also is important to recognize the validity of potential fulfillment of prophecy. That is, the actual fulfillment of an event can be conditioned on the response of the people at the time the event is to be fulfilled. The response of those to whom the prophecy is directed can determine whether or not the prophecy will be fulfilled at that time.

3

BIBLICAL MEANING OF "FULFILLMENT"

Charles H. Dyer

Romantic love and the fulfillment of biblical prophecy share one trait in common. Most people claim to "know it when they see it," but few can provide a coherent explanation of what it actually is. The interpretation of biblical prophecy lies at the heart of dispensationalism, but how to determine when a prophetic utterance was—or will be—fulfilled is still more art than science. This chapter cannot hope to provide a definitive answer on the biblical meaning of fulfillment, but the goal is to raise critical issues that do affect our approach to prophecy.

THE USE OF "FULFILL"
DOES NOT ALWAYS INDICATE FULFILLMENT

One major approach used by many to determine whether or not a prophecy has been fulfilled is to look for a "fulfillment formula" such as "and so was fulfilled what the Lord had said through the prophet." Others would broaden this to include any time the word *plēroō* (fulfilled) is used when referring to the Old Testament.[1] Is the presence of the word *plēroō*, either by itself or in a "fulfillment formula," a good indication that the New Testament writer is pointing to the fulfillment of Old Testament prophecy? Not necessarily—for three reasons.

The Word Plēroō Does Not
Always Refer to Fulfilled Prophecy

Plēroō occurs ninety times in the New Testament, but only twenty-eight occurrences seem to be part of an introductory formula. Most of the remaining sixty-two occurrences have no connection with prophecy. *Plēroō* has five separate ranges of meaning in the New Testament.[2] Only one of these five refers to the fulfillment of prophecy. Some examples of the varied uses of *plēroō* help to illustrate how broadly the word was used.

"To fill [something] with content." The first range of meaning for *plēroō* focuses on an object that has been filled fully with something else. Christ told a parable based on catching fish in a net. "When [the net] was full [*plēroō*], the fishermen pulled it up on the shore" (Matt. 13:48). In Christ's parable the net was "filled full" with all sorts of fish. In the days preceding Christ's crucifixion Mary anointed Christ's feet with perfume. When she did, "the house was filled [*plēroō*] with the fragrance of the perfume" (John 12:3).

"To fulfill a demand or claim." The second range of meaning for *plēroō* focuses on satisfying the righteous demands or claims imposed by God. The apostle Paul described to the Romans how "the righteous demands of the law might be fully met [*plēroō*] in us, who do not live according to the sinful nature but according to the Spirit" (Rom. 8:4). Later in the same book Paul wrote that "he who loves his fellowman has fulfilled [*plēroō*] the law" (Rom. 13:8). Matthew has the same sense in mind when he records Christ's words to the multitudes: "Do not think that I have come to abolish the Law or the Prophets; I have not come to abolish them but to fulfill [*plēroō*] them" (Matt. 5:17). Christ is *not* saying that He came to fulfill prophecies made about Him in the Old Testament. The contrast in the text is between abolishing or breaking the law and "fulfilling" or practicing the law (vv. 17, 19).[3]

"To fill up completely a specific measure." The third range of meaning for *plēroō* focuses on completely reaching a set quantity, duration, or amount. Christ told His disciples that "Jerusalem will be trampled on by the Gentiles until the times of the Gentiles are fulfilled [*plēroō*]" (Luke 21:24). The Jews in Damascus tolerated Saul's persuasive preaching only so long. "After many days had gone by [lit. 'been fulfilled' (*plēroō*)], the Jews conspired to kill him" (Acts 9:23). The Tribulation martyrs who cry out to God for justice are told to "wait a little longer, until the number of their fellow servants and

brothers who were to be killed as they had been was completed [*pl̄eroō*]" (Rev. 6:11).

"To complete." Sometimes *pl̄eroō* conveys the idea of finishing or bringing an action or activity to a conclusion. Luke ends Christ's message to the multitudes by stating, "When Jesus had finished saying [lit., 'had completed' (*pl̄eroō*)] all this in the hearing of the people, he entered Capernaum" (Luke 7:1). Paul commands Archippus at Colossae, "See to it that you complete [*pl̄eroō*] the work you have received in the Lord" (Col. 4:17).

"To complete [or] to fulfill prophetic sayings which were spoken with divine authority." It is this fifth range of meaning for *pl̄eroō* that impacts most directly on our understanding of the fulfillment of Bible prophecy. This usage of *pl̄eroō* usually occurs with some type of fulfillment formula. And, yet, less than one-third of the occurrences of the word *pl̄eroō* in the New Testament fit this category. The mere presence of *pl̄eroō* is not enough to indicate fulfillment of prophecy. "Clearly, to apply our English denotations of the word 'fulfill' to its occurrences in the biblical text will sometimes result in an interpretation unintended by its author."[4] But even if the word *pl̄eroō* by itself cannot be used to determine the fulfillment of biblical prophecy, can we be on more solid interpretive ground when the word occurs as part of a "fulfillment formula"? Again, the answer is, not necessarily.

The Use of Plēroō in a "Fulfillment Formula"
Does Not Always Refer to Fulfilled Prophecy

Though the presence of the word *pl̄eroō* by itself may not point to the fulfillment of Bible prophecy, some believe that the occurrence of *pl̄eroō* within a "fulfillment formula" does indicate prophetic fulfillment.[5] Certainly the use of *pl̄eroō* in a fulfillment formula must be given close examination. In fact, twelve variations of a fulfillment formula employing *pl̄eroō* occur in the New Testament. Each of these needs to be stated briefly (in my own translation):

1. "In order that it might be fulfilled [*pl̄eroō*] which was spoken by the Lord through the prophet" (Matt. 1:22; 2:15).
2. "In order that it might be fulfilled [*pl̄eroō*] which was spoken by _____" (Matt. 4:14 [Isa.]; 21:4 [the prophet]; 27:35 [the prophet].
3. "Then was fulfilled [*pl̄eroō*] that which was spoken by Jeremiah" (Matt. 2:17; 27:9).

4. "So that it might be fulfilled [*plēroō*] which was spoken by _____" (Matt. 2:23 [the prophets]; 8:17 [Isa.]; 12:17 [Isa.]; 13:35 [the prophet]).

5. "In order that might be fulfilled [*plēroō*] the Scriptures" (Matt. 26:56; Mark 14:49).

6. "And was fulfilled [*plēroō*] the Scripture" (Mark 15:28; James 2:23).

7. "Today is fulfilled [*plēroō*] this Scripture" (Luke 4:21).

8. "That may be fulfilled [*plēroō*] all things that have been written" (Luke 21:22; 24:44).

9. "In order that the word of _____ might be fulfilled [*plēroō*]" (John 12:38 [the prophet]; 18:32 [Jesus]).

10. "In order that the Scriptures might be fulfilled [*plēroō*]" (John 13:18; 17:12; 19:24; 19:36).

11. "In order that might be fulfilled [*plēroō*] the word that has been written/that he said" (John 15:25; 18:9).

12. "It was necessary to have been fulfilled [*plēroō*] this Scripture" (Acts 1:16).

It is obvious in these formula statements that the New Testament writer links the life of Christ with the Old Testament. But does every occurrence of such a formula point to the fulfillment of prophecy? In several instances the answer seems to be no.[6]

Hosea 11:1 was not a prediction of Jesus Christ. In Hosea 11:1–2 the prophet continues God's indictment against the nation of Israel for her sin by contrasting God's faithfulness with Israel's rebellion. "When Israel was a child, I loved him, and out of Egypt I called my son. But the more I called Israel, the further they went from me. They sacrificed to the Baals and they burned incense to images" (Hos. 11:1–2). The calling of Israel "from Egypt" is a reference to the Exodus—an event that occurred more than 700 years before Hosea penned his message. In Hosea's indictment Israel was the *disobedient son* who departed from God to serve idols. Three verses later Hosea completes his word picture by announcing God's judgment on this disobedient nation. "Will they not return to Egypt and will not Assyria rule over them because they refuse to repent?" (Hos. 11:5).

The only reason many have viewed Hosea 11:1 as some sort of veiled prophecy is the "fulfillment formula" Matthew uses when he quotes this verse in Matthew 2:15. Joseph, Mary, and the young child left Bethlehem and fled to Egypt when it was revealed to them that

Herod planned to kill Christ. They stayed in Egypt "until the death of Herod. And so was fulfilled [*plēroō*] what the Lord had said through the prophet: 'Out of Egypt I called my son.'" Does the use of (*plēroō*) with a fulfillment formula in this passage demand that one find some hidden prophecy in Hosea 11:1?

When God calls His son "out of Egypt" in Hosea 11 the event is history, not prophecy. Hosea is looking back 700 years to the first Exodus from Egypt. He is not looking forward 700 years to Christ's return from Egypt following the death of Herod. How then is Matthew using *plēroō* with his fulfillment formula? The answer is found both in an understanding of the range of meanings for (*plēroō*) and in an understanding of the argument of the book of Matthew.

Matthew wrote to the Jews, and much of his gospel is devoted to proving to his Jewish readers that Jesus Christ is their Messiah. In the first part of the book Matthew draws a series of parallels between Jesus and the nation Israel. In effect, Matthew seeks to prove that Jesus is the Messiah because he is the embodiment of all that the nation of Israel as God's son should have been. He succeeded where the nation as a whole had failed. The parallels can be charted as follows:

Israel's History	Christ's Life	Point of Comparison/Contrast
Israel was called from Egypt as a "child" (Hos. 11:1).	Christ was called from Egypt as a child (Matt. 2:15).	Israel was a disobedient child; Christ was not (Hos. 11:2–5).
Israel was "baptized" as a nation in the Red Sea (Ex. 14; 1 Cor. 10:1–2).	Christ was baptized by John the Baptist (Matt. 3).	Israel disobeyed God within three days after the Red Sea baptism (Ex. 15:22–26). Christ was "my Son, whom I love; with him I am well pleased" (Matt. 3:17).
Israel went into the wilderness where she was tempted for forty years (Exodus–Numbers).	Christ went into the wilderness where He was tempted for forty days (Matt. 4).	Israel failed her temptations and incurred God's wrath; Christ successfully passed every temptation.
Israel went to Mount Sinai to receive God's law (Ex. 19ff).	Christ "went up on a mountainside" and explained the law (Matt. 5–7).	Israel broke the law before Moses could carry the tablets down from the mountain (Ex. 32); Christ said, "Do not think that I have come to abolish the Law or the Prophets; I have not come to abolish them but to fulfill them" (Matt. 5:17).

The mere presence of *plēroō* in Matthew 2:15 does not require one to force a prophecy of Christ into Hosea 11:1. One must first look at Hosea 11:1 to see what the passage means in its own context. Only after determining the meaning in its context should one go to the New Testament to see how the writer is using the passage. Matthew used Hosea 11:1 because his purpose was to show that Christ succeeded as God's Son while Israel failed as God's son. Christ "realized the full potential" or "filled completely" God's designs for Israel when He called them from Egypt. Thus, Matthew was not using *plēroō* to point out a veiled prophecy in Hosea. Instead, he was looking back and focusing on the contrasts between Israel's failures as God's son and Christ's obedience as God's Son. Hosea had only Israel in view in his prophecy, and even though Matthew uses *plēroō* with a fulfillment formula, Matthew's quote of Hosea 11:1 does not make the passage a predictive prophecy.

Jeremiah 31:15 is not a prediction of the death of babies in Bethlehem. A second example of *plēroō* being used in a fulfillment formula that is not referring to the fulfillment of a predictive prophecy can be found in Matthew 2. Matthew records the death of the babies in Bethlehem at the hand of Herod's soldiers and concludes, "Then what was said through the prophet Jeremiah was fulfilled: 'A voice is heard in Ramah, weeping and great mourning, Rachel weeping for her children and refusing to be comforted because they are no more'" (Matt. 2:17–18). But was the death of babies in Bethlehem the fulfillment of Jeremiah's prophecy?

Jeremiah 30–33 are four chapters of hope in a book of judgment. In these four chapters the prophet looks beyond the coming Babylonian captivity and offers hope to the people of Israel. Jeremiah 31 records the prophet's announcement that God will make "a new covenant with the house of Israel and with the house of Judah" (Jer. 31:31). But before the announcement of the new covenant Jeremiah describes God's plans to restore the land of Israel and to gather His people from captivity.

In Jeremiah 31:15 Jeremiah records the sad lament in the city of Ramah as he describes "Rachel weeping for her children." Ramah is located approximately six miles north of Jerusalem on the main internal roadway that snakes along the spiny ridge of Israel from Shechem in the north to Beersheba in the south. After Jerusalem fell to the Babylonians Ramah became the staging area where prisoners were brought for processing before being "carried into exile to Babylon." Jeremiah had been brought in chains to Ramah after the fall of Jerusalem (Jer. 40:1). His use of "Rachel" was both poignant and appropriate. The city of Ramah was in the tribal allotment of Benjamin (Josh. 18:25)—one of the two children born to Rachel. And Rachel died giving birth to Benjamin, just after she breathed his name, Ben-Obi, "son of my trouble" (Gen. 35:18).

Jeremiah personifies as "Rachel" the older women of Judah who were deemed too old, too weak, or too poor to be of use in captivity. These were the individuals whom the Babylonians chose not to carry into exile (Jer. 40:7). But these women were overcome with grief instead of gratitude because they watched their own sons being carried off to Babylon in chains. That is the "mourning and great weeping" described by Jeremiah.

Jeremiah's purpose in chapter 31 is to offer hope to those who have seen their sons carried into captivity. Thus, after describing their sorrow, Jeremiah offers assurance: "This is what the Lord says: 'Refrain your voice from weeping and your eyes from tears, for your work will be rewarded,' declares the Lord. 'They will return from the land of the enemy. So there is hope for your future,' declares the Lord. 'Your children will return to their own land'" (vv. 16–17). In Jeremiah 31 the prophet is clearly referring to mothers who are weeping as their children are taken into captivity. And the point of the passage is a message of hope—those taken away will be returned.

Is Jeremiah 31:15 even a remote prediction of the death of babies in Bethlehem? If so, it's a prophecy that names the wrong city (Ramah versus Bethlehem), the wrong action (captivity versus death), and the wrong outcome (return from captivity versus no return from death). The only point of comparison is the sadness felt in the hearts of both groups of women. And it is that point of comparison that Matthew is making by using *plēroō*. He is *not* saying that Jeremiah was predicting the death of babies in Bethlehem. Instead, he is indicating that the measure of grief experienced by the women in Ramah who watched their sons being carried off into captivity was "seen in full" or "filled completely" by the women in Bethlehem who watched their sons being slaughtered. Once again, even though Matthew uses *plēroō* with a fulfillment formula, the passage being quoted was not a prediction being fulfilled at that time.

THE USE OF ANALOGOUS LANGUAGE
DOES NOT ALWAYS INDICATE FULFILLMENT

If the word *fulfill* (either by itself or in a fulfillment formula) cannot serve as an absolute guide for determining when a prophecy is fulfilled, what other means are available? Some have looked for analogous language to help determine prophetic fulfillment. That is, some feel that when a New Testament writer applies Old Testament language to the church or to current realities, he is pointing to the fulfillment of those Old Testament prophecies or types. A. Berkeley Mickelsen provides an excellent summary of this position when he uses Ezekiel 40–48 as an example to show how the passage is fulfilled today.

> Because of what God did in Christ, there will be no return to the shadows, but rather there will be the worship of God on a transcendently higher level. Holding to the one people of God in the New Testament consisting of Jew and Gentile (see Rom. 11; the words *laos, oikos, doulos, hagios;* Matt. 21:43 and I Peter 2:9–10; Eph. 2:1–3:6), an interpreter should apply these materials to the worship of God in the time of consummation. The twelve tribes stand for the unity of the people of God. If the interpreter keeps a *literal* base (e.g. worship = worship; Palestine = Palestine) while at the same time he makes use of *the principles of correspondence and analogy* (People of God = Jew and Gentile in Christ, cf. Ezek. 43:7–9 which speaks of God's dwelling [*shaken*] in the midst of the children of Israel for ever, with Rev. 7:9, 15 which speaks of God's dwelling [*skeno-o*] with those from all nations and tribes and peoples and tongues; Rev. 21:3 which speaks of the tabernacle of God *with men*: "And He will dwell [*skeno-o*] *with them*"), he will achieve very satisfactory results.[7]

One major premise that lies behind the use of analogous language as a means for determining the fulfillment of prophecy is the unity of the people of God. Those who practice fulfillment by analogy insist that promises made to the people of God in the Old Testament (Israel) can find fulfillment in the people of God in the New Testament (the church).

> The New Testament unfolds the significance of the new people of God, the body of Christ, his Church. Any treatment of prophecy which ignores what Jesus Christ did in breaking down the barrier between Jews and Gentiles or tries to reconstruct that barrier has dismissed one of the key effects of Jesus' atoning death. The house or household of God is a structure of great importance.[8]

No one questions the fact that the New Testament uses much analogous language. Paul tells the Ephesians that the church is rising "to become a holy temple" (Eph. 2:21). Peter tells his readers that they, "like living stones, are being built into a spiritual house to be a holy priesthood, offering spiritual sacrifices acceptable to God through Jesus Christ" (1 Peter 2:5). The list of examples could be expanded, but these serve as good illustrations of the type of analogous language employed by the New Testament writers. However, the key question remains: By using such language did the writers intend for the readers to assume that Old Testament prophecies concerning Israel are now being fulfilled in the church?

Analogies Can Indicate
More Than Fulfillment of Prophecy

The chief fallacy in identifying fulfillment through the use of analogous language is the assumption that a New Testament writer can only use an analogy to indicate fulfillment. But people use quotations, comparisons, or analogies for a large number of reasons. "People who write books or magazine articles often quote other writings. They do it to support what they themselves are saying, to give an example or illustration of their viewpoint, to summarize their points, or to make comparisons or parallels between their material and that of someone else."[9] In what sense are the New Testament writers using analogies from the Old Testament?

The apostle Paul uses several analogies or illustrations in his epistle to the Ephesians. In Ephesians 2:21 he refers to the church as a "holy temple." But what indication in the context is there that Paul intends his readers to understand this as the fulfillment of Ezekiel's prophecy of a glorious temple? Earlier in the chapter Paul alludes to the fact that Christ "has destroyed the barrier, the dividing wall of hostility" (Eph. 2:14). The barrier described by Paul was a physical one that stood in the outer court of Herod's Temple in Jerusalem. This barrier had inscriptions in Latin and Greek that warned Gentiles not to enter the inner courts of the Temple. "No man of another nation to enter within the fence and enclosure round the temple. And whoever is caught will have himself to blame that his death ensues."[10] Paul uses the physical barrier in Herod's Temple as an analogy of what Christ has done in allowing Gentiles equal status with Jews in gaining full access into God's presence. But this barrier did not exist in Solomon's Temple, nor does it exist in Ezekiel's detailed description of the future temple (Ezek. 40:17–19). Thus, Paul's analogy of the temple barrier comes from the Temple standing in Paul's day, not from Old Testament prophecies.

In Ephesians 2 Paul uses two analogies from the Temple. First, the wall of partition is broken down, allowing Gentiles and Jews equal access. Second, both Gentiles and Jews are being built into a unified temple of God. The first analogy came from Herod's Temple.

Is it not more likely to assume that Paul also based the second analogy on the physical Temple in existence in his day rather than on the future temple promised by Ezekiel?

One must be careful in reading too much meaning into an analogy. For example, Paul refers to the Body of Christ—composed of Jews and Gentiles—as "one new man" in Ephesians 2:15. But later in Ephesians he exhorts the believers to "put off your old self [man]" that is corrupted by sinful desires and to put on "the new self [man]" created to be like God (Eph. 4:22–24). In chapter 4 Paul makes a distinction between the kind of person one was before he or she came to Christ and the new way of life he or she is now to put on because of this relationship to Christ. The use of the "new man" analogy in 4:24 is so distinct from its use in 2:15 that the NIV translates it "new self" in 4:24. Yet the Greek phrase is identical in both verses (*kainon anthropon*). The point is that Paul can (and does) use analogous language in different ways—sometimes he even uses the same analogy in two different ways in the same book. We must guard against forcing Paul into a rigid mold where every analogy must be interpreted in exactly the same way. This is true whether Paul is using the analogy of the "new man" or the "temple." *The mere presence of an analogy does not automatically argue for the fulfillment of Old Testament prophecy.*

Analogies Must Be Interpreted in Light of the Author's Intended Purpose

The second danger in looking for "fulfillment by analogy" is the danger in focusing on one word or phrase to the exclusion of the New Testament writer's larger purpose in the book or failing to interpret any analogy in light of the author's larger body of writings. Paul's analogy of the church as a "holy temple" in Ephesians 2:21 is a good example of the danger one can face if he or she interprets an analogy in isolation. While it might be *possible* that Paul intended his readers to see in this a fulfillment of Ezekiel 40–48, is this consistent with Paul's other writings?

The one place where Paul gave a clear analysis of the relationship between Israel and the church as they relate to God's Old Testament promises is Romans 9–11. Paul had ample opportunity to share with his readers that the church had permanently replaced Israel and was now the eternal beneficiary of God's Old Testament promises. Yet in this crucial passage Paul maintains an ethnic distinction between Israel and the church and announces that God still has a future for Israel. J. Lanier Burns captures the importance of Paul's clear meaning: "In summary, if Jews and Gentiles are 'one and continuous' without ethnic distinctions, then there is no point in the urgency of the initial question about rejection and the progression to the future salvation of all Israel (v. 26)."[11]

Rather than looking for the fulfillment of Old Testament prophecies in Paul's use of analogies, it seems better to start with Paul's clear teaching on the future of Israel. "Israel has experienced a hardening in part until the full number of the Gentiles has come in. And so all Israel will be saved" (Rom. 11:25–26). Any interpretation of Paul's analogous use of Old Testament imagery must be consistent with his other clear writings.

Analogous language by itself is too imprecise to serve as a guide to the fulfillment of Old Testament prophecies. Does a New Testament writer's use of analogous language point to the fulfillment of prophecy or can the writer be alluding to the Old Testament for other literary purposes? Zuck identifies at least ten ways New Testament writers use the Old Testament.

1. To point up the accomplishment or realization of an Old Testament prediction
2. To confirm that a New Testament incident is in agreement with an Old Testament principle
3. To explain a point given in the Old Testament
4. To support a point being made in the New Testament
5. To illustrate a New Testament truth
6. To apply the Old Testament to a New Testament incident or truth
7. To summarize an Old Testament concept
8. To use Old Testament terminology
9. To draw a parallel with an Old Testament incident
10. To relate an Old Testament situation to Christ[12]

Of the ten ways New Testament writers use the Old Testament, only one relates to the fulfillment of prophecy. In the other nine the New Testament writers quote or allude to Old Testament people, events, and actions and use them to illustrate or illuminate their own messages to the church. These points of comparison relate more to the literary purposes of the New Testament writers than they do to prophetic purposes hidden in the pages of the Old Testament.[13] One cannot determine the fulfillment of Bible prophecy merely on the basis of New Testament allusions to the Old Testament.

THE HISTORICAL, LITERAL INTERPRETATION
OF THE PROPHECY MUST DETERMINE FULFILLMENT

The two previous sections explored approaches to identifying the fulfillment of prophecy that began in the New Testament. That is, each approach started in the New Testament by observing some type of correspondence between events in the New Testament and specific passages in the Old Testament. If the New Testament used the word *plēroō* in connection with an Old Testament passage or if it employed analogous language from the Old Testament, then each approach assumed that the Old Testament passage was fulfilled in the action, event, institution, or person being described in the New Testament. Whereas this approach seems to work in some instances, in others the Old Testament passage bears little resemblance to the New Testament "fulfillment" it is supposed to be predicting. The problem is that the word *plēroō* can mean far more than the "fulfillment" of a prophecy, and the New Testament writers use the word in a variety of ways when citing the Old Testament. In the same way the New Testament writers employ analogous language to accomplish a number of literary purposes, only one of which is to indicate the fulfillment of prophecy.

What then is the proper approach to discovering the fulfillment of an Old Testament prophecy? It is this writer's contention that the proper approach to discovering the biblical fulfillment of a prophecy must begin in the Old Testament. One cannot determine the fulfillment of prophecy until one first knows whether a passage is prophetic and, if it is, what the parameters are that will constitute a biblical fulfillment. The remainder of this chapter will offer some guidelines for approaching biblical prophecy.

Prophetic Literature Must Be Interpreted Using the Same Hermeneutical Principles Applied to Other Literature

The basic question to be asked when approaching a passage of Scripture is, What does the passage mean? That is, How does one determine the meaning of a text? Conservative evangelicals argue for grammatical-historical-literal interpretation for most of Scripture.[14] However, some change their approach when it comes to "prophetic" passages. This can produce a form of hermeneutical circular reasoning. Such individuals interpret Old Testament prophecies as if they are symbolic because they believe that is how the New Testament interprets the Old Testament text. But if the "fulfillment" has no clear correspondence to the actual prophecy, how is one to know that the

Old Testament was, in fact, predicting that specific event? How, then, is one to know when to interpret literally and when to interpret symbolically?

It appears that a symbolic interpreter determines that the New Testament fulfillment of a given passage must be interpreted symbolically by watching for the word *plēroō* in the New Testament or looking for analogous language. In other words, he assumes that a New Testament writer's use of *plēroō* or analogous language is "proof" that the writer is saying that the passage is now being fulfilled. With this proof in hand, he is able to pour the symbolic meaning back into the Old Testament passage.

A better approach is to begin with the Old Testament passage itself and to determine the meaning of the passage in its original historical context. Is the passage pointing toward the future? If so, to what is the passage pointing? What is the possible range of fulfillment from the perspective of the original audience? Several examples can show how this approach to fulfillment works.

The fulfillment of Genesis 3:15. One of the first "prophecies" in the Bible came when God cursed the serpent in the Garden of Eden following the sin of Adam and Eve. God said, "And I will put enmity between you and the woman, and between your offspring and hers; he will crush your head, and you will strike his heel" (Gen. 3:15). Whereas the first part of the verse could picture the antipathy that would develop between humans and snakes, the second part of the verse seems to look beyond a mere animosity. Instead of referring to all the woman's offspring ("seed"), God announces that "he" (an individual, not all the woman's offspring) will crush "your" (this particular serpent's) head. Adam and Eve would have understood this as a prediction of the serpent's demise by one of their offspring. The prophecy did not specify who the offspring would be or when he would defeat the serpent. As far as Adam and Eve were concerned this could have been fulfilled by any physical descendent beginning with the birth of Cain.

Further revelation could narrow the scope of meaning, but it could never substitute a different meaning. To do so might imply that God misled those to whom the original revelation was given or suggest that God is unable to communicate clearly to His people. From our vantage point in the progress of biblical revelation we know that the ultimate objects of the prophecy were Christ and Satan. Beginning with the killing of the babies in Bethlehem and extending through the temptations in the wilderness to the betrayal by Judas, Satan did all in his power to thwart Christ. The final "bruising of the heal" was likely the crucifixion of Christ. The resurrection showed the triumph of the Son of God over this Satanic foe. The "crushing of the serpent's head" describes the lake of burning sulfur where he will spend eternity in torment (Rev. 20:10).

The prophecy of Genesis 3:15 seems clearly to have its ultimate fulfillment in this conflict between Christ and Satan. Yet no New Testament passage uses *plēroō* to say that this was (or will be) its fulfillment. The fulfillment is determined by understanding the meaning of the prophecy in its historical context and then looking for the corresponding individuals or events that satisfy all the particulars of the prophecy.

One final observation on the prophecy of Genesis 3:15 is in order. Though most see the prophecy as being fulfilled in the conflict between Christ and Satan, one could come to a different conclusion if he or she looked for the fulfillment of prophecy based on the use of analogous language. At the end of his letter to the Romans Paul alludes to the prophecy of Genesis 3:15: "The God of peace will soon crush Satan under your feet" (Rom. 16:20). If fulfillment of prophecy is based on analogous language, then Paul would be saying that the "offspring" of the woman is the church, and the church (not Christ) is the instrument that will crush Satan. Was Paul announcing that the church would be the one who would crush Satan and thus fulfill the prophecy? The answer seems to be no. Even though Paul is obviously alluding to Genesis 3:15, he phrases the passage in a way that lets his readers know that it is God (not the church) who will crush the head of the serpent. Paul is stressing to his readers that the church will share in Christ's victory over Satan—but the church does not fulfill the prophecy. God crushes the serpent's head. In this case analogous language does *not* point to the fulfillment of prophecy.

The fulfillment of Zechariah 9:9. This passage lies within the first of two "oracles" that comprise the second half of Zechariah's book. The first oracle (Zech. 9–11) focuses generally on the first coming of the Messiah, whereas the second oracle (Zech. 12–14) focuses generally on the second coming of the Messiah.

In Zechariah 9:1–8 the prophet describes God's judgment on Israel's enemies. Some feel that these verses were fulfilled historically in the conquests of Alexander the Great. However, in Zechariah 9:9 the prophet announces the coming of Israel's king to Jerusalem. "Rejoice greatly, O Daughter of Zion! Shout, Daughter of Jerusalem! See, your king comes to you, righteous and having salvation, gentle and riding on a donkey, on a colt, the foal of a donkey." Zechariah wrote during the postexilic period following Israel's return from the Babylonian captivity. The last king of Israel had been torn off his throne and carried in chains to Babylon by Nebuchadnezzar more than seventy-five years earlier. No king had sat on the throne since.

Zechariah announces to Jerusalem that her king would arrive to bring deliverance. Yet the king would not ride into Jerusalem as a proud warrior on a war horse. Instead, the king would appear as the righteous and gentle ruler who would ride into Jerusalem on "a donkey, on a colt, the foal of a donkey." Zechariah's point seems to be that Israel's king would possess the ideal characteristics of righteousness and gentleness.

When one first reads Zechariah 9:9 it appears as though the king rides into Jerusalem on two animals. He rides on a "donkey," and he also rides on "a colt, the foal of a donkey." Most have understood this as a good example of synonymous parallelism in Hebrew poetry. The animal in the second line is parallel to (and identical with) the animal named on the first line. The king will ride in on a donkey, that is, on a young donkey (a colt). Hebrew parallelism is clearly attested, and this is certainly a valid understanding of the passage. However, it is also possible to interpret the two lines as synthetic parallelism to allow for the possibility of two animals being present.

In Matthew 21 Christ prepares for His triumphal entry into Jerusalem during the passion week. As they ascend the Mount of Olives from the east, Christ gives specific instructions to His disciples. "Go to the village ahead of you, and at once you will find a donkey tied there, with her colt by her. Untie them and bring them to me" (v. 2). Though Jesus rode only on the colt (Mark 11:2; Luke 19:30), both animals had cloaks placed on them and were part of the royal procession into Jerusalem (Matt. 21:7). The specifics of Zechariah's prophecy are fulfilled in Christ's triumphal entry into Jerusalem.

Matthew indicates that all the events of the Triumphal Entry "took place to fulfill what was spoken by the prophet" (Matt. 21:4). Zechariah's prophecy of a Triumphal Entry into Jerusalem was fulfilled by Christ. But do we know it was fulfilled because Matthew used the word *plēroō*? Mark and Luke both record the incident (Mark 11; Luke 19) but neither quote from Zechariah's prophecy or use the word *plēroō*. Would the prophecy have been any less a fulfillment without Matthew's statement? The prophecy was fulfilled because all the particulars of the prophecy correspond to the actual events that transpired on the day Christ rode into Jerusalem, not because one of the gospel writers used the word *plēroō*.

Genesis 3:15 and Zechariah 9:9 can be understood according to the normal principles of hermeneutics. The process for determining the fulfillment of both is (a) determine what each prophecy meant in its original, historical context and (b) look for a historical incident that corresponds to the meaning of the text. When the particulars of the text are paralleled in a historical event, then the prophecy is fulfilled.

Distinguish Between Meaning and Significance in Fulfillment

One of the issues that must be addressed in discussing the fulfillment of prophecy is the question of why New Testament writers quoted from or alluded to the Old Testament. In some instances they are clearly associating the events that transpired in their time with specific predictions made in the Old Testament, which means that these events were the fulfillment of Old Testament prophecies. But at other times the New Testament writers cite Old Testament passages that clearly have no prophetic import. For example, in 1 Corinthians 10 Paul draws on Israel's failure during the Exodus to provide lessons on life for the believers in Corinth. He even says that the accounts "were written down as warnings for us, on whom the fulfillment [lit., 'ends'] of the ages has come" (1 Cor. 10:11).

One way to distinguish between fulfilled prophecy and the application of God's truth to different audiences is to distinguish between *meaning* and *significance*.[15] The term *meaning* focuses specifically on the author's intended understanding of the text. A text has only one meaning.

> For the Lord himself will come down from heaven, with a loud command, with the voice of the archangel and with the trumpet call of God, and the dead in Christ will rise first. After that, we who are still alive and are left will be caught up together with them in the clouds to meet the Lord in the air. And so we will be with the Lord forever. (1 Thess. 4:16–17)

When Paul penned those words he had only one specific event in mind. The meaning of the words corresponds to a specific time when the dead will rise and those alive will be caught up into the air to meet Christ.

But while a text can have only one meaning, it can have many applications. *Significance* refers to the application of a text's meaning to various groups of individuals. As Virkler writes, "To affirm that scriptural texts have a single *meaning* in no way negates the fact that meaning may have a variety of *applications* in different situations."[16]

Paul's prediction in 1 Thessalonians 4 has only a single meaning, but it has had significance for believers throughout the ages. Why? Because the potential existed for the passage to be fulfilled from Paul's day till today.

New Testament writers draw applications from the Old Testament and apply them to the church. The Old Testament can have significance for events in the New Testament, but that does not mean that the meaning of the Old Testament passage is bound up in the New Testament events. Thus, Paul could relate Israel's failure in the wilderness to the church in Corinth because the events surrounding Israel in the wilderness held great significance for the Corinthian church in its struggle with sin. This is consistent with Paul's admonition to Timothy that "all Scripture is God-breathed and is useful for teaching, rebuking, correcting and training in righteousness" (2 Tim. 3:16).

Biblical fulfillment occurs when the meaning of a specific Old Testament prophecy finds its exact correspondence in a New Testament person, activity, or event.[17] If the New Testament writer looks back to the Old Testament and draws significance from the Old Testament for his specific audience, this is application of the Old Testament, not fulfillment of the Old Testament.

Recognize the Validity of Potential Fulfillment

Fulfillment of prophecy is sometimes conditional on the response of those to whom the prophecy is directed. God sent Jonah to Nineveh, and Jonah's prophetic message was very direct. "Forty more days and Nineveh will be overturned" (Jonah 3:5). Yet forty days later Nineveh was still standing. Why? Because inherent in God's message was the implicit promise that God could change the outcome based on the response of the people. "A divine prophecy of doom is not necessarily absolute, but—who knows?—may turn out to be conditional if it creates in the recipients a change of heart and life."[18]

A number of prophecies develop the idea of conditional (or potential) fulfillment. One of the most dramatic statements on potential or conditional fulfillment comes from God through the prophet Jeremiah. In explaining the illustration of the potter refashioning the marred pot, God says, "If at any time I announce that a nation or kingdom is to be uprooted, torn down and destroyed, and if that nation I warned repents of its evil, then I will relent and not inflict on it the disaster I had planned" (Jer. 18:7–8). However, this concept of potential fulfillment is not limited just to prophecies of doom. God also applies it to promises of blessing: "And if at another time I announce that a nation or kingdom is to be built up and planted, and if it does evil in my sight and does not obey me, then I will reconsider the good I had intended to do for it" (vv. 9–10).

God's fulfillment of blessings or cursings can be conditioned on the response of those to whom the message is given. In effect, some prophecies can have the potential for fulfillment at a particular time, but that potential may or may not be realized, depending on how the people respond to the message.

It is this writer's opinion that one example of potential fulfillment in the New Testament is John the Baptist. God closed the Old Testament with an announcement that a "messenger" would be sent to prepare the way for the Lord (Mal. 3:1). Then God identified the messenger: "See, I will send you the prophet Elijah before that great and dreadful day of the Lord comes" (Mal. 4:5). From the passage one could not be sure if Elijah would physically return from heaven to prepare the way for the Lord or if God would send another individual "like Elijah" to prepare the way for the Lord.[19] But God did announce that a messenger would appear before the final day of judgment to prepare the way for the Lord.

Before Christ's public ministry began, God sent John the Baptist to Israel. John was not the physical incarnation of Elijah. When the religious leaders asked him, "Then who are you? Are you Elijah?" (John 1:21), John told them that he was not. However, John had the *potential* to fulfill Malachi's prophecy concerning Elijah. Thus, Jesus could turn to the crowd that was following Him and say, "And if you are willing to accept it, he is the Elijah who was to come. He who has ears, let him hear" (Matt. 11:14–15). "'If ye are willing' (*ei thelete*) must not be supposed to mean that it does not much matter. That it matters very much indeed is shown by the concluding refrain, 'He that hath ears to hear, let him hear' (xiii. 9, 43). They are a warning against neglect of the fulfillment of prophecy."[20]

But did Jesus in fact say that John was the fulfillment of Malachi's prophecy concerning Elijah? The addition of the phrase, "if you are willing to receive it," implies that the answer is conditional. Stanley Toussaint provides an excellent analysis and summary of this crucial clause:

> He goes on to show the potential of the coming of the kingdom. The kingdom would come *if* they would receive it. The conditional particle "if" (ei) makes the condition one of assumed reality. It is certain that if they should receive it John would be the fulfillment of Malachi 4. There is scarcely a passage in Scripture which shows

more clearly that the kingdom was being offered to Israel at this time. Its coming was contingent upon one thing: Israel's receiving it by genuine repentance. Because of this John is not here said to be Elijah. He fulfilled Isaiah 40:3 and Malachi 3:1, but not Malachi 4:5–6 because the latter passage is dependent upon the response of the people. Malachi 4:6 says that he shall turn the heart of the fathers to the children and the heart of the children to their fathers; John did not do this. John is the forerunner of the King. He could be Elijah if Israel would but respond correctly. If John were Elijah the kingdom would be Israel's.[21]

John the Baptist's *potential* fulfillment of Malachi's prophecy of Elijah provides an excellent case study on the nature of biblical fulfillment. Several points are in order. First, neither the use of the word *plēroō* nor the use of analogous language are the basis for making John the fulfillment of Malachi's prophecy. Second, the correspondence between Malachi's prophecy and John the Baptist strongly suggest that the prophecy would be fulfilled when all the particulars of the prediction were met. John arrived (a) before the great and dreadful day of the Lord, (b) to preach repentance, and (c) before the Lord was revealed. Third, the fulfillment of the prophecy in John was conditioned on the response of the people. "If you are willing to accept it, he is the Elijah" (Matt. 11:14). However, Christ goes on to show that the people had *not* accepted the ministry of John the Baptist ("for John came neither eating nor drinking, and they say, 'He has a demon'"[v. 18]). Thus, all the particulars of Malachi 4:1 were not fulfilled in John the Baptist, so he was not the fulfillment of Malachi 4:6.

Since John did not completely fulfill the prophecy, we should then expect another prophet to arise who will. In fact, Revelation 11 describes "two witnesses" who will prophesy in Jerusalem prior to Christ's second coming. The fact that they have "power to shut up the sky so that it will not rain during the time they are prophesying" (Rev. 11:6) recalls the deeds of Elijah.[22] On the word of Elijah God withheld rain from Israel for more than three years (1 Kings 17:1; 18:1). These witnesses in Jerusalem are able to withhold rain during the time they are prophesying, which is 1,260 days—three-and-a-half years. God will fulfill Malachi's prophecy by again sending his witnesses before the "great and dreadful day of the Lord."

CONCLUSION

When is an Old Testament prophecy fulfilled? The answer must begin in the Old Testament. Before one can determine when a prophecy is fulfilled, one must first know *exactly* what is being predicted. The meaning of the prophecy must be determined within its original context. Later revelation can add more specificity to a prophecy (i.e., the "offspring" of the woman in Gen. 3:15 can later be specified as Christ), but a "fulfillment" cannot contradict the original meaning of a prophecy in its historical context.

Determining prophetic fulfillment by the use of the word "fulfill" (*plēroō*) is not an adequate approach. The word can mean more than "to fulfill a prophecy," and one can get into great danger by forcing a "fulfillment" onto an Old Testament prophecy just because the New Testament writer used the word *plēroō*. Even the use of *plēroō* in a "fulfillment formula" does not prove that the New Testament writer is indicating that a prophecy is being fulfilled.

Determining prophetic fulfillment by the use of analogous language in the New Testament is also an unreliable guide. The New Testament writers use many analogies. First, analogies may sometimes be based on current realities rather than on Old Testament prophecies (Herod's Temple as opposed to Ezekiel's temple in Eph. 2). Second, even if a New Testament writer alludes to the Old Testament, one must determine *why* the writer is making the analogy and *how* he is using the Old Testament. Most allusions to the Old Testament are not intended to show the fulfillment of prophecy.

The only safe approach to determining the fulfillment of prophecy is first to understand the prophecy in its original context. Then one must examine the New Testament to see if the prophecy corresponds to the later events that actually transpired. Biblical fulfillment occurs when the meaning of a specific Old Testament prophecy finds its exact correspondence in a New Testament person, activity, or event.

One must also recognize the validity of potential fulfillment of prophecy. That is, the actual fulfillment of an event can be conditioned on the response of the people at the time the event is to be fulfilled. The response of those to whom the prophecy is directed can determine whether or not the prophecy will be fulfilled at that time. Jonah's prophecy to Nineveh, God's prophecy to Judah through Jeremiah, and Malachi's prophecy of Elijah (and the coming of John the Baptist) are three prominent examples.

If one expects a prophecy to be fulfilled when all the particulars of that prophecy are met and if one allows for the potential fulfillment of prophecy based on the response of the recipients, then one finds the New Testament to be remarkably consistent. The coming of John the Baptist and Christ signal God's announcement/offer of the kingdom to Israel. But the actual fulfillment was contingent on their acceptance. Israel did not accept Jesus as their Messiah, and the Davidic kingdom promises were not fulfilled. Following the resurrection of Christ the apostles again offer the kingdom to Israel (Acts 2 and 3). Once again the offer was contingent on their acceptance of Jesus as their Savior and Messiah. Again Israel failed to respond properly and again the kingdom for Israel was postponed. In the book of Revelation God pictures a third period when the kingdom will be announced/offered to Israel. This time Israel will respond and Jesus will return to earth to reign as King, seated on the throne of David. The Old Testament prophecies ultimately will be fulfilled exactly as God promised.

Notes

1. Thus, an interpreter like Louis Berkhof (*Principles of Biblical Interpretation* [Grand Rapids: Baker, 1950], 153) writes, "Prophecies should be read in the light of their fulfillment, for this will often reveal depths that would otherwise have escaped the attention. . . . If [the interpreter] should simply ask, in such cases, to what event the prophet refers, he would be in danger of narrowing the scope of the prediction in an unwarranted manner." According to Berkhof's approach one should start with the New Testament references that indicate a prophecy was "fulfilled" and then read the fulfillment back into the Old Testament prophecy.
2. *TDNT* (Grand Rapids: Eerdmans, 1968), 6:290–98.
3. It is this meaning of *plēroō* that Moulton and Milligan (*The Vocabulary of the Greek New Testament Illustrated from the Papyri and Other Non-Literary Sources*, reprint ed. [Grand Rapids: Eerdmans, 1974], 520) see as the common meaning in the New Testament. They interpret the word as to "accomplish a duty."
4. Henry A. Virkler, *Hermeneutics: Principles and Processes of Biblical Interpretation* (Grand Rapids: Baker, 1981), 205.
5. Thus, Archer and Chirichigno (*Old Testament Quotations in the New Testament: A Complete Survey* [Chicago: Moody, 1983], 147), when examining Matthew's use of Hosea 11:1, write, "But Hos 11:1 seems to refer to the Israelite nation of Moses' day, whereas Mt 2:15 states that the return of the infant Jesus with Mary and Joseph to Judea and Galilee was a fulfillment of Hos 11:1. . . . It should be observed that fulfillment (*hina plēroō the to hrema*) implies that the Exodus deliverance of national Israel was a prophetic event for which the coming of the Messiah as personal Israel was the antitypical fulfillment."
6. So Roy B. Zuck (*Basic Bible Interpretation* [Wheaton, Ill.: Victor, 1991], 267) writes, "In these verses the Old Testament incidents or statements were 'fulfilled' not in the sense of prophecies being realized but in the sense that they were 'filled with more (a higher) meaning.'"
7. A. Berkeley Mickelsen, *Interpreting the Bible* (Grand Rapids: Eerdmans, 1963), 297–98.

8. Ibid., 301. Earlier Mickelsen wrote, "The unity of the New Testament people of God with those who preceded, while at the same time maintaining their separate identity in ways of approaching God, is part of the logic of promise and fulfillment" (p. 241).

9. Zuck, *Basic Bible Interpretation*, 260.

10. C. K. Barrett, *The New Testament Background: Selected Documents* (New York: Harper & Row, 1961), 50.

11. J. Lanier Burns, "The Future of Ethnic Israel in Romans 11," in *Dispensationalism, Israel and the Church: The Search for Definition*, Craig A. Blaising and Darrell L. Bock, eds. (Grand Rapids: Zondervan, 1992), 209.

12. Zuck, *Basic Bible Interpretation*, 260–70.

13. So J. Barton Payne (*Encyclopedia of Biblical Prophecy* [New York: Harper & Row, 1973], 128) writes, "The NT epistles thus repeatedly quote OT prophecies, though not in reference to their actual fulfillments."

14. Thus, Berkhof (*Principles of Biblical Interpretation*, 67–132) devotes a chapter to grammatical interpretation and a second chapter to historical interpretation. Mickelsen (*Interpreting the Bible*, 99–177) discusses "context," "language," and "history and culture" in his section on general hermeneutics.

15. Thus, E. D. Hirsch, Jr. (*Validity in Interpretation* [New Haven: Yale Univ., 1967], 8), writes, "*Meaning* is that which is represented by a text; it is what the author meant by his use of a particular sign sequence; it is what the signs represent. *Significance*, on the other hand, names a relationship between that meaning and a person or a conception, or a situation, or indeed anything imaginable."

16. Virkler, *Hermeneutics*, 199.

17. Zuck (*Basic Bible Interpretation*, 242) states it thus: "Fulfillment should be seen in accord with the words of the prediction."

18. Leslie C. Allen, *The Books of Joel, Obadiah, Jonah and Micah*, NICOT (Grand Rapids: Eerdmans, 1976), 226.

19. Thus, Pieter A. Verhoef (*The Books of Haggai and Malachi*, NICOT [Grand Rapids: Eerdmans, 1987], 340–41) writes, "In the history of exegesis many Jewish and Christian interpreters maintained that the historical prophet Elijah will return in person. . . . In the light of the NT application it is not necessary to expect the coming again in person of the historical prophet Elijah. He was introduced in our text as a typical representative of the OT prophets."

20. Alfred Plummer, *An Exegetical Commentary on the Gospel According to S. Matthew*, reprint ed. (Minneapolis: James Family Christian Publishers, n.d.), 163.

21. Stanley D. Toussaint, *Behold the King: A Study of Matthew* (Portland: Multnomah, 1980), 153.

22. The witnesses actually parallel the ministries of Israel's two greatest Old Testament prophets—Moses and Elijah. Not only do they withhold rain as did Elijah, but they also "have power to turn the waters into blood and to strike the earth with every kind of plague as often as they want" (Rev. 11:6). The picture of Moses announcing the plagues that devastated Egypt comes to mind. The association between Moses and Elijah is not surprising. In Malachi 4 the prophet, in describing the coming day of judgment, first exhorts his readers to "remember the law of my servant Moses" (Mal. 4:4). He then announces the coming of Elijah (Mal. 4:6). On the Mount of Transfiguration Moses and Elijah appear with Christ (Matt. 17:3).

In defining the doctrine of the kingdom, it is important to observe that the Scriptures themselves give a detailed description of various spheres of kingdom, including the universal kingdom where God rules over all creation, the kingdom of God revealing God's rule over moral creatures (such as holy angels and elect human beings), the kingdom of David, the present mystery form of the kingdom, and the millennial kingdom. Each of these spheres is distinct as described in the Scriptures. Ignoring scriptural distinctions leads to erroneous conclusions in the doctrine of the kingdom and confuses our understanding of God's promises.

4

BIBLICAL KINGDOMS COMPARED AND CONTRASTED

John F. Walvoord

T he concept of a divine rule over the affairs of the world is a major doctrine of the Bible and is assumed or stated from Genesis to Revelation. Such a concept is in keeping with the doctrine of the sovereignty of God and the infinite attributes of God, who is all-powerful, all-wise, who controls human history, and who ultimately will bring all creation and its creatures into subjection to Himself.

The proper place to begin this study is to analyze how the Scriptures use the concept of a kingdom and what is meant by it. Many works on the divine kingdom ignore the important biblical background that describes the precise character of God's government of the world. Although there is general agreement among orthodox scholars that God is sovereign, varied interpretations of the divine kingdom affect the total historic and prophetic understanding of Scripture, producing a wide range in the statement of the doctrine.[1]

It is imperative that our doctrine of the divine kingdom be based upon Scripture. One must begin with the conviction that the Bible is inspired of God and is accurate in its revelation of spiritual truth. Until there is agreement that the Bible is authoritative, there can be no agreement on the doctrine of the kingdom.

The main concept of the kingdom is quite simple. A *kingdom* is a rule by a king (or other ruler) who exerts his authority over people and often over a territory. In the scriptural concept of kingdom, God may be king in every sense of the term without necessarily forcing recognition of this from the human race. It is, therefore, essential to examine what the Scriptures themselves have to say about the various forms of the divine kingdom.

THE BIBLICAL CONCEPT OF A DIVINE KINGDOM

The kingdom idea is, of course, illustrated in every political government. Beginning with Noah, human government was authorized by God (Gen. 9:9). Biblical illustrations abound, such as the major empires of the past—Egypt, Assyria, Babylon, Medo-Persia, Greece, and Rome. Many smaller kingdoms also are recognized. These are political entities with the power sometimes assumed by the king, sometimes achieved through battle, and sometimes granted by the consent of the people. Simply defined, a *kingdom* is a sphere of rule. Both the examples on a human level and scriptural references to different forms of kingdom provide insight to the concept of a divine kingdom.

A survey of existing literature on the subject of the kingdom of God reveals that many scholars treat this subject without paying much attention to what the Bible actually teaches on the subject. If a theology of the divine kingdom is represented as biblical, it must take into consideration that different spheres of government are revealed in the Bible, not only in human government but also in divine government. Because there is difference of opinion in theology concerning the historical past as well as the future, which is outlined in prophecy, major differences have arisen concerning the nature of the divine kingdom. In order to resolve these, we need to examine carefully what the Bible actually teaches on various forms of the divine kingdom.

FORMS OF THE DIVINE KINGDOM

The Universal Kingdom of God

In Scripture, God is often revealed to be the ruler over the entire creation, whether animate or inanimate. Having created the world, God by His infinite nature retains control over it, even though much of its operation is governed by natural law or even the action of moral creatures who choose a path of activity. Psalm 45:6 states, "Your throne, O God, will last for ever and ever; a scepter of justice will be the scepter of your kingdom." This government (kingdom) is declared to last forever, overshadowed by a just God who governs the universe.

The psalmist expresses a similar view in Psalm 103:19: "The Lord has established his throne in heaven, and his kingdom rules over all." Such a universal kingdom requires universal recognition. In Psalm 145:10–13, the statement is made, "All you have made will praise you, O Lord; your saints will extol you. They will tell of the glory of your kingdom and speak of your might, so that all men may know of your mighty acts and the glorious splendor of your kingdom. Your kingdom is an everlasting kingdom, and your dominion endures through all generations."

It is important to note the beginning, extent, and climax of this kingdom. It began at creation. God the Creator became supreme governor of all creation. It continues all through biblical history and prophecy and finally merges with the eternal kingdom of God in the eternal state. In Daniel 4:3 Nebuchadnezzar proclaimed, "How great are his signs, how mighty his wonders! His kingdom is an eternal kingdom; his dominion endures from generation to generation." What is true of the unlimited extent of the universal kingdom, and its beginning and duration, is not found in other forms of the kingdom.

The Kingdom of God

Especially in the New Testament, revelation is given concerning the kingdom of God. We may define this as "God's rule over all moral creatures, that is, angels and men who are willingly subject to Him." The kingdom of God differs from the universal kingdom as a kingdom because it distinguishes between those who are spiritually related to God and those who are not. Central in the importance of understanding this aspect of the kingdom is the statement of John 3:3 that it is necessary to be born again to enter the kingdom of God: "I tell you the truth, no one can see the kingdom of God unless he is born again." The kingdom of God includes all the elect of the human race (those who have been born again), as well as holy angels (Heb. 1:4–14). Although angels are not born again in the sense that humans can be, there was a point in time when there was a separation of the holy angels from the demon world, including Satan. From the time of that separation, Scripture seems to point to the eternal security of the holy angels, much as a believer becomes secure in Christ from the moment that he is born again—when he receives eternal life.

With this in view, it becomes apparent that the kingdom of God began with the creation of moral creatures (i.e., angels) and encompasses all history, including God's salvation of human beings throughout the entire past and future history of the world.

The concept of the kingdom of God is not entirely clear in the Old Testament. Obviously, under God's Old Testament rule many men and women were pious believers in God; but many others were not. The scope of God's divine kingdom was not revealed clearly until the New Testament period when Jesus Christ revealed grace and truth. "Grace and truth came through Jesus Christ" (John 1:17). Old Testament saints were born again (genuine children of God); and the concept of a kingdom of God extends back to the first believers, Adam and Eve, and can be traced through the godly Abel (in contrast to wicked Cain). The kingdom of God also exists into eternity, as stated in 2 Peter 1:11, even though it began in time, since the citizens of it exist forever in the new Jerusalem.

In the New Testament the term *kingdom of heaven* is also used. The great majority of biblical scholars assume that the kingdom of heaven is the same as the kingdom of God and usually dismiss the idea of a difference without considering the evidence. In Matthew 13, however, in the parables of the kingdom of heaven, some of the parables seem to imply that the kingdom includes a merely professing element. For instance, in the parable of the weeds and the wheat (Matt. 13:24–30, 36–43), the field containing both is said to be the kingdom of heaven. This would imply that there are those who are indistinguishable from true believers but whose true character will be revealed at the time of harvest. In like manner, the parable of the net (Matt. 13:47–50) indicates that the net symbolized the kingdom of heaven, including both good and bad fish, which will be separated at the time of judgment.

This concept of profession is never mentioned in passages on the kingdom of God. The usual reason given for Matthew's choice of the term *kingdom of heaven* is that there was a reluctance on the part of Jews to use the term *kingdom of God.* However, Matthew does use the term *kingdom of God* in five passages. And in all five of these cases, the kingdom of God (Matt. 6:33; 12:28; 19:24; 21:31, 43) is limited to those who are saved.

The concept of a sphere of profession alongside the sphere of reality, regarding salvation, is common in thinking today and also is found in the New Testament. Where Matthew uses the term *kingdom of God,* apparently he selects this term deliberately because it refers to the sphere of salvation.

Another argument against distinguishing the kingdom of God from the kingdom of heaven, of course, is that some of these "kingdom of heaven" passages in Matthew are parallel to passages in the other Gospels where the term *kingdom of God* is used. There is an explanation if the kingdom of God is subsumed by the kingdom of heaven. This usage does not prove that they are exactly the same thing. A person might refer to someone as from Dallas. He could mean the city of Dallas, Dallas County, or Dallas Seminary. Regardless of what was meant, the term Dallas covers these three concepts.

These arguments support the idea that there is a sphere of profession in the spiritual kingdom. However, distinguishing between the kingdom of heaven and the kingdom of God does not have any significant effect upon the doctrine of the kingdom or upon the overall relationship of the doctrine of the kingdom to prophecy.[2] George Ladd is in error when he attempts to make the kingdom of heaven a major feature of dispensationalism.[3] The concept of the kingdom of heaven is not a dispensational idea any more than is the concept of the kingdom of God. The kingdom of God is found in every dispensation; likewise, every dispensation has an element of mere profession without reality. Understanding the term kingdom of heaven is an exegetical problem, not a theological one, and should not be made more significant than it actually is. Dispensationalism does not depend on recognition of the professing element in the kingdom, nor does it depend on distinguishing between the kingdom of heaven and the kingdom of God.

As with other kingdoms, it is important to determine the beginning and end of the sphere of the kingdom in view. The kingdom of God began with the creation of holy angels and includes all human beings who will enter the sphere of salvation. The ultimate destiny of this kingdom is that it will merge with the everlasting kingdom in the new Jerusalem (2 Peter 1:11), which will be entirely composed of those who are elect angels and elect humans.

The Kingdom of David

One prominent feature of the Old Testament is the revelation of the kingdom of David. King David was part of the development of the theocratic kingdom in the Old Testament, wherein God was ruler over the people of Israel through appointed kings, the first of which was Saul. In contrast to Saul, however, who was demanded by the people with God's consent, David was selected by God. The kingdom of David is supported by the Davidic covenant (2 Sam. 7:5–16; 1 Chron. 17:3–15). To David it was promised that he would be the first in a series of rulers over his kingdom and his house, that is, his physical descendants; this kingdom would continue forever through a king who would come later. David found this remarkable, and God put it in unmistakable terms: "Your house and your kingdom will endure forever before me; your throne will be established forever" (2 Sam. 7:16).

Even though the Davidic kingdom was an outgrowth of the theocratic program, it began with David. Included in the sphere of rule of the Davidic throne were all the people living within the geographic bounds of Israel, which probably included some foreigners. This kingdom was not limited to those who were born again and thus was not soteriological.

Almost all conservative expositors agree that Christ is the appointed one who will fulfill the Davidic covenant, but there are many differences of opinion in the eschatological systems of the interpreters as to how this covenant is fulfilled. These differences have led to considerable controversy over the exact character of the fulfillment of the Davidic promise.

The Kingdom in Its Mystery Form

When Christ began His public ministry, it was natural for the children of Israel to ask whether this was the predicted kingdom of the Old Testament. There seems to have been a universal lack of comprehension that there were two comings of Christ and that His first coming had to do with suffering and death and His second coming with a glorious reign (1 Peter 1:10–12). The disciples and the people of Israel who put their trust in Christ, as recorded in the Gospels, fully expected that He would bring in the prophesied Davidic kingdom of the Old Testament. They expected that Israel would be delivered from Roman oppression and become the prominent nation that the Old Testament indicated. Matthew, writing after the death, resurrection, and ascension of Christ, explained why Christ did not bring in the prophesied Davidic kingdom. His answer is that in the present age, before the second coming and since the first coming of Christ, another form of the kingdom is being established that was not clearly revealed in the Old Testament, namely, a mystery form of the kingdom. This is detailed in chapter 13 of Matthew's record.

The New Testament designates as a "mystery" a truth that was not revealed in the Old Testament but is revealed in the New Testament (Col. 1:26). Some expositors, even among those who are not premillennial, are beginning to recognize that the Old Testament in its prophetic outlook leaps the present age from the first coming of Christ to the events just before the Second Coming without dealing specifically with what is commonly called "the church age" or "the age of grace." This age is an unrevealed period as far as Old Testament prophecy is concerned, though some prophecies that deal with the after-Cross situation obviously relate to today.

Christ introduced His various revelations in Matthew 13 by using parables. When the disciples asked the question, "Why do you speak to the people in parables?" Jesus answered them, "The knowledge of the secrets of the kingdom has been given to you, but not to them" (v. 11). The mystery of the kingdom of heaven is that, although Christ is absent from earth for most of the time between His first and second coming, God will nevertheless have a rule over those who are followers of Christ.

The kingdom of heaven in its mystery form does not correspond precisely to any of the other kingdoms. It is not specifically the kingdom of God (though it includes the kingdom of God) because there are some in it who apparently are not saved. The kingdom of heaven is not totally triumphant, but it contains both good seed and bad seed, which grow together until the time of harvest (vv. 24–30). One parable indicates that this kingdom will grow like a mustard seed, a very small seed, to a tree (vv. 31–32). The kingdom of heaven is likened to dough permeated by yeast (leaven), which seems to represent evil (v. 33). Also, those included in the kingdom of heaven are pictured as some good fish and some bad fish, as described in the parable of the net (vv. 47–50). The kingdom as it exists today is a mystery that was not revealed in the Old Testament.

There are other mysteries, or elements, revealed about the present age that are outlined in many other Scriptures, and it constitutes a major area of divine revelation in the New Testament. In the present age Israel is blinded to the fact that Jesus is their Messiah but will have this blindness lifted when the Rapture occurs and the time of the fullness of the Gentiles ends (Rom. 11:25; 16:25; Eph. 6:19; Col. 4:3). In the present age the church is a mystery not revealed in the Old Testament as the bride of Christ (Eph. 5:23–32), in contrast to Israel that in the Old Testament is pictured as the unfaithful wife of Jehovah (Hos. 4:1–16). In the present age Christ indwells the believer, something that the Old Testament does not anticipate (Gal. 2:20; Col. 1:26–27). Christ Himself is part of the divine revelation of the New Testament because God was in Christ. Even though this was hidden in the incarnation process temporarily, He nevertheless embodies all that God is (1 Cor. 2:7; Col. 2:2, 9).

In the present age there is also the mystery of godliness (1 Tim. 3:16). Another mystery referred to is the lawlessness that will have its ultimate expression in the man of sin (2 Thess. 2:7–9). The seven stars of Revelation (1:20) also are called a mystery, something that the Old Testament did not anticipate. The final mystery mentioned in the New Testament is Babylon (Rev. 17:5, 7). Babylon, of course, was recognized in the Old Testament, both in its political and religious forms, but the truths explained in Revelation 17–18 were not revealed in the Old Testament. All of these mysteries demand extensive exploration and study.

The kingdom, in its mystery form, is not the universal kingdom; it is not the millennial kingdom; it includes the present form of the kingdom of God. It has its own special characteristics beginning with Christ in His incarnation and continuing until the rapture of the church.

The Millennial Kingdom

Both the Old Testament and the New testify to the fact that when Christ comes back in His second coming He will establish a kingdom on earth. According to Revelation 20:1–6 there will be a millennial kingdom. Belief in a future millennial reign of Christ on earth is limited to the premillennial interpretation of the Davidic covenant (and of Scripture as a whole). If we accept Revelation 20 at face value, as a prediction of the future, we also believe that the second coming of Christ will precede the thousand-year kingdom.

The culmination of the Davidic kingdom and fulfillment by Christ is stated in many passages of Scripture, including Jeremiah 23:5–8. Because this is such a strategic passage and covers so many of the issues determining the nature of the Davidic kingdom, it needs to be studied in detail.

> "The days are coming," declares the Lord, "when I will raise up to David a righteous Branch, a King who will reign wisely and do what is just and right in the land. In his days Judah will be saved and Israel will live in safety. This is the name by which he will be called: The Lord Our Righteousness. So then, the days are coming," declares the Lord, "when people will no longer say, 'As surely as the Lord lives, who brought the Israelites up out of the land of the north and out of all the countries where he had banished them.' Then they will live in their own land."

In this passage it is predicted that this future son of David will reign and prosper. And he will execute judgment and righteousness in the earth.

This will take place at a time when Judah and Israel will both be dwelling safely under the protection of the Messiah who is defined as "The Lord Our Righteousness." This will be fulfilled in connection with the second coming of Christ. This passage states that the Lord will reassemble the children of Israel from all over the world and that they will dwell in their own land in the kingdom that follows His arrival. It appears that this day has not yet arrived because the children of Israel are not dwelling safely; they have not been reassembled from all over the world from all the countries where they were driven; nor have they assumed their full possession of the land.

Ezekiel 39 adds the further statement that ethnic Israel not only will be brought back to their land, but that none of them would be left in the lands of their captivity: "Then they will know that I am the Lord their God, for though I sent them into exile among the nations, I will gather them to their own land, not leaving any behind" (Ezek. 39:28).

In keeping with this, we conclude that the kingdom of David is a political kingdom that ultimately will be ruled over by Christ, just as David ruled it in history. This kingdom will be populated by the people of Israel when they come back and possess their Promised Land. It is linked in time to the second coming of Christ and the ending of Israel's captivity in various countries around the world.

All agree that Christ is the appointed Son of David to rule over Israel. He is also the King of the universe and the King who reigns over the kingdom of God. In connection with His universal reign or His reign over the elect, Christ is active now. However, Christ is not ruling politically over national Israel today because most Jews do not acknowledge Him as their king and do not subject themselves to Him or His laws. This has become an issue in current interpretations of the kingdom of God.

Ultimately, of course, all forms of the kingdom are merged in the new heaven and new earth, except that God will continue to rule over the unsaved who will not be there. The kingdom of God will be operative over all the saints from all dispensations.

In summarizing the character of these kingdoms, it should be noted that they have a different beginning and a different ending and that they have different spheres of rule. The universal kingdom covers all. The kingdom of God includes only those who are saved of angels and men. The kingdom of David referred only to the people of Israel and, in particular, to those living in the land of Israel. What was true in history also will be true in prophecy, for Israel is going to be restored to its land.[4] These spheres of kingdom cannot be merged, but each constitutes its own rule, has its own special characteristics, and has its own subjects.

THE AMILLENNIAL DOCTRINE OF THE KINGDOM

The idea that prophecy cannot be interpreted literally, as advanced by the School of Theology at Alexandria, Egypt, in the third century, affected seriously the interpretation of eschatology. At that time, the principle of nonliteral interpretation influenced all areas of theology. In the following centuries, the church largely was able to rescue all major doctrines except eschatology. In the fourth and fifth centuries Augustine took the position that the Bible ordinarily should be interpreted in its normal, historic, literal, and grammatical sense; eschatology was a special case (i.e., eschatology could not be interpreted literally).

Amillennial theologians are not consistent, however, when it comes to interpreting eschatology. While the amillennial view denies that there is a literal future Millennium, those who hold this view ordinarily accept the idea that the Second Coming is literal and that heaven and hell are literal. In other words, they do not make all eschatology nonliteral, only certain areas. The reasoning followed by Augustine and later theologians in accepting amillennialism is totally inadequate in the present climate of eschatological discussion. It would be very interesting to see what Augustine would do with a modern work that defends premillennialism.

This inconsistent interpretation of prophecy has led to a nonliteral approach to the kingdom. Amillennial interpreters combine various forms of "kingdom" into one concept, namely, a kingdom of God. This "kingdom of God" includes the characteristics of the universal kingdom, the kingdom of salvation, the Davidic kingdom, and the mystery form of the kingdom. To this they added, of course, the millennial kingdom, not interpreting it literally but finding it fulfilled in the present age. Some amillennialists now are trying to find other explanations, such as the intermediate state or the new heaven and new earth, for the fulfillment of millennial promises. As with Augustinians, the main approach of amillennialism today continues to regard the Millennium as being fulfilled in the present age by Christ ruling in the heart.

In keeping with this general conclusion that all the kingdoms are phases of one kingdom idea, many hold that soteriology is the one factor that binds them all together. Accordingly, such interpreters conclude that God's main purpose in the universe is soteriological. Saving the elect becomes not only the purpose of the kingdom of God (which is the sphere of salvation according to Scripture), but also of the kingdom of David, the mystery form of the kingdom, and the fulfillment of the millennial kingdom in the present age. The various forms of kingdom all are reduced to a phase or aspect of God's saving program.

The Scriptures, of course, do not support the idea that God's only purpose in the world is to save the elect. The Bible reveals that He is manifesting His glory, His perfections, both in the natural world and in the plan of salvation. In His revelation concerning His sovereign control and guidance of the political empires of the world, beginning with Egypt and climaxing in Rome, soteriology is not the primary objective. Accordingly, even Reformed theologians who are amillennial often will concede that the actual supreme goal of God in creation was to manifest His infinite perfections. Salvation is obviously a major part of this revelation, but not the totality. The whole theory that all kingdoms should be reduced to the soteriological equivalent is not what the Bible teaches in its doctrine of the various kingdoms.

The concept that all the kingdoms are phases of one kingdom, thus failing to note biblical distinctions, is seldom supported biblically. Rather, it is assumed, and often without any attempt to adjust the definition of the kingdom to what the Scriptures actually teach.[5] Such an approach builds upon the assumption that the Davidic kingdom is basically soteriological and points to Christ. This eliminates any real physical, political kingdom of David if his kingdom is viewed as exclusively soteric. By downplaying the idea of a physical, political Davidic kingdom, the argument for a future millennial kingdom following Christ's second advent is weakened. It may be concluded that the amillennial understanding of the kingdom has been influenced, in large measure, by failing to distinguish the various ways that the word *kingdom* is used in the Scriptures, specifically not recognizing the difference between the Davidic kingdom and the kingdom of God.

THE HISTORIC PREMILLENNIAL VIEW

Dispensational theology has viewed the Millennium as a fulfillment of the Davidic covenant of Christ ruling over national Israel—a key feature in the fulfillment of God's plan. By way of contrast, the historic premillennial system does not necessarily see the Millennium as a fulfillment of political, spiritual promises to David with special reference to Israel, but simply as a future thousand-year period in the outworking of God's plan. The concept of Israel's place in the Millennium is minimized in contrast to dispensational premillennialism. Historic premillennialism is distinguished from amillennialism in that premillennialists teach that there will be a specific thousand-year period (the Millennium) following the second advent of Christ and occurring before the eternal state.

THE KINGDOM OF GOD
IN RELATION TO DISPENSATIONS

Many theologians have agreed that there are at least two major theological covenants—the covenant of grace and the covenant of redemption. These express recognition of the fact that God in eternity past determined the program of salvation and the death of Christ in relationship to it. Both covenants reveal God's central purpose in saving the elect and often are associated with what is known as covenant theology.

Theologians, however, have also recognized biblical covenants as distinct from the theological covenants listed above. The biblical covenants relate to God's outworking of His plan for the world in human history and set forth various rules of life for God's people. These often correlate with what are known as dispensations. There is, first of all, the rule of the Garden of Eden, where God gave Adam simple instructions to obey. The will of God, however, was rejected when Adam and Eve ate of the forbidden fruit.

Another example of a biblical covenant is found after the flood. A new covenant (Gen. 9:9) was inaugurated that introduced human government and capital punishment.

With the introduction of Abraham in Genesis 12, a series of great promises were given that is called the Abrahamic covenant. Abraham was told that he would become a great man, the father of a great nation. His seed, later identified as Israel, was promised to be a race descending from him; and God promised that all nations would be blessed through Abraham's posterity (Gen. 12:1–3).

Abraham is a great man in Scripture. He has been the progenitor of the nation Israel as well as some other races, and through Abraham have come the prophets, the writers of Scripture, the twelve apostles, and Jesus Christ Himself. Accordingly, salvation stems from the Abrahamic covenant, which continues to impact human affairs and programs in the world, but the fulfillment of the covenant requires more than salvation.

The Abrahamic covenant was followed by the Mosaic covenant, given through Moses to Israel following the Exodus. This rule of life had three major divisions: (1) the commandments, God's will in moral issues (Ex. 20:1–26); (2) the judgments affecting the social civil life of Israel (Ex. 21:1–24:11); and (3) the religious ordinances (Ex. 24:12–31:18). Together these instructions included more than 600 laws to govern Israel's conduct. There was no evidence that God required any nations other than Israel to follow the Mosaic Law, and He did not judge the other nations for not observing it. The Mosaic Law gave God's people specific instruction and guidance.

Unfortunately, the Mosaic Law itself did not bring spiritual growth to Israel. Instead, it revealed their disobedience. It taught them of their need for Christ, with the grace of God as the only possibility for salvation. In the New Testament the rule of grace is revealed more clearly. There was grace, of course, in the Old Testament because all forgiveness stems from the grace of God that, in turn, stems from the death of Christ on the cross for the sins of the world. In the present age, however, grace is not only a method of salvation (as it was in other dispensations), but it also is identified as a rule of life.

Premillennialists also believe in a future reign of Christ in the millennial kingdom following the Second Coming. Each of these dispensations, or rules of life, vary; and yet they all are related to a God who does not change His basic moral standards but does change the application and requirements extended to believers and to the world. The distinguishable variations in these requirements define a stewardship, or dispensation.[6] What God requires in each dispensation is revealed in the Scriptures.

This basic idea—progressive revelation that changes what God expects of man—is generally recognized by conservative theologians. Some object to the word *dispensations,* but they recognize that there are these different rules of life. Believers today do not go back to Jerusalem to celebrate the feasts or offer the sacrifices. They do not condemn a person for gathering sticks on Saturday, which under the Mosaic Law required a death sentence. In other words, it is impossible to interpret the moral code of the Bible without recognizing that though there are some things that do not change, such as salvation and basic morality, there are changes in what God requires of His people in different dispensations.

In the early twentieth century, C. I. Scofield, in his reference Bible, delineated seven dispensations, or rules of life. He also believed in the premillennial return of Christ. He believed that the millennial kingdom would differ from the Mosaic Law, as well as the present age, in its rule of life and that the millennial kingdom would follow the Second Coming. About this time, however, a good deal of controversy arose over the doctrine of dispensations that really did not relate to the doctrine itself.

The dispensational issue is important in trying to determine the doctrine of the kingdom of God. In order to bring clarity to a rather confusing situation, it first should be observed that dispensations are rules of life. They are not ways of salvation. There is only one way of salvation and that is by grace through faith in Jesus Christ. Even though this was not revealed in great detail in the Old Testament, it has been revealed more clearly in the New Testament (e.g., Rom. 4). There is no reason to believe that the rules of life in the Bible were in themselves ways of salvation, though obedience to these rules of life might demonstrate that a person is saved.

Dispensationalism (differing stewardships) actually is an ancient doctrine going back even to the first century.[7] In many theologies it is considered a good word, expressing the difference in rules of life for different periods of biblical revelation. It is unfortunate that the word itself has caused division and confusion so that some dispensationalists avoid it for fear of stirring up needless controversies.

In some circles dispensationalism even has been considered heretical. Because of this, there may be an attempt to redefine dispensationalism to make it less offensive to those of other beliefs, such as amillennialists and even nondispensational premillennialists. One of the tendencies has been to soften and to somewhat blur the distinction between the various dispensations. There also may be some associated with dispensationalism who believe that present theological research demands a change in some commonly held dispensational tenets.

It should be observed that there are similarities in the various dispensations. Even though Israel and the church have separate programs, they also have similarities. However, what is true for Israel in the past and for Israel in the future is not the present rule of life, and premillennialists, at least, defend the idea that the present age is not the Millennium.

In current theological circles it is being debated whether the definition of dispensationalism should be modified or changed. My colleagues, Craig Blaising and Darrell Bock at Dallas Theological Seminary, have attempted to present a new definition of dispensationalism.[8] Both Blaising and Bock assert that they accept the doctrinal statement of Dallas Seminary that affirms premillennialism, pretribulationism, and a future rule of Christ over the nation Israel in the millennial kingdom. They say that they are just as dispensational as ever, but they believe that we need to broaden the definition of certain aspects of God's present work.

Essential to their argument is their definition of the kingdom of God, but it is rather significant that they do not define this. This absence of clear definition permits them to move from one kingdom to another and to transfer attributes, situations, and revelation from one form of the kingdom to another. For instance, Darrell Bock, throughout his whole chapter on the reign of the Lord Christ never defines the word *kingdom,* except as God's rule over the earth, and in his discussion he freely moves from the universal kingdom to the kingdom of God to the kingdom of David and the millennial kingdom as if they all are interchangeable. He concludes that Christ in heaven is on the throne of David, arriving at this conclusion by ignoring the scriptural guidelines that separate these kingdoms and their spheres of rule.[9]

The subject is somewhat confusing because Jesus Christ is King over all these kingdoms; that is, He rules over the world. As Creator, He rules over the kingdom of God, that is, those who are saved. He is the future Davidic ruler of Israel, and He is the King of kings and Lord of lords in the millennial kingdom. He retains these rights and privileges as He operates in God's government. However, the error comes when these kingdoms are merged or blurred.

In modern life, spheres of kingdom have to be observed even though they affect the same person. For instance, if a person is guilty of breaking the law, the first question that must be settled is, what law? It could be a federal offense; if a person violated federal law, the case would have to be tried in federal courts. It could be a state law, which would have to be tried in a state court. It could be a law of a given city, which would have to be tried in the city courts. These are not the same courts. Each court would have its own sphere of influence, sphere of authority, and specific laws.

In my own experience, when I was president of Dallas Theological Seminary, I had certain rights and responsibilities based on the constitution of the seminary. However, at the same time I was chairman of two other nonprofit organizations. When I sat on the board of one of these organizations, I was still president of Dallas Seminary, but that was irrelevant to what I was doing because I had to be guided by the constitution under which I was working. In other words, Dallas Seminary did not become this organization, and this organization was not merged with Dallas Seminary. This idea of merging spheres of rule is a basic fallacy that has seemingly permeated this concept of progressive dispensationalism.

Just because Jesus Christ is the King over all these kingdoms does not mean that the kingdom of David has been inaugurated. In a sense, the millennial kingdom already would have begun if Christ were ruling on the Davidic throne. Though they admit that Christ is not ruling over Israel today, progressive dispensationalists want to identify the present work of God as a fulfillment of the Davidic promises. This, of course, is similar to what the amillennialists hold who also make the throne of David a throne in heaven today.

By contrast, classic dispensationalists regard Christ as the appointed Son of David who will reign over Israel but conclude that the actual beginning of His reign will coincide with the beginning of the millennial kingdom. Even David had been appointed king (1 Sam. 16:1–3) well before he actually began his kingly reign over Israel (2 Sam. 2:4).

Accordingly, classic dispensationalists feel that progressive dispensationalism, as it is called, is built upon a foundation of sand and that it is lacking specific scriptural proof. The "search for definition" that characterizes progressive dispensationalism actually ends without any clear definition. Nevertheless, progressive dispensationalists still do expect a premillennial return of Christ and the pretribulational Rapture before the end-time trouble. Likewise, they affirm that the full measure of Christ's reign over Israel will be fulfilled in the millennial kingdom. In a word, whereas the men represented by this new movement are recognized scholars who try to uphold fundamental doctrines of Scripture, they are, nevertheless, building their view on an inadequate definition of the kingdom concept in the Bible.

It is rather significant that in seeking responses from scholars for inclusion in the book *Dispensationalism, Israel and the Church*, three men were selected, none of whom was a classic dispensationalist. Naturally, these critics found this innovation a change in their direction (which they approved). It should be said, however, that many chapters in the book do not touch upon the definition of dispensations or dispensationalism itself, but upon peripheral matters, on which perhaps there could be some general agreement between dispensationalists and nondispensationalists.

CONCLUSION

In conclusion, it should be observed that the definition of *divine kingdoms* is of great importance and should be based on biblical definitions that fully recognize the character, history, and uniqueness of the kingdom being considered. Scripture observes these distinctions, and any disregard of what the Scriptures reveal will lead to erroneous conclusions.

NOTES

1. See Wendell Willis, ed, *The Kingdom of God in 20th Century Interpretation* (Peabody: Hendrickson, 1987).
2. See Charles C. Ryrie, *Dispensationalism Today* (Chicago: Moody, 1965), 170–73.
3. George E. Ladd, *Crucial Questions About the Kingdom of God* (Grand Rapids; Eerdmans, 1952), 193.
4. Ezekiel 47–48 teaches that each tribe will be assigned a specific portion of the Holy Land and Christ will reign over them as the Son of David.
5. Examples of this can be seen in the book by John Bright, *The Kingdom of God* (New York: Abingdon-Cokesbury, 1953).
6. See Ryrie, *Dispensationalism Today,* 29.
7. Consider the issues that the early church wrestled with in Acts 10, 11, and 15.
8. See the publication *Dispensationalism, Israel and the Church: The Search for Definition,* Craig A. Blaising and Darrell L. Bock, eds. (Grand Rapids: Zondervan, 1992).
9. Darrell L. Bock, "The Reign of the Lord Christ," in *Dispensationalism,* Blaising and Bock, eds., 37–67.

D ispensationalists have differed in their understanding of the church's relationship to the new covenant. Does it relate to Israel alone, to Israel and to the church, or to Israel with some spiritual blessings accruing to the church? In order to answer this question, first it is important to examine what the new covenant actually promised. The new covenant builds on the prior Abrahamic and Davidic covenants. The Abrahamic covenant includes the land promises, and the Davidic covenant promises national identity. The new covenant relates to the work of God in the hearts of His people so that they fully obey His word and receive the blessings of obedience. Second, we consider how Jesus and the New Testament writers described the new covenant. Do they indicate that the church fulfills the provisions of the new covenant as described in Jeremiah 31? Finally, we need to evaluate whether or not the church today demonstrates (either actually or potentially) the new covenant quality of life.

5

THE NEW COVENANT

John R. Master

E ver since Origen designated the first-century canonical writings the New Testament¹ many Christians have commonly assumed a direct relationship between the church and the new covenant of Jeremiah 31:31–34.

"The time is coming," declares the Lord, "when I will make a new covenant with the house of Israel and with the house of Judah. It will not be like the covenant I made with their forefathers when I took them by the hand to lead them out of Egypt, because they broke my covenant, though I was a husband to them," declares the Lord. "This is the covenant I will make with the house of Israel after that time," declares the Lord. "I will put my law in their minds and write it on their hearts. I will be their God, and they will be my people. No longer will a man teach his neighbor, or a man his brother, saying, 'Know the Lord,' because they will all know me, from the least of them to the greatest," declares the Lord. "For I will forgive their wickedness and will remember their sins no more."

Dispensationalists especially must examine and articulate this relationship, as it has implications for the distinction between the church and Israel and for the understanding and fulfillment of Old Testament promises.

What is the relationship of the church to the new covenant of Jeremiah 31:31–34? Within dispensationalism some have held to *two* new covenants: a new covenant for Israel prophesied in Jeremiah 31:31–34 and a separate new covenant mentioned in 2 Corinthians 3:6 and in the book of Hebrews.[2] These people believe that the two new covenants are distinct, as are the church and Israel.

Others have held to a single new covenant fulfilled by Israel, but with spiritual blessings for the church.[3] In other words, the new covenant is given to Israel but the spiritual blessings "spill over" to the church. The new covenant, in this view, is still solely for Israel, but there are "spiritual blessings" for the church from this covenant.

Many now hold that the church in some sense is "fulfilling" some aspects of the new covenant in the present dispensation. According to this view, the new covenant was given to Israel (Jer. 31:31–34), but the writers of the New Testament see a "fulfillment" of the new covenant by the church. This view generally suggests that there is, in the present church age, both an "inaugurated" and a partial fulfillment of the new covenant. In addition to the present inaugurated aspect of fulfillment of the new covenant, there will be a future "completed" fulfillment for Israel. According to their view, there are "already" and "not yet" aspects to the new covenant's fulfillment.

A dispensational understanding of the new covenant assumes that the New Testament writers do not change the meaning of the original prophecy, as correctly understood in its historical context. They may, however, provide additional information concerning "fulfillment" not found in the Old Testament prophecy as it was originally understood in its context.[4] Any one of the three views mentioned above fulfills this criterion.

But is the church actually fulfilling the new covenant of Jeremiah 31:31–34? Attempting to examine this question requires investigating at least three others: What did the new covenant actually promise in its context? How do New Testament authors refer to the new covenant? And how does the church age fit the description of the provisions of the new covenant?

PROMISE OF THE NEW COVENANT

The Abrahamic Promises

Foundational to any discussion of the new covenant of Jeremiah 31:31–34 is its relationship to the promise given to Abram in Genesis 12:1–3. The Lord told Abram to leave his country and his family. Then the Lord said, "I will make you into a great nation and I will bless you; I will make your name great, and you will be a blessing. I will bless those who bless you, and whoever curses you I will curse;

and all the peoples on earth will be blessed through you." Out of this promise to Abram come God's covenants with Israel regarding a land, a seed, and a blessing. The fulfillment of these subsequent covenants is directly related to the fulfillment of the promise to Abram to become a great nation. The land promise implicit in the promise to make Abram a great nation (Gen. 12:2), therefore, is subsequently confirmed by God's unconditional covenant (Gen. 15).

The Land Covenant

The promise of land for Israel (the Palestinian covenant) is often associated with Deuteronomy 30:3ff. If the land promises were based solely on the promises of God in Deuteronomy, these might seem conditional because of the conditional nature of the blessings and cursings section (Deut. 27–30) in which the land promise is found. Therefore, it may be better to use the unconditional, unilateral covenant God made with Abram (Gen. 15) as the basis for Israel's right to the land blessings.

Genesis 15, by contrast, gives no indication of conditionality. In fact, the very nature of the events described point to God's pledge of Himself alone to fulfill the covenant He made with Abram. God alone was active in the covenant ratification. Abram was in a deep sleep as God's presence passed between the parts of the dead animals.

The Davidic Covenant

Just as it was hard to conceive of the concept of a nation, in the culture of Abram's day, without a land, it was equally difficult to conceive of a nation without a leader. The Davidic covenant (2 Samuel 7:16; cf. 1 Chron. 17:14; Ps. 89) confirms the provision of a king, guaranteeing an eternal throne to a descendant of David. An eternal throne would seem to imply the need for an eternal ruler. Jesus, the descendant of David, will rule forever over the kingdom unilaterally covenanted to David by God (Matt. 1; Luke 1; Rom 1:3; etc.). The promises to Abram concerning both the land and a leader thus find their certainty of fulfillment in God's unilateral and unconditional covenants recorded in Genesis 15 and 2 Samuel 7:16. The Palestinian covenant (Gen. 15) and the Davidic covenant (2 Sam. 7:16) are God's subsequent unilateral and unconditional covenantal provisions to ensure the fulfillment of His promise of blessings to Abram (Gen. 12:2–3).

Along with the promise (Gen. 12) to make Abram a great nation, God promised that Abram's great nation would bring promised blessings to all the peoples of the earth. These two events are directly connected in the Genesis 12 promise. To simply say, without specific revelation, that the universal blessings to "all peoples on the earth" are independent of the national promise made to Abram and his descendants may violate the unitary nature and context of the promise to Abram. The blessings and cursings of Abram ("you," Gen. 12:3) take place through the blessings and cursings of the nation promised to Abram. The blessing of all the people of the earth is related to the promise of making Abram a great nation in his seed, the Messiah. Abram's being made a great nation is foundational for the blessings to the nations.

In order for Abram's people to experience the blessings of the messianic kingdom, however, they would need to obey God (Deut. 27–30). A simple reading of the Old Testament text shows that the Israelites were anything but obedient, and God did have to judge them finally by sending them out of the land. Has Israel's disobedience, in the Old Testament and subsequently in their rejection of Jesus as Messiah, brought about their being replaced in the program of God by the church? Romans 9–11 as well as a simple reading of the Old Testament prophecies related to Israel would seem to argue against this conclusion by speaking of a future for a redeemed ethnic Israel. If obedience was necessary and yet the nation's history was marked by disobedience, how would God's covenanted promises be fulfilled with certainty?

The New Covenant

The guarantee of blessings and the necessity of Israel's obedience are reconciled in the new covenant of Jeremiah 31:31–34. The third major covenant directly associated with the fulfillment of the promise made to Abram (Gen. 12), Jeremiah 31:31–34 specifically identifies the new covenant by name (v. 31). Allusions to it may be found in other texts, but the term *new covenant* is found only in this text in the Old Testament. This covenant is specifically said to be different from the covenant "made with their forefathers when I took them by the hand to lead them out of Egypt" (v. 32). The new covenant is thus different from and a replacement for the Mosaic covenant.

But what is to be different from the Mosaic covenant? In the new covenant the Lord said, "I will put my law in their minds and write it on their hearts" (v. 33). Under the new covenant the house of Israel and the house of Judah would obey the law of God. The new covenant would be different from the Mosaic covenant it replaces in that it would guarantee a unilateral divine change in its recipients so that they will obey the commands of God. The problem of the conditional nature of the land blessings is thus overcome by the promise of a divine work that brings about such an inner transformation that obedience results and the covenant conditions are met. The need for this inner transformation and the work of God was even mentioned by Moses in Deuteronomy 30:6, well before the revelation of the new covenant to Jeremiah.

In Jeremiah's prophecy, what "law" would be in their minds and on their hearts? Contextually would not Jeremiah's readers have thought of the commands of God given through Moses? Is there any indication that new commands are demanded or even implied? The term *my law* is the Hebrew word *tôratî,* which, to Jeremiah's audience, would have signaled the instruction God had given to His people through Moses and the prophets. The difference between the Mosaic covenant and the new covenant did not lie specifically in a difference in commands but rather in the people's response, which would, under the new covenant, be the work of God in the individual's life so that each would obey (*tôratî*). "From beginning to end the prophet stresses divine initiative."[5] Interestingly, there is no mention of a change in the laws of God, only in their actual obedience to them.

Although the new covenant is not specifically related to the ministry of the Holy Spirit, such an inference would not seem strange or unnatural. "The purport of Jer. 31.31ff., even though it does not speak of the spirit, is in effect no different from that of Isa. 32.15ff.; 11.9 or Ezek. 36.26ff., namely a new possibility, created by God himself, of realizing the will of God in human life. Zech. 12.10; Joel 2.18ff.; 3.1f. also point in this direction."[6] God intends to work in the lives of the Israelites so that they will finally and fully obey the commands of God that will lead to their entering into the fullness of God's blessings and the blessings of the Promised Land.[7]

Ezekiel 36 would further support a relationship between the new covenant and the Holy Spirit. In Ezekiel 36 particular reference is made to the Spirit of God (v. 27), although, since the term *new covenant* is not used in the Ezekiel passage, the connection with the new covenant of Jeremiah 31 is circumstantial (however generally, if not universally, acknowledged). The context of Ezekiel, though, relates to the children of Israel's doing the will of God, as does Jeremiah 31. Furthermore, Ezekiel 36:28 indicates that, when this occurs, Israel will be dwelling in the land, thus tying this promise to Israel's enjoying the blessings of the Promised Land.

In the Old Testament, the emphasis of the new covenant seems to relate to the work of God in the lives of the Israelites that will make them obedient to the commands of God as found in the Old Testament.[8] The people would do the will of God and enjoy the blessings of God. In particular, they would receive the blessings of the land that were dependent, according to Deuteronomy (cf. Leviticus 26), on covenant faithfulness to the Lord. The new covenant did not merely make such obedience possible; it guaranteed obedience, apparently through the ministry of the Holy Spirit.

The need for obedience on the part of the people to enjoy the promises of the kingdom given to Abram gives the new covenant an important role. It is the unilateral and unconditional covenant that guarantees, by the grace of God, that His people will be obedient. Thus, through the three major covenants God has taken the responsibility upon Himself to provide the land, the leaders, and the obedient people.

THE NEW TESTAMENT WRITERS
AND THE NEW COVENANT

How then did the New Testament authors understand the new covenant? Do the New Testament writers understand the new covenant in the same eschatological sense for Israel as a simple reading of the Old Testament text might suggest?

Since the new covenant in the Old Testament is so closely tied to the blessings of God for Israel and her obedience to the Lord, which was necessary for those blessings, how the new covenant is used in the New Testament has significant theological implications. If believers in the church are fulfilling the new covenant promises, how is this taking place? Has the church been incorporated into (added to) the new covenant with distinctive blessings? Has the church replaced Israel as the fulfillment of the new covenant? Were the Old Testament prophecies related to the land to be understood as spiritual blessings?

The term *new covenant* is specifically mentioned in the synoptic gospels (Matt. 26:28; Mark 14:24; Luke 22:20), in Paul's letters (Rom. 11:27; 1 Cor. 11:25; 2 Cor. 3:6), and in the book of Hebrews. Jesus spoke of the new covenant in the upper room, where He celebrated the Passover feast with His disciples just before His crucifixion. With their Old Testament background, the disciples surely would have viewed Jesus' mention of the new covenant in light of the Jeremiah text. Luke 22:20 says that the "cup," representing the new covenant in His blood, is poured out (cf. 1 Cor. 11:25).[9] Jesus identified His death and the shedding of His blood as the ratification of the new covenant (cf. Ex. 24:8; Heb. 9:16).[10]

The Gospel accounts of the Last Supper and the mention of the new covenant are related to an eschatological setting.[11] "For I tell you I will not drink again of the fruit of the vine until the kingdom of God comes" (Luke 22:18; cf. Matt. 26:29; Mark 14:25). "For I tell you, I will not eat it again until it finds fulfillment in the kingdom of God" (Luke 22:16). All three synoptic authors put the cup of the new covenant in this eschatological context relating to the "kingdom." Only Luke specifically includes the eating of the Passover in this same context.

In the synoptic gospels, the blood (Christ's violent, sacrificial death) and not the covenant (although the covenant is related to the blood) is specifically said to be "for" the disciples. The new covenant was ratified by Christ's death on the cross.[12] Yet because a covenant has been "cut" does not mean that it is fully operational. God "cut" a covenant with Abraham regarding the land (Gen. 15), which has not yet been fulfilled. There may or may not be a period of time between the cutting of the covenant and its realization in human experience, when it becomes functional.

Paul's use of the new covenant has similar eschatological overtones. In writing to the Corinthian church, Paul had to deal with problems relating to the celebration of the Lord's Supper. Rather than manifesting a unity of the body, the behavior of the Corinthians was promoting the opposite. They were already being judged (1 Cor. 11:30) for their selfish behavior because they failed to recognize this unity of the Body of Christ.

To remind them of the Lord's teaching, Paul cites Jesus' words to the apostles in the upper room (v. 24). Whichever manuscript tradition is followed, common to all is the phrase "for you" (*hupēr humōn*). Paul's quotation of Jesus specifically identifies the breaking of the bread as a memorial of His death for the believers in Corinth. The expression "for you," however, is not found in Paul's mention of the cup of the new covenant (v. 25; cf. Luke 22:20). The absence of this expression with the mention of the cup might indicate that the bread is a memorial specifically for them but that the cup does not relate as directly to them but rather to God's covenant faithfulness to Israel's future. Both the bread and the cup are to be used "in remembrance of Me" (1 Cor. 11:24–25).

First Corinthians 11:26 then combines the eating of the bread (Jesus' death) and the drinking of the cup to present a retrospective ("you proclaim the Lord's death") and prospective outlook ("until he comes") and to develop ideas Paul has just set forth (*gar*). The Lord's Supper looks both backward and forward, to what Christ has done and to what He will do. And, in fact, the actual participation at a common meal would reflect His present provision as they experienced, in fellowship together, the physical provision of God. In this way God's work past (death on the cross), present (physical and spiritual blessings), and future (the new covenant) would be in the mind of the believer celebrating the Lord's Supper.

If, in reading what the New Testament says about the new covenant, one understands the new covenant in the same sense as presented in the Old Testament by Jeremiah and Ezekiel, then the new covenant would have its future realization after the second coming of Christ to establish the messianic kingdom for Israel. When Christ returns, Israel will be transformed into an obedient people who will receive the blessings of God promised to Abram and his descendants in the Old Testament. This understanding would fit well with the future emphasis Paul spells out in verse 26 of 1 Corinthians 11 ("until He comes"). The church's remembrance would be a constant reminder of God's faithfulness to His covenant promises (an idea of apparently great significance in Rom. 9–11). God's faithfulness to Israel would be an evidence that God would be faithful to His church.

In 2 Corinthians 3:6, Paul speaks of being made "competent as ministers of a new covenant." As Wright notes, "It is now generally agreed that the overall theme of the section . . . is Paul's defence, not of his apostolic ministry in itself, but of a particular style or character of that ministry."[13] The major emphasis, then, of this section is not a supposed contrast between the Mosaic Law and the present dispensation of grace but is related to the style of Paul's ministry. Assuming that Paul is defending his "style" of ministry may shed some helpful light on the contrast between "letter" (*gramma*) and "Spirit" (*pneuma*) found in this verse.

This same contrast between "letter" and "Spirit" also is found in Romans 7:6, where the expression *palaiotēti grammatos,* translated in the NIV as "the old way of the written code," is used in contrast to "the new way of the Spirit." Here "the old way of the written code" does not appear to be synonymous with the Mosaic Law itself but with how the law was being used. In Romans 7, *palaiotēti grammatos* is viewed negatively. This misuse of the Mosaic Law contrasts with Paul's immediately following positive comments concerning the law. In Romans 7:6, Paul seems to be contrasting a way of service that is not based upon the ministry of the Spirit of God with a ministry based on the Spirit of God. This contrast is not simply an Old Testament (law) versus New Testament (grace) distinction because the Holy Spirit was just as necessary for spiritual life and service in the Old Testament as in the New Testament. The problem is the misuse of the law based on a misunderstanding of the law and not the law itself.

> This same perspective may be found in 2 Corinthians 3:6:
> But what about verse 6b? The contrast between 'the letter' and the 'spirit' (better 'the Spirit') we take in contrast not between the Old Testament law which is written and a spiritual religion which knows no law, but between the legalistic relation of the Jews of Paul's time to God and to His law and the new relation to God and His law established by the Holy Spirit and resulting from Christ's work. In the absence of the Spirit the law was misused and comes to be for those who misuse it simply 'letter' (cf. what was said above on Rom. 7:6b), and this law without the Spirit 'killeth' (verse 6c—cf. Rom. 7:10).[14]

Referring to 2 Corinthians 3:6, Smith simply says, "Clearly one should avoid interpreting *gramma* to mean Scripture."[15]

In 2 Corinthians 3:6, the contrast between "letter" and "Spirit" is a contrast between a ministry based on works and self-effort and a ministry dependent upon the Spirit of God. A ministry not related to the Holy Spirit always brings death, because without the Spirit there is no divine life. Paul and others were servants of a new covenant, and they were ministering in the power of the Spirit. That is why his "style" of ministry would have been different from those still teaching works as the key to a relationship to God. Paul did not reject the Mosaic Law, just its misuse.

Why then does Paul mention "new covenant" (note the anarthrous construction possibly stressing "quality" more than "identity") in 2 Corinthians 3:6? Is it a reference to the new covenant of Jeremiah 31:31–34? This association normally is assumed by most commentators. Often, however, this connection is made because "letter" is thought to refer to the Old Testament Mosaic Law. If "letter" does not refer to the Old Testament but to a ministry based on works, then the mention of the new covenant would point to Paul's divinely empowered ministry as opposed to a ministry related to the works of men.

The text does not say that the new covenant is now being fulfilled, only that Paul and others are the ministers (*diakonous*) of the covenant. The idea of being a "servant of" does not seem to point to the necessity of or even the implication that they are "fulfillers" of something (cf. 2 Cor. 6:4; 11:15, 23).[16]

Additionally, understanding Paul to be claiming fulfillment of the new covenant raises significant questions. If the new covenant of Jeremiah 31:31–34 promises the certainty of experiential obedience to the commands of God ("Torah"), why did Paul continue to experience sin (1 Timothy 1:15; cf. Phil. 3:12)? How could the Corinthians be so sinful if the new covenant were presently fulfilled in them? A better understanding may view Paul's claim simply that God had made him "adequate" (*hikanosen*) to serve, not fully and perfectly obedient. In other words, to take 2 Corinthians 3:6 as a statement of the actualization and fulfillment of the new covenant of Jeremiah 31 fails to deal adequately with the original statements in Jeremiah, with the immediate historical context and specific point of Paul's argument about the style of his ministry, and with the situation of the church's experience.

Some would continue to argue that the eschatological age has actually begun with the ministry of Christ. In their view, the promises of God are now receiving an inaugurated or partial fulfillment until Jesus returns to destroy all of the sinful aspects of "this present evil age." When Christ returns we will experience more fully and completely the blessings of the eschatological age. In the meantime, the new covenant of Jeremiah is functioning and yet believers are not yet fully sanctified. But such a transitional stage demands new revelation not found in the Old Testament contexts relating to the new covenant. According to the Old Testament the new covenant goes beyond partial fulfillment of obedience because even under the Mosaic covenant, by God's grace, there was partial fulfillment or obedience. How does a partial fulfillment of the new covenant now differ from the partial obedience experienced under the Mosaic covenant?

Of course, from a dispensational perspective, Paul was ministering in some sense "a" new covenant in that every new dispensation is related to a new covenant. Each dispensation is, in fact, a covenantal arrangement that establishes the stewardship requirements of each dispensation. The dispensations of "human government" and of the "Mosaic Law," or any dispensation including the "church age," involve "new covenants." By definition, a change in dispensations results from a change in stipulations (with the implied or specifically articulated blessings and cursings). The former covenant relationship is replaced with an updated and revised covenant. In some cases this involves the updating of the historical prologue section of the covenant as well. Every new dispensation involves some "new covenant," not only the present church age.

In Romans 11:27 Paul refers to the new covenant by quoting from it. The new covenant quotation is part of a composite citation of Isaiah 59:20–21a and Jeremiah 31:34c. Both of the references, in their Old Testament contexts, speak of a time when Israel's sins would be forgiven and the people would be obedient to the Word of God. In other words, both texts deal with a people of God (Israel) who obey the Lord, unlike the former disobedient generations. Both texts speak of the unilateral and unconditional work of God to bring this about ("I have put," "I will put"). There is a thematic and theological connection between these two Old Testament texts in their contexts.

While one must acknowledge the volume of discussion about the meaning of the term *Israel* in the expression "all Israel will be saved," the term in Romans 11:26 may be best understood to refer to a future for a redeemed, ethnic Israel. Understanding the text in this fashion would indicate that Paul is using the Isaiah and Jeremiah texts as they would have been naturally understood by the readers of the Old Testament (at least before the church age), to speak of a time of perfect national obedience and consequent national blessing. The fulfillment of the new covenant is associated with the coming of Messiah to set up His kingdom for His sanctified/glorified people.

To this point, the passages that refer to the new covenant of Jeremiah 31 follow a common thread. All refer to a time when the messianic kingdom is introduced and the people of God are glorifying God through their obedience, brought about by a sovereign work of God. Only if one asserts that 2 Corinthians 3:6 teaches the fulfillment of the new covenant of Jeremiah 31 by the church (which this author doubts), does the future fulfillment of the new covenant for national Israel come into question.

The book of Hebrews, however, is a major focal point in the discussion of the church's relationship to the new covenant. Besides the extended quotation of Jeremiah 31:31–34 in chapter 8, the author mentions the new covenant a number of other times (Heb. 9:15; 10:16–17; 12:24).

The historical situation underlying the book of Hebrews sets the stage for the use of the new covenant in Hebrews 8. Apparently the author envisioned the possibility of some of his readers returning to current Jewish practices. To do so, in the author's mind, would be to go backwards in their spiritual lives to something inferior. Judaism, as it was being practiced, was a religion of works and not of pure grace. The author argues that even the Mosaic revelation, upon which apostate Judaism was based, was only a temporary system to be replaced by the new covenant. The revelation through Jeremiah that there would be a new covenant proved that the Mosaic covenant was not God's final word on His relationship with believers. The temporary nature of the Mosaic Law proved that God had something better (permanent) for His people. Certainly the revelation of God in the coming of Christ and the beginning of the church age would have been in perfect accord with the temporary nature of the Mosaic Law.

The rhetorical skill of the author in his use of Old Testament citations is evident. Since the author is quite careful in exactly how the Old Testament is quoted, to take the statement of Hebrews 8:13 to mean that the new covenant is now being fulfilled is to make the author say something he has avoided saying. In chapter 8, the author does not specifically say that the Mosaic Law has been done away for all time. The author's point is simply that the Old Testament actually spoke of the temporary nature of the Aaronic priesthood and the Mosaic Law. Once the new covenant was announced by Jeremiah, the Mosaic covenant was "growing old" and was "ready to disappear" (Heb. 8:13).

The author of Hebrews also follows a line of argument concerning the priesthood. The Mosaic covenant and the Aaronic priesthood are connected, just as are the new covenant and the Melchizedekian priesthood. When there is a change in the priesthood, there must also be a change of law (Heb. 7:12). The Melchizedekian priesthood and the new covenant are coextensive. When the new covenant and the Melchizedekian priesthood have begun to function, there is no going back to the Aaronic priesthood and the Mosaic Law (Heb. 7:17–19).

Hebrews 5:5–6 seems to indicate that at the resurrection (cf. Acts 13:33) Jesus was appointed by His Father to be a priest after the order of Melchizedek. The Gospels indicate that Jesus' death meant the "cutting" of the new covenant, a point supported by the author of Hebrews (Heb. 9:15). The death of Christ, being the focal point of God's redemptive program for all mankind, is also the point in time when provision was made for the realization of Jeremiah's new covenant. The provision of the new covenant and the Melchizedekian priesthood go hand in hand and are connected to the death and resurrection/ascension of Christ.

Based on these observations, it is no wonder that many argue that the promises for Israel (i.e., Jer. 31:31–34; etc.) are being fulfilled by the church and that the church is understood to be the new Israel. If Jesus is presently functioning as the Melchizedekian high priest, the new covenant must be in operation (though the argument could be reversed). If this were the case, a return to an Aaronic priesthood and Mosaic Law program would be impossible for the people of God, even for a redeemed ethnic Israel. Therefore, many reject a future Jewish form of the kingdom.

Those who hold this view on the new covenant but who might allow for a future for a redeemed ethnic Israel would not see the redemption of ethnic Israel as a return to some form of the Mosaic Law because it would have been permanently set aside by the new covenant and Melchizedekian priesthood. Others would argue as follows: The Old Testament indicates that the kingdom for Israel is related to at least some aspects of the Mosaic Law; the New Testament teaches that the Mosaic Law is forever set aside; therefore, the promises given to Israel in the Old Testament should be understood as being fulfilled in some fashion by the church, the new Israel. This approach would "spiritualize" the fulfillment of the promises made to Israel and have them fulfilled by the church. They would further argue that the New Testament thus gives us a divine interpretation of the Old Testament text. The New Testament, in this view, reveals to us what God originally intended the Old Testament text to mean, and thus they would claim to be understanding the text in a normal or literal fashion.

THE CHURCH AND THE NEW COVENANT

It remains, then, to "prove" that what has been provided by Christ's death and resurrection is actually realized/operational and experienced by the church today. If Christ is presently functioning as the Melchizedekian high priest and the new covenant is being fulfilled, it seems that the most one could say about the new covenant being fulfilled today is that it is partial or inaugurated,[17] unless one adopted the view that the church fulfills the promises made to Israel.

But such an understanding presents clear problems. If the new covenant is being fulfilled, ought not believers in the church age to demonstrate a greater obedience of faith than did the Old Testament saints living under the Mosaic covenant (cf. Heb. 11; 1 Cor. 10)? As the New Testament indicates, believers today are not completely doing the will of God. Are the lives of today's saints more spiritual than David's or Jeremiah's? Paul's suggestion that the unnatural branches will be cut off if they fail to believe as Israel did in the Old Testament (Rom. 11:19–21) would seem to imply a potential parallel between the unfaithfulness of Israel in the Old Testament and that of believers in the present age. Would such unbelief be appropriate for believers experiencing the fulfillment of the new covenant?

Furthermore, the great commission's command to "teach" is hard to reconcile with the new covenant's promise that they would not need to "teach" under its blessings (Jer. 31:34). These observations argue against anything more than a partial fulfillment of the new covenant in the present church age. This may explain why the author of Hebrews does not specifically say that the new covenant is being fulfilled or that Christ is presently ministering as Melchizedekian High Priest in the church age. All Hebrews specifically says is that we have "such a" High Priest (Heb. 8:1).

The new covenant is cited again in Hebrews 10:16–17. The context of the quotation relates to the finished work of Christ. In verse 14, the author describes Jesus as having "made perfect forever those who are being made holy." The emphasis on the work of Christ is related to *making people perfect forever.* This would seem to point to a future time when the child of God is glorified and freed from all sin. At the present time the child of God is being sanctified (*tous hagiazomenous*), but the emphasis of Christ's death being focused on, in the context of Hebrews 10:16–17, relates to the "making perfect forever" (*teteleiōken eis to diēnekes*). The emphasis is on the finality of Christ's once-for-all work of providing for the perfection of believers in contrast to the present offerings of the Jewish priests (Heb. 10:11) and the failure to reach perfection under this system (Heb. 10:1).

This would tie in well with the eschatological emphasis of the new covenant found in Jeremiah and the eschatological association of the new covenant and Christ's coming indicated by Paul in Romans 11:27, 1 Corinthians 11:26, and in the synoptic gospels. In context, the Hebrews 10:16–17 quotation from Jeremiah would serve as the "proof text" that Jesus has provided, through His death, the perfection God had promised in the Old Testament. He has also provided for the future perfection of believers in the church age.

Hebrews 10:18 states that where and when this forgiveness is realized, there is no longer any sacrifice for sin. If this final consummation has occurred, then the idea of a sin offering mentioned in Ezekiel (cf. Ezek. 44:29; 45:17, 19, 23) is anachronistic if it is considered to be yet future. For this reason, many would argue that the Old Testament teaching on a future temple must be understood to be fulfilled, in some sense, in the person and work of Christ in the church, in order to avoid conflicting with the New Testament's teaching (which is given a place of priority in the interpretive scheme) about Christ's death as the final offering for sin.

In Jeremiah 31:34 the reason for God's no more remembering their sins is based on God's work in their lives, ensuring that they do not sin. Therefore, the cessation of the offering for sin is, in Jeremiah, tied to the actual cessation of sinning. It is hard to relate this situation to the present age. The saints in Corinth and Peter's behavior before the churches of Galatia argue against the idea of the believer in this age not sinning. First John explicitly states that believers sin. Paul's own personal experience evidences this reality. In light of this, the teaching of Hebrews might better be understood not as relating to what believers were experiencing in that day, but what, through the work of Christ, is yet future. This would tie in well with the style of the author whose argument is dealing with the danger of returning to the Jewish practices of his day. He wanted his readers to move ahead in their spiritual growth in Christ.

Hebrews 12:24 also mentions the new covenant. Interestingly the term "new" (*neas*) is not the same term for "new" (*kainēs*) the author has used earlier (Heb. 8:8, 13; 9:15). The term *neas* is used only in this verse in the book of Hebrews, and this is the only time the term is used for what most identify as Jeremiah's new covenant. Generally the distinction in the meaning of these terms has been that *kainēs* stresses newness in quality, whereas *neas* stresses newness in respect to time, although this distinction may not always be valid. The change in terminology has been explained in various ways. Bruce suggests that the change is because of rhythm.[18] The author could also have used *neas* because he wanted to stress the recent "cutting" of the covenant. In any case, the mention of Jesus' mediation of a "new covenant" points to His greatness and the superiority of His ministry to Judaism. To come to "Jesus the mediator of a new covenant" does not demand that the covenant is presently being fulfilled any more than an Old Testament saint's coming to the God of the Davidic covenant meant that the Davidic covenant was being fulfilled in the Old Testament.

CONCLUSION

A brief examination of the primary texts related to the new covenant of Jeremiah 31:31–34 places the covenant in an eschatological context. It does not appear that any believer has entered into all the blessings promised in the new covenant in this life since all still sin (cf. Rom. 7). The new covenant focuses on the divine causation of spiritual obedience. It guarantees, in its original context, the surety of the full and complete salvation that God promises to the house of Israel and the house of Judah. They would then obey God's instruction (*tôratî*).

In addition to this promise of sinlessness is the statement that at the time of its fulfillment, at least in the fullest sense, all will know the Lord. None will need to teach another (Jer. 31:34). The present ministry of the church in teaching (Matt. 28:19–20; Eph. 4:7–16) would seem to argue for some "future" fulfillment (even if one were to argue for some "present" fulfillment of Jeremiah 31:31–34) because the complete fulfillment of the new covenant seems to eliminate the need for teaching.

If one argues for some sort of present fulfillment of the new covenant, what is it? It would appear to be limited to the statement, "I will forgive their wickedness and will remember their sins no more" (Jer. 31:34; LXX 38:34). The term *forgive* (*hieōs*) in the LXX occurs in the New Testament only in Matthew 16:22 and Hebrews 8:12. It translates the Hebrew term *slat*. The form of the term *remember* (*mnēsthō*) in the LXX occurs only in Hebrews 8:12 and translates the Hebrew term *zākār*. The writers of the New Testament do not seem to pick up the "forgiveness" terminology of Jeremiah 31:34 in the New Testament as it relates to the death of Christ except in the Hebrews 8:12 quotation of Jeremiah 31.[19] Why is this the case if the church is receiving in an initial sense or in some other way the benefits of the new covenant?

What then is a suggested relationship of the church to the new covenant of Jeremiah 31:31–34? The church is united to the mediator of the new covenant. The new covenant has been cut. The actualization of the new covenant in the lives of believers, however, is yet future, when Christ returns and the house of Israel and the house of Judah are transformed by God's grace to obey completely the commands of God. Believers today also have the promise of a similar future transformation (Rom. 8:30; 1 John 3:2).

The new covenant specifically mentioned in the Scriptures is yet future for a redeemed and sanctified Jewish people. Theologically there are many new covenants because each dispensation is a new covenant. There is no need to apply the promises of Israel's new covenant to the church because the same spiritual promises are specified for the church (Rom 8:30; 1 John 3:2; etc.). If the church is fulfilling the new covenant, why then are Old Testament saints (who were not enjoying the greater blessings provided by the new covenant) an illustration of godly living for believers in the church age (who supposedly are enjoying the greater benefits of the new covenant)? Are church saints today living more godly lives than the Old Testament saints lived?

Church saints have a covenantal relationship with God that differs from the Old Testament saints living under the Mosaic stewardship. This relationship is not the same as the relationship that Israel will yet have with her Lord when He establishes His kingdom on earth. This suggestion seems to better follow the consistent eschatological emphasis of the passages dealing with Jeremiah's new covenant and its emphasis on the future aspect of and completeness of the experience of salvation. The faithfulness of God to His covenant promises for Israel (cf. Romans 9–11) guarantees His faithfulness to His promises of final glorification for the church saints (Rom. 8:28–39). That the church does not fulfill the new covenant of Jeremiah 31:31–34 ensures the certainty of God's promises for the church. A fundamental conviction of the church is that God does not change His unconditional unilateral promises to His people in any age, whether to the descendants of Jacob or to believers in the church.

Notes

1. Walter C. Kaiser Jr., *Toward an Old Testament Theology* (Grand Rapids: Zondervan, 1978), 231–32.
2. Lewis Sperry Chafer, *Systematic Theology* (Dallas: Dallas Seminary Press, 1948), 7:98–99; Charles C. Ryrie, The Basis of the Premillennial Faith (Neptune N.J.: Loizeaux, 1953), 105–25.
3. *Scofield Study Bible* (New York: Oxford, 1967), 1317, note on Heb. 8:8.
4. Paul D. Feinberg, "Hermeneutics of Discontinuity," in *Continuity and Discontinuity: Perspectives on the Relationship Between the Old and New Testaments,* John S. Feinberg, ed. (Westchester: Crossway, 1988), 109–28.
5. Bernhard W. Anderson, "The New Covenant and the Old," in *The Old Testament and Christian Faith,* Bernhard W. Andersen, ed. (New York: Harper & Row, 1963), 230.
6. Walther Eichrodt, *Theology of the Old Testament* (Philadelphia: Westminster, 1967), II:58–59.
7. Robert L. Saucy (*The Case for Progressive Dispensationalism* [Grand Rapids: Zondervan, 1993], 32) recognizes that the new covenant promises "ultimate perfection," although he sees this as being "worked out gradually in our lives."
8. R. E. Clements' statement (*Old Testament Theology* [Atlanta: John Knox, 1978], 103) moves in this direction by recognizing the unilateral nature of the covenant but falls short of the divine causality of the text: "he will himself, by his action within the human heart, give the power and strength to fulfil them (cf. Ezek. 36:26–7)."
9. I. Howard Marshall, *Commentary on Luke* (Grand Rapids: Eerdmans, 1983), 805–6.
10. For a brief discussion of the textual problems with this verse, see Marshall, *Commentary on Luke,* 799–800.

11. Though seeing the church as fulfilling the new covenant, Howard C. Kee ("After the Crucifixion—Christianity Through Paul," in *Christianity and Rabbinic Judaism,* Hershel Shanks, ed. [Biblical Archaeology Society, 1992], 90) recognizes the eschatological significance of the Last Supper: "At his final meal, according to the Gospel accounts, the disciples were told in symbolic language that was to become part of the eucharistic words employed by the Church down to the present day that Jesus would be taken from them for a time but that he and they would be reunited in the new age when God's rule would triumph over the world (Mark 14:25; Matthew 26:29)."

12. D. A. Carson, "Matthew," in *Expositor's Bible Commentary* (Grand Rapids: Regency, 1984), 8:537.

13. N. T. Wright, *The Climax of the Covenant* (Minneapolis: Fortress, 1992), 176.

14. C. E. B. Cranfield, "St. Paul and the Law," *Scottish Journal of Theology* (March 1964), 57.

15. D. Moody Smith, "The Pauline Literature," in *It is Written: Scripture Citing Scripture,* D. A. Carson and H. G. M. Williamson, eds. (Cambridge: Cambridge Univ., 1988), 282.

16. The use of "servant" followed by a genitive is found in passages such as Romans 15:8; 16:1; 2 Corinthians 11:15, 23; Ephesians 3:7; Colossians 1:7; and 1 Timothy 4:6.

17. This view could be supported by the observation that believers are not yet fully obedient to the Lord.

18. F. F. Bruce, *The Epistle to the Hebrews* (Grand Rapids: Eerdmans, 1964), 379.

19. When one looks at the Greek words used to translate the Hebrew terms of Jeremiah in other Old Testament texts, one still does not find these other Greek terms playing a central role in the terminology of the New Testament writers relating to the work of Christ for the believer today. "The Christian Church, from the earliest times, claimed the promise of Jer 31:31–34 and understood itself to be the people of the new covenant. It also thought of itself as a new people (1 Pet 2:1–10): Israel to which the Gentiles now belong. It comes as somewhat of a surprise then to find so little said in the NT about a new covenant" (Jack R. Lundbom, "The New Covenant," in *Anchor Bible Dictionary,* David Noel Freedman, ed. (New York: Doubleday, 1992), 4:1090.

C lassical dispensationalism has always insisted on a consistent distinction between Israel and the church, which, in turn, actually came from a consistent usage of a literal, or plain, hermeneutic. The basis for such a distinction is seen in the biblical definition of Israel, along with a clear understanding of Israel's election and the divine purposes of that election. The evidences for such a distinction include knowing four things: when the church was born and the role of Spirit-baptism for the existence of the church; the prerequisites of Messiah's ministry before the church could come into existence; the mystery character of the church; and the seventy-three usages of *Israel* in the New Testament, which, in turn, leads to a correct exegesis of Galatians 6:16. The conclusion is also supported by a study of the biblical usage of *seed of Abraham* and an exegesis of Romans 2:25–29.

6

ISRAEL AND THE CHURCH

Arnold G. Fruchtenbaum

W hatever differences there may be within classic dispensationalism, the one area of uniform agreement is the consistent distinction between Israel and the church.
Demonstrating that such a distinction is a necessary conclusion from biblical evidence is the purpose of this chapter.

DEFINITION OF ISRAEL

As used in this chapter, the term *Israel* is viewed theologically
as referring to all descendants of Abraham, Isaac, and Jacob, also
known as the Jews, the Jewish people, Israelites, Hebrews, etc.[1] The
term is not limited to the present political and national state in the
Middle East, which is merely a part of the whole; nor is it limited to
those who adhere to the religion of Judaism only.

THE ELECTION OF ISRAEL

In dealing with the concept of election, a distinction must be
made between individual election and national election. The former
is soteriological and results in the salvation of that individual. This
type of election extends to both Jewish and Gentile individuals; and
any person who has ever believed, either Jew or Gentile, was the
object of God's individual election. However, the concern of Israelology is national election because only Israel is called an elect nation.

National election does not guarantee the salvation of every individual within the nation since only individual election can do that. Nor does national election guarantee the physical salvation of every member of the nation. What national election does guarantee is that God's purpose(s) for choosing the nation will be accomplished and that the elect nation will always survive as a distinct entity. It guarantees the physical salvation of the nation and, in the case of Israel, even a national salvation. It is the national election of Israel that is the basis of Israel's status as the Chosen People.

The Fact of Israel's Election

The book of Deuteronomy, more than the other four books of Moses, emphasizes this factor. The earliest reference to Israel's election is Deuteronomy 4:37: "And because he loved thy fathers, therefore he chose their seed after them, and brought thee out with his presence, with his great power, out of Egypt."

In this verse, Moses makes three points. First, the basis of God's election was His love for the Fathers—Abraham, Isaac, and Jacob—with whom He made a covenant. Second, on that basis, God "chose their seed after them." On the basis of that covenant relationship, God chose Israel to be His elect nation. Third, on the basis of that election He delivered Israel out of Egypt.

Later, in Deuteronomy 7:6–8 God states that He chose Israel and declared them "a holy people," not because of any innate righteousness, as Deuteronomy 9:4–6 indicates, but because "Jehovah thy God hath chosen thee" (7:6). The concept of "holiness," like "sanctification," means "a setting apart." By God's choosing of Israel, she was set apart from all other nations to be "a holy people." Furthermore, Israel was chosen to be God's "own possession" and this "above all peoples that are upon the face of the earth" (7:6). This statement separates the nation and people of Israel from all other nations and so Israel alone is the elect nation.

The concept of Israel as a nation that is God's special possession is reaffirmed twice. The first time is in Deuteronomy 14:2: "For thou art a holy people unto Jehovah thy God, and Jehovah hath chosen thee to be a people for his own possession, above all peoples that are upon the face of the earth." Israel's status as "a holy people" is based on the fact that God "hath chosen thee to be a people for his own possession, above all peoples that are on the face of the earth." Israel is declared a people chosen by God, i.e. the Chosen People. The second reaffirmation of God's choosing Israel is Deuteronomy

26:18. And because Israel is "a people for his own possession," she was expected to keep the commandments of God (see also Ex. 19:6).

In Deuteronomy 7:7–8, Moses spelled out the basis for Israel's election, both negatively and positively. Negatively (v. 7), it was not because of Israel's great numerical size, for the exact opposite was really true. Positively (v. 8), Israel was chosen for two reasons: first, because God loved Israel in spite of her small size; and, second, because God has a covenant relationship with the Fathers, the three patriarchs and, therefore, God must keep His oath made to them. It is for this very reason that God rescued Israel through the Exodus.

Still later in Deuteronomy 10:15–16, Moses states, "Only Jehovah had a delight in thy fathers to love them, and he chose their seed after them, even you above all peoples, as at this day. Circumcise therefore the foreskin of your heart, and be no more stiff-necked."

God chose Israel to be an elect nation, not true of any other nation in this world. However, national election does not guarantee the salvation of every individual member of that nation. Individual salvation is based on individual election on God's part and faith on man's part. In verse 16, individual members of the elect nation are encouraged to "circumcise therefore the foreskin of your heart." Whereas circumcision of the flesh is a sign of one's membership in the elect nation, circumcision of the heart is a sign of individual election.

The Reasons and Purposes of Israel's Election

Though Israel was chosen on the basis of God's love, there was purpose and reason to Israel's election. One purpose of God's election was for Israel to be "a kingdom of priests and a holy nation" (Ex. 19:6). Israel had a priestly tribe, the tribe of Levi, but the nation as a whole was also to be a priesthood. The historical function of a priest was to represent man to God. The tribe of Levi represented Israel before God; and the nation Israel was to represent the Gentile nations before God.

A second reason was that God chose Israel to be the recipient of His revelation and to record it. For this reason, Israel received the law of Moses (Deut. 4:5–8; 6:6–9; Rom. 3:1–2).

A third reason was to propagate the doctrine of the One God (Deut. 6:4).

A fourth reason was to produce the Messiah (Rom. 9:5; Heb. 2:16–17; 7:13–14).

THE DISTINCTION BETWEEN
ISRAEL AND THE CHURCH

Some theologians insist that at some point the church receives the promises given to Israel and thus becomes the "New Israel" (known as replacement theology). Some believe the terms *church* and *Israel* are used virtually "interchangeably,"[2] most citing Galatians 6:16 and some, Romans 9:6—the extent of their biblical support. The purpose of this section is to examine those passages often used to teach that the church is spiritual Israel.

Dispensationalists have correctly seen the consistent distinction the Bible makes between Israel and the church, but have not always used the best terminology in trying to show the nature of this distinction. A common distinction some dispensationalists make is to describe Israel as an "earthly people" with "earthly promises," while the church is a "heavenly people" with "heavenly promises." However, such a distinction is not correct, nor is it necessary to dispensationalism. Each entity has both an earthly future with earthly promises and a heavenly future with heavenly promises. The distinction between Israel and the church is a biblical one, and there are clear distinctives in God's program for each, but the contrast between earthly and heavenly is not one of them.

The Evidences for the Distinction
of Israel and the Church

The first evidence is the fact that the church was born at Pentecost, whereas Israel had existed for many centuries. There is no biblical evidence that the church existed in the Old Testament. The use of the future tense in Matthew 16:18 shows that it did not exist in gospel history either: "And I also say unto thee, that thou art Peter, and upon this rock I will build my church; and the gates of Hades shall not prevail against it." This church, born at Pentecost, is the Body of Christ, "And he is the head of the body, the church: who is the beginning, the firstborn from the dead; that in all things he might have the preeminence" (Col. 1:18).

Entrance into the Body of Christ is by Spirit baptism: "For in one Spirit were we all baptized into one body, whether Jews or Greeks, whether bond or free, and were all made to drink of one Spirit" (1 Cor. 12:13). So when did Spirit baptism into Christ's Body actually begin? According to Acts 1:5, Spirit baptism was still future as of that point: "for John indeed baptized with water; but ye shall be baptized in the Holy Spirit not many days hence." The answer is that Spirit baptism began in Acts 2:1–4. This passage does not state that the events of Pentecost included Spirit baptism; however, Acts 11:15–16 indicates that Spirit baptism did occur then.

Peter, while defending his actions of going into the house of a Gentile (Acts 10), points out that the Gentile believers received the same experience of Spirit baptism as did the Jews (11:15). Peter explained that the "Holy Spirit fell on them" (the Gentiles), as the Holy Spirit once fell "on us [the Jewish believers] at the beginning." Then Peter states (11:16) that the prophecy of Jesus in Acts 1:5 was fulfilled in Acts 2:1–4.

The second evidence is that certain events in the ministry of the Messiah were essential to the establishment of the church—the church does not come into being until certain events have taken place. These events include the resurrection/ascension of the Messiah to become head of the church

> which he wrought in Christ, when he raised him from the dead, and made him to sit at his right hand in the ₙeavenly places, far above all rule, and authority, and power, and dominion, and every name that is named, not only in this world, but also in that which is to come: and he put all things in subjection under his feet, and gave him to be head over all things to the church, which is his body, the fullness of him that filleth all in all. (Eph. 1:20–23)

The church, with believers as the body and Christ as the head, did not exist until after Christ ascended to become its head. And it could not become a functioning entity until after the Holy Spirit provided the necessary spiritual gifts. According to Ephesians 4:7–11, these spiritual gifts could only be provided after the ascension:

> But unto each one of us was the grace given according to the measure of the gift of Christ. Wherefore he saith, When he ascended on high, he led captivity captive, And gave gifts unto men. (Now this, He ascended, what is it but that he also descended into the lower parts of the earth? He that descended is the same also that ascended far above all the heavens, that he might fill all things.) And he gave some to be apostles; and some, prophets; and some, evangelists; and some, pastors and teachers.

The third evidence is the mystery character of the church. A New Testament *mystery* is a truth not revealed in the Old Testament (Eph. 3:3–5, 9; Col. 1:26–27). At least four defining characteristics of the church are described as a mystery. (1) The body concept of Jewish and Gentile believers united into one body is designated as a mystery in Ephesians 3:1–12. (2) The doctrine of Christ indwelling every believer, the Christ-in-you concept, is called a mystery in Colossians 1:24–27 (cf. Col. 2:10–19; 3:4, 11). (3) The church as the Bride of Christ is called a mystery in Ephesians 5:22–32. (4) The Rapture is called a mystery in 1 Corinthians 15:50–58. These four mysteries describe qualities that distinguish the church from Israel.

The fourth evidence that the church is distinct from Israel is the unique relationship between Jews and the Gentiles, called one new man in Ephesians 2:15: "having abolished in his flesh the enmity, even the law of commandments contained in ordinances; that he might create in himself of the two one new man, so making peace." This *one new man,* separate from both Israel and the Gentiles, is comprised of believing members from both. The same three groups are distinguished from each other in 1 Corinthians 10:32: "Give no occasion of stumbling, either to Jews, or to Greeks, or to the church of God."

The fifth evidence for the distinction between Israel and the church is found in Galatians 6:16. Since this is a key text for replacement theology it will be examined in the following section.

Perhaps one more observation can be made. In the book of Acts, both Israel and the church exist simultaneously. The term *Israel* is used twenty times and *ekklesia* (church) nineteen times, yet the two groups are always kept distinct.

The Use of Israel in the New Testament

The term *Israel* is used a total of seventy-three times in the New Testament. Replacement theologians state that the church is the new Israel. Cox even claimed that the two terms are used interchangeably.[3] As the following list shows, however, such a bold claim is unwarranted from the evidence:

Matt. 2:6	Q.[4] Micah 5:2, "shepherd of my people Israel"
Matt. 2:20	The family's return to "the land of Israel"
Matt. 2:21	Same as above
Matt. 8:10	Centurion, "so great faith, no, not in Israel"
Matt. 9:33	Response of multitudes, "never so seen in Israel"
Matt. 10:6	Go only to "lost sheep of the house of Israel"
Matt. 10:23	Work of the disciples in "the cities of Israel"
Matt. 15:24	Messiah to "lost sheep of the house of Israel"
Matt. 15:31	The multitudes "glorified the God of Israel"
Matt. 27:9	Q. Zechariah 11:12–13, Messiah sold for thirty pieces of silver by "the children of Israel"

Matt. 27:42	Jesus mocked as "the king of Israel"
Mark 12:29	Q. Deuteronomy 6:4: "Hear O Israel"
Mark 15:32	Jesus mocked as "the king of Israel"
Luke 1:16	John to get "children of Israel to turn"
Luke 1:54	Messiah to give help "to Israel his servant"
Luke 1:68	A reference to God as "the God of Israel"
Luke 1:80	John in desert until "his showing unto Israel"
Luke 2:25	Messianic hope as "the consolation of Israel"
Luke 2:32	Messiah to be "the glory of thy people Israel"
Luke 2:34	Messiah, "falling and rising of many in Israel"
Luke 4:25	Historical reference to the "widows in Israel"
Luke 4:27	Historical reference to the "lepers in Israel"
Luke 7:9	Centurion, "so great faith, no, not in Israel"
Luke 22:30	Authority over "the twelve tribes of Israel"
Luke 24:21	Jesus the one they hoped would "redeem Israel"
John 1:31	Messiah "manifest to Israel" through John
John 1:49	Nathanael described Jesus as the "King of Israel"
John 3:10	Jesus called Nicodemus "the teacher of Israel"
John 12:13	Triumphal entry Jesus called "the King of Israel"
Acts 1:6	The disciples ask, "Lord, dost thou at this time restore the kingdom to Israel?"
Acts 2:22	Peter to unbelieving Jews, "Ye men of Israel"
Acts 2:36	Same audience as above reference
Acts 3:12	Peter to unbelieving Jews, "Ye men of Israel"
Acts 4:10	Peter declares to "all the people of Israel"
Acts 4:27	Israel and Gentiles guilty of the crucifixion
Acts 5:21	Unbelievers "senate of the children of Israel"
Acts 5:31	Peter offers "repentance to Israel" (unbelievers).
Acts 5:35	Gamaliel addressing Sanhedrin, "Ye men of Israel"
Acts 7:23	Stephen, "the children of Israel" in Moses' time
Acts 7:37	Same as above
Acts 7:42	Same as above
Acts 9:15	Paul, to Gentiles and to "the children of Israel"
Acts 10:36	Peter, Jesus came "unto the children of Israel"
Acts 13:16	Paul, to unbelieving Jews, "men of Israel"
Acts 13:17	Paul, "this people Israel" at the Exodus.
Acts 13:23	Paul, Messiah fulfilled "promise . . . unto Israel"
Acts 13:24	Paul, John preached "to all people of Israel"
Acts 21:28	"Men of Israel" is the mob who attacked Paul.
Acts 28:20	Paul in chains for "the hope of Israel"
Rom. 9:4	Paul, the privileges God gave the "Israelites"

Rom. 9:6	Paul, two Israels—believing and unbelieving Jews
Rom. 9:27	Contrast, unbelieving Israel/believing remnant
Rom. 9:31	Unbelieving Israel "did not arrive at that law"
Rom. 10:19	Paul, Israel received and rejected message
Rom. 10:21	God still reaches out to unbelieving Israel
Rom. 11:1	Paul, an "Israelite" nationally and ethnically
Rom. 11:2	Paul, "Elijah . . . pleaded with God against Israel"
Rom. 11:7	Paul, contrast unbelieving Israel/remnant
Rom. 11:25	Paul, the "blindness" that had "befallen Israel"
Rom. 11:26	Prophecy that all (ethnic) Israel will be saved.
1 Cor. 10:18	"Israel after the flesh," national ethnic Israel
2 Cor. 3:7	"The children of Israel" at the time of Moses
2 Cor. 3:13	Same as above
2 Cor. 11:22	Paul, unbelieving Jews and he are both "Israelites"
Gal. 6:16	Paul, "the Israel of God" (see this chapter)
Eph. 2:12	The "commonwealth of Israel" contrasted with the Gentiles and with the "one new man" (the church)
Phil. 3:5	Paul affirms that he came from "the stock of Israel"
Heb. 8:8	A quotation of the new covenant of Jeremiah
Heb. 8:10	Same as above
Heb. 11:22	Historical reference to the Israel of the Exodus
Rev. 7:4	A reference to the twelve tribes of Israel
Rev. 21:12	Same as above

Of these seventy-three citations, the vast majority refer to national, ethnic Israel. A few refer specifically to Jewish believers who still are ethnic Jews. Generally, only three of these passages are used by replacement theologians to support their thesis that the church equals Israel. On two of these references (Rom. 9:6; 11:26) they are not unanimous, for some replacement theologians also have concluded that these verses speak of national, ethnic Israel. The key verse for replacement theologians is Galatians 6:16 (which we will examine in the next section).

"The Israel of God" of Galatians 6:16

The purpose of this section is to examine Galatians 6:16, a passage routinely cited by replacement theologians as evidence that the church is the "spiritual" Israel. An important emphasis of the book of Galatians is correcting those Gentiles who were attempting to please God through trying to keep the law. The ones deceiving them were Judaizers demanding adherence to the law of Moses. To them, a

Gentile had to convert to Judaism as part of salvation through the Messiah.

In Galatians 6:15, Paul states that the important thing for salvation is the work of God in forming a new creature, not reliance on circumcision or uncircumcision. In addition to identifying the physical rite, Paul also uses circumcision and uncircumcision (Gal. 2:7–9) to refer to two groups of people—Jews and Gentiles.

> When they saw that I had been intrusted with the gospel of the uncircumcision, even as Peter with the gospel of the circumcision (for he that wrought for Peter unto the apostleship of the circumcision wrought for me also unto the Gentiles); and when they perceived the grace that was given unto me, James and Cephas and John, they who were reputed to be pillars, gave to me and Barnabas the right hands of fellowship, that we should go unto the Gentiles, and they unto the circumcision.

Individuals out of those two groups who responded to the grace message of faith in Christ then would become "church saints," united as one in Christ. In Galatians 6:16, Paul pronounces a blessing on members of the two groups who would experience the work of divine grace apart from human works such as circumcision, "And as many as shall walk by this rule, peace be upon them, and mercy, and upon the Israel of God."

Paul writes about "them" and "the Israel of God." Are these the same? In the epistle to the Galatians Paul already has mentioned (as indicated above) both Gentile and Jewish believers. From an ethnic or national standpoint believers are called from two distinctly different backgrounds. Replacement theologians generally affirm that both terms refer to the same group and thus conclude that the church is called the Israel of God. However, in order to accept the proposition that the terms *them* and *the Israel of God* both describe the same group, one must ignore the primary meaning of *kai* (and) in the expression "and upon the Israel of God."

The identity of the Israel of God. There are two main views concerning this verse. The first insists that *the Israel of God* is the church as a whole while the other limits it to Jewish believers. The first view is described as follows:

> The first is the claim that "the Israel of God" is simply a term descriptive of the believing church of the present age. . . . The Israel of God is the body who shall walk by the rule of the new creation, and they include believing people from the two ethnic bodies of Jews and Gentiles.[5]

121

S. Lewis Johnson, former professor of Greek and New Testament Exegesis at Dallas Theological Seminary, has done a detailed study of Galatians 6:16. In his introduction, Johnson makes the following observation:

> In spite of overwhelming evidence to the contrary, there remains persistent support for the contention that the term Israel may refer properly to Gentile believers in the present age. . . . The primary support is found in Galatians 6:16. . . .
> I cannot help but think that dogmatic considerations loom large in the interpretation of Galatians 6:16. The tenacity with which this application of "the Israel of God" to the church is held in spite of a mass of evidence to the contrary leads one to think that the supporters of the view believe their eschatological system, usually an amillennial scheme, hangs on the reference of the term to the people of God, composed of both believing Jews and Gentiles. Amillennialism does not hang on this interpretation, but the view does appear to have a treasured place in amillennial exegesis.
> In speaking of the view that the term refers to ethnic Israel, a sense that the term *Israel* has in every other of its more than sixty-five uses in the New Testament and in its fifteen uses in Paul, in tones almost emotional William Hendriksen, the respected Reformed commentator, writes, "I refuse to accept that explanation." . . .
> What I am leading up to is expressed neatly by D. W. B. Robinson in an article written about twenty years ago: "The glib citing of Gal. vi:16 to support the view that 'the church is the new Israel' should be vigorously challenged. There is weighty support for a limited interpretation." We can say more than this, in my opinion. There is more than weighty support for a more limited interpretation. There is overwhelming support for such. In fact, the least likely view among several alternatives is the view that "the Israel of God" is the church.[6]

Johnson has observed that an impressive list of names support the view, but that the linguistic "bases of the interpretation are few and feeble." Their interpretations demand that *kai* "before the term 'the Israel of God' is an explicative or appositional *kai*."[7]

Johnson rejects this view on three grounds. The first is for grammatical and syntactical reasons.[8] In order to accept the explicative or appositional interpretation one must resort to a secondary or lesser meaning of *kai*: "It is necessary to begin this part of the discussion with a reminder of a basic, but often neglected, hermeneutical principle. It is this: in the absence of compelling exegetical and theological considerations, we should avoid the rarer grammatical usages when the common ones make good sense."[9]

Because the uncommon usage serves well the view that the term *the Israel of God* is the church, that seems to be the rationale for interpretation, in spite of grammatical usage. An extremely rare usage has been made to replace the common usage, even in spite of the fact that the common and frequent usage of *and* makes perfectly good sense in Galatians 6:16.[10]

Johnson points out that if Paul's intention was to identify the them as being *the Israel of God,* then the best way of showing this was to eliminate the *kai* altogether. The very presence of the *kai* argues against the *them* being *the Israel of God.* As Johnson notes, "Paul, however, did not eliminate the *kai.*"[11]

The second ground for rejecting this view is for exegetical considerations that deal with context and usage:

> From the standpoint of biblical usage this view stands condemned. There is no instance in biblical literature of the term *Israel* being used in the sense of the church, or the people of God as composed of both believing ethnic Jews and Gentiles. Nor, on the other hand, as one might expect if there were such usage, does the phrase *ta ethne* (KJV, "the Gentiles") ever mean the non-Christian world specifically, but only the non-Jewish peoples, although such are generally non-Christians. Thus, the usage of the term *Israel* stands overwhelmingly opposed to the first view.[12]

For those who would cite Romans 9:6 as evidence, this verse is no support for such a view, for the distinction is between Jews who believe and Jews who do not: "Paul is here speaking only of a division within ethnic Israel. Some of them are believers and thus truly Israel, whereas others, though ethnically Israelites, are not truly Israel, since they are not elect and believing. . . . No Gentiles are found in the statement at all."[13] Even many replacement theologians agree with this view of Romans 9:6 and do not use it to support their view of Galatians 6:16.

A cursory reading of the context reveals that Paul in distinguishing between physical status and spiritual status for those is Christ. Although the Judaizers were emphasizing physical qualifications, Paul states that one's position in Christ depends exclusively on spiritual qualifications. Notice that Paul does not even talk about the church, but refers to position *in Christ* (Gal. 6:15). Certainly Paul does not seek to demean or eradicate physical differences, he merely states that they have no bearing on whether or not one is in Christ.

Just as earlier Paul states that gender distinctives and social status are irrelevant to position in Christ (Gal. 3:28), so in Galatians 6:15 he explains that circumcision also means nothing. And just as physical differences do not keep persons from being in Christ, so physical similarities cannot put them in Christ. All Jews belong to ethnic Israel. And Gentiles do not. So there is no basis for concluding that Paul intends to imply to his readers that *Israel* can refer to Gentiles, whether or not they are in Christ.

The third ground for rejecting this view is theological: "there is no historical evidence that the term *Israel* was identified with the church before A.D. 160. Further, at that date there was no characterization of the church as 'the Israel of God.' In other words, for more than a century after Paul there was no evidence of the identification."[14] Johnson summarizes the rejection of the first view:

> To conclude the discussion of the first interpretation, it seems clear that there is little evidence—grammatical, exegetical, or theological—that supports it. On the other hand, there is sound historical evidence against the identification of *Israel* with believing or unbelieving Gentiles. The grammatical usage of *kai* is not favorable to the view, nor is the Pauline or New Testament usage of *Israel*. Finally, . . . the Pauline teaching in Galatians contains a recognition of national distinctions in the one people of God.[15]

The second view is that *the Israel of God* is the believing Jewish remnant within the church. This is Johnson's own view and is the common dispensational view:

> The second of the important interpretations of Galatians 6:16 and "the Israel of God" is the view that the words refer simply to believing ethnic Israelites in the Christian church. Does not Paul speak of himself as an Israelite (cf. Rom. 11:1)? And does not the apostle also speak of "a remnant according to God's gracious choice" (cf. 11:5), words that plainly in the context refer to believing Israelites? What more fitting thing could Paul write, it is said, in a work so strongly attacking Jewish professing believers, the Judaizers, than to make it most plain that he was not attacking the true believing Jews? Judaizers are anathematized, but the remnant according to the election of grace are "the Israel of God."[16]

Another place where Paul distinguishes between two categories of ethnic Israel is Romans 9:6, making a distinction between elect and nonelect Israel. It appears logical to view "the Israel of God" (Gal. 6:16) as believing Jews in contrast to unbelieving Jews called "Israel after the flesh" (1 Cor. 10:18).

Johnson supports this view on the same three grounds that he rejected the first view. On grammatical and syntactical grounds, Johnson states that "there are no grammatical, or syntactical considerations that would be contrary" to this view, and, furthermore, the "common sense of *kai* as continuative, or conjunctive is followed."[17] In other words, it uses the primary meaning of *kai*.

> Exegetically the view is sound, since "Israel" has its uniform Pauline ethnic sense. And further, the apostle achieves a very striking climactic conclusion. Drawing near the end of his "battle-epistle" with its harsh and forceful attack on the Judaists and its omission of the customary words of thanksgiving, Paul tempers his language with a special blessing for those faithful believing Israelites who, understanding the grace of God and its exclusion of any human works as the ground of redemption, had not succumbed to the subtle blandishments of the deceptive Judaizers. They, not the false men from Jerusalem, are "the Israel of God," or, as he calls them elsewhere, "the remnant according to the election of grace" (cf. Rom. 11:5).[18]

As for theological grounds, Johnson says,

> And theologically the view is sound in its maintenance of the two elements within the one people of God, Gentiles and ethnic Jews. Romans 11 spells out the details of the relationship between the two entities from Abraham's day to the present age and on to the fulfillment in the future of the great unconditional covenantal promises made to the patriarchs.[19]

It appears evident that there are major difficulties with trying to support the view that "the Israel of God" in Galatians 6:16 means the church, made up of believing Jews and Gentiles:

> If there is an interpretation that totters on a tenuous foundation, it is the view that Paul equates the term "the Israel of God" with the believing church of Jews and Gentiles. To support it, the general usage of the term *Israel* in Paul, in the New Testament, and in the Scriptures as a whole is ignored. The grammatical and syntactical usage of the conjunction *kai* is strained and distorted—and the rare and uncommon sense accepted when the usual sense is unsatisfactory—only because it does not harmonize with the presuppositions of the exegete. And to compound matters, in the special context of Galatians and the general context of the Pauline teaching, especially as highlighted in Romans 11, Paul's primary passages on God's dealings with Israel and the Gentiles, are downplayed. . . . The doctrine that the church of Gentile and Jews is the Israel of God rests on an illusion. It is a classic case of tendentious exegesis.[20]

The conclusion is that the church is never called a "spiritual Israel" or a "new Israel." The term Israel is either used of the nation or the people as a whole, or of the believing remnant within. It is never used of the church in general or of Gentile believers in particular. In fact, even after the Cross there remains a threefold distinction. First, there is a distinction between Israel and the Gentiles as in 1 Corinthians 10:32 and Ephesians 2:11–12. Second, there is a distinction between Israel and the church in 1 Corinthians 10:32. Third, there is a distinction between Jewish believers (the Israel of God) and Gentile believers in Romans 9:6 and Galatians 6:16.

The Seed of Abraham

Another argument used in replacement theology to teach that Israel is the church is that Gentile believers are referred to as the "seed of Abraham" (Gal. 3:29) and therefore can be equated with Israel, which also is identified as the seed of Abraham. It should be noted that the term *seed of Abraham* is used in four different senses in the Scriptures. First, it refers to the physical seed of Abraham. This is the natural offspring who are physical descendants of Abraham, which also logically includes Arabs. However, in the Old Testament, the term always refers to the physical descendants of Abraham who are Jews. But the term *seed of Abraham* is not limited to referring to the physical seed. Second, it refers to the Messiah who is the unique individual Seed of Abraham (Heb. 2:16–17). Third, it is a reference to the believers today; the church is the spiritual seed of Abraham (Gal. 3:29). This seed includes Jews who are physical descendants of Abraham and Gentiles who are not physical descendants of Abraham but who have Abraham's faith. But we must ask: "Is this spiritual seed of Abraham ever called 'Israel'"? The answer is, no. Those who are the spiritual seed are partakers of Jewish spiritual blessings but are never said to become partakers of the physical, material, or national promises. Fourth, the term *seed of Abraham* sometimes identifies the righteous remnant of Israel (Isa. 41:8; Rom. 9:6).

Ethnic Jews who have accepted the Lord Jesus Christ as their Messiah—Jewish Christians—are the Israel of God, and they are spiritual seed of Abraham. Other groups also are Abraham's spiritual seed, but none of these groups ever is referred to as Israel.

The Seed of Jacob

What replacement theologians need to prove their case is a statement in Scripture that all believers are of "the seed of Jacob." Such teaching would indicate that the church is spiritual Israel or that Gentile Christians are spiritual Jews. This is exactly what they do not have. Not all physical descendants of Abraham are Jews, but all physical descendants of Jacob are. The very term *Israel* originated with Jacob and not with Abraham. If there were even one verse that showed that the church is the seed of Jacob, replacement theologians could support one of their key contentions. This they cannot do. They only resort to passages that speak of the seed of Abraham, which, by itself, is insufficient to prove their contention, since the use of "Israel" is more restrictive than the use of "Abraham."

Romans 2:25–29

Another passage used to teach the Israel-equals-the-church interpretation is Romans 2:25–29, where Paul contrasts mere outward conformity with inward conformity:

> For circumcision indeed profiteth, if thou be a doer of the law: but if thou be a transgressor of the law, thy circumcision is become uncircumcision. If therefore the uncircumcision keep the ordinances of the law, shall not his uncircumcision be reckoned for circumcision? and shall not the uncircumcision which is by nature, if it fulfill the law, judge thee, who with the letter and circumcision art a transgressor of the law? For he is not a Jew who is one outwardly; neither is that circumcision which is outward in the flesh: but he is a Jew who is one inwardly; and circumcision is that of the heart, in the spirit not in the letter; whose praise is not of men, but of God.

Paul's focus in this passage was the Pharisaic concept that all who were circumcised automatically would become part of God's kingdom. Paul recognized that certain privileges accompanied circumcision. But circumcision did not establish the covenant; it was only the sign of the covenant that was already established. Circumcision did not establish the covenant, but it brought blessings that were dependent upon obedience. If a Jewish person pleaded exemption from judgment because he was a member of the covenant nation (shown by his circumcision), it then follows that the only way judgment could have been avoided was by keeping the law. The mere act of circumcision did not exempt the Jew from judgment if he failed to keep the law. Mere ritual will not bring justification.

Just as water baptism does not save any Gentile, circumcision will not save any Jew. Jeremiah taught that circumcision without spiritual transformation is no better than uncircumcision. Paul taught the other side of the coin: uncircumcision with transformation is circumcision. In Romans 2:25 he spells out the principle: a rite without reality is unrighteousness. A Jew cannot be saved by his circumcision since he could not keep the law anyway. Conversely verse 26 points out that reality without rite is righteousness. If a Gentile could keep the law, but lacked circumcision, that lack of circumcision would not condemn him. Verse 27 states that, in fact, the righteous uncircumcision will judge the unrighteous circumcision. The obedience of the uncircumcised Gentile can judge the disobedience of the circumcised Jew.

Having said that circumcision cannot save because ritual does not bring justification, Paul shows, in Romans 2:28–29, why circumcision itself does not avail. Mere physical birth cannot save. Neither can mere physical circumcision save. Physical circumcision is outward, whereas God demands inward circumcision—that which is of the heart. Such inward circumcision is praised by God. When Paul states "whose praise is not of men, but of God" (v. 29), he plays upon the meaning of certain words. Since the term *Jew* has the root meaning of "praise," verse 29 can be paraphrased, "whose Jewishness is not of men but of God." The real meaning of Jewishness is the praise of God. Therefore, a true Jew is one who is a Jew both outwardly and inwardly—not outwardly only.

The Romans 2:25–29 passage does not teach that Gentiles become spiritual Jews. Paul concluded his discussion of the Gentiles in Romans 2:16. In Romans 2:17–3:20 he considers the Jewish question. In this section he employs the same reasoning as in Romans 9–11. He distinguishes between Jews who do not believe and Jews who do believe. This is not a distinction between Jews and Gentiles, nor between Israel and the church, but between the remnant and the nonremnant—between the Jewish believer and the Jewish unbeliever. He shows that a Jew who is not a believer, whose Jewishness is merely outward, is not exempt from divine judgment, for he too has fallen short of the righteousness of God. He has had greater revelation, but that carries with it greater responsibility to that revelation. His failure to keep the law shows that he is not living up to the righteous standard of God. Therefore, he, like the Gentile, has fallen short of God's righteous standards. So he, like the Gentile, is under divine condemnation of sin. Paul points out that the true Jew is not a Jew who has only outward circumcision. A true Jew is a "completed" Jew, a "full" Jew, one who has had both types of circumcision— outward and inward.

These verses must be kept in their context, which is that Paul is dealing with Jews and making a distinction between Jews who believe and Jews who do not believe. He is not teaching that every Gentile Christian is a spiritual Jew. Rather, he is teaching that every Jew is not a full Jew. A completed Jew is one who has had both circumcisions, the circumcision of the flesh, which is outward in obedience to the Abrahamic covenant, and an inward circumcision of the heart as an act of obedience to the new covenant. McClain comes to the same conclusion:

> Paul shows that there is such a thing as being a Jew merely in outward form. But God demands an inward reality and would not recognize any man as a Jew unless he has that. Some people think this statement teaches that every Christian is a Jew, but what it really teaches is that every Jew is not a Jew. No man can be a Jew unless he is born outwardly as a son of Abraham, and also inwardly in spirit; therefore, a man born only outwardly of Abraham is not a true Jew.[21]

A true Jew—a full Jew—is a Jew who is a Jew both outwardly and inwardly. This is a Jew who has responded to the revelation of God and has accepted Christ as Messiah. This person is an ethnic Jew who also is a member of the church. And that person belongs to two groups simultaneously, both Israel and the church. But these are never blended.

CONCLUSION AND SUMMARY

The New Testament consistently differentiates between Israel and the church, which is the very position historically embraced by dispensationalists. The differentiation has been demonstrated by the New Testament use of the terms *Israel* and *the seed of Abraham*. The conclusion is further supported by revelation concerning the beginning of the church in Acts 2 and the mystery form of the church, Christ's body. This church has been gifted by the ascended Christ and is comprised of Gentile believers and a believing remnant from ethnic Israel.

NOTES

1. Lewis Sperry Chafer, *Systematic Theology* (Dallas: Dallas Seminary Press, 1947), 7:205–6.
2. William E. Cox, *Amillennialism Today* (Nutley, N.J.: Presb. & Ref., 1966), 46–47.
3. Ibid.
4. In this list "Q." stands for "quotation."

5. S. Lewis Johnson, "Paul and 'The Israel of God': An Exegetical and Eschatological Case-Study," in *Essays in Honor of J. Dwight Pentecost*, Stanley D. Toussaint and Charles H. Dyer, eds. (Chicago: Moody, 1986), 183.

6. Ibid, 181–82. Quoting William Hendriksen, *Exposition of Galatians, New Testament Commentary* (Grand Rapids: Baker, 1868), 247; and D. W. B. Robinson, "The Distinction Between Jewish and Gentile Believers in Galatians," *Australian Biblical Review* 13 (1965), 29–48.

7. Johnson, "Paul and 'The Israel of God,'" 184.

8. Ibid., 187–88.

9. Ibid., 187.

10. Ibid., 188.

11. Ibid.

12. Ibid., 189.

13. Ibid.

14. Ibid., 191.

15. Ibid.

16. Ibid., 185.

17. Ibid., 192.

18. Ibid.

19. Ibid.

20. Ibid., 195.

21. Alva J. McClain, *Romans: The Gospel of God's Grace* (Chicago: Moody, 1973), 86.

A distinctive tenet of dispensational interpretation is the recognition of prophetic postponement. This phenomenon can be demonstrated in Old Testament texts where we recognize unfulfilled aspects of the messianic program for national Israel. Daniel 9:26–27, as a much contested model for demonstrating time intervals in eschatological passages, reveals historical, structural, and grammatical justification for the validity of the postponement approach. Daniel's model is found to inform the sequence and theme selection of the synoptic gospel accounts of the Olivet Discourse, and in part to have shaped the literary form, themes, language, and general structure of the book of Revelation. However, Daniel 9:26–27 is but one of many postponement passages. These can be defined as either eschatological Day of the Lord or eschatological messianic.

———————

7

PROPHETIC POSTPONEMENT IN DANIEL 9 AND OTHER TEXTS

J. Randall Price

D ispensationalism always has recognized that the New Testament revelation of two phases to the messianic advent has necessitated an interruption in the fulfillment of the restoration program unconditionally guaranteed to national Israel (Jer. 31:31–37). This is evidenced by the observation in the Old Testament that this restoration included the two inseparable elements of spiritual redemption (cf. Isa. 9:1–7; 53–55; Ezek. 36:25–27; 37:14, 23) and national restoration (cf. Isa. 9:8; 56:1–8; Ezek. 36:24, 28; 37:24–28). The first advent work of the Messiah provided spiritual redemption for ethnic Israel (Matt. 1:21; cf. Luke 2:11); but being rejected on a national scale, i.e., the nation as represented by its national leadership (Matt. 23:37, cf. Acts 3:13–15, 17; 4:25–27), necessitated the Messiah's second coming to complete the promise of national restoration (Matt. 23:39; cf. Acts 1:6–7).

THE RECOGNITION OF POSTPONEMENT

Jesus had instructed His disciples concerning two phases (messianic redemption and restoration) following the preview of the messianic kingdom (Matt. 16:28; Mark 9:1; Luke 9:26–27) at Jesus' transfiguration (Matt. 17:1–8; Mark 9:2–8; Luke 9:28–36). The appearance of Elijah with Jesus (Matt. 17:4–5; Mark 9:4–5), coupled with Jesus' statements concerning His rising from the dead (Matt. 17:9;

Mark 9:9–10), had confused the disciples and provoked the question, "Why then do the scribes say that Elijah must come first?" (Matthew 17:10; Mark 9:11). Jesus' reply was made with respect to the two phases when He answered, "Elijah *is coming* to restore all things [cf. Mal. 4:5]; but I say to you, that Elijah *already came,* and they did not recognize him, but did to him whatever they wished. So also the Son of Man is going to suffer" (Matthew 17:11–12; Mark 9:12–13). In other words, just as the messianic forerunner's coming had two phases: John the Baptizer (one to suffer and die), and Elijah the Prophet (one of restoration and glory), so also would the Messiah's coming. The response to the forerunner foreshadowed the response to the Messiah and necessitated the postponement of the fulfillment specifically promised to national Israel.

The Early Jewish-Christian Interpretation of Postponement

This interruption in the divine program of Israelite redemptive history was also interpreted in early Jewish-Christian theology as a postponement of the messianic blessings originally promised to the nation. This recognition of postponement is explicit in the earliest post-Pentecostal preaching of the apostles. For example, in Acts 3:18 we read of the fulfillment of the messianic blessings of redemption in the first phase of Jesus' advent in the words, "But the things which God announced beforehand by the mouth of all the prophets, that His Messiah should suffer, He has thus fulfilled." This redemptive proclamation is then tied in the text (vv. 19–21) to the second phase of advent, which further fulfills the messianic blessings of restoration: "Repent therefore and return, that your sins may be wiped away, in order that times of refreshing may come from the presence of the Lord; and that He may send Jesus, the Messiah appointed for you, whom heaven must receive until the period of restoration of all things about which God spoke by the mouth of His holy prophets from ancient time."

The phrases "times of refreshing" and "period of restoration of all things," are expressions for the messianic era or the promised restoration of national Israel to the divine ideal (cf. Isa. 2:2–4; 4:2–6; 11:6–9; 62:1–12; etc.).[1] The latter term ("restoration") is especially related to national Jewish *repentance* toward the redemptive work of Messiah, since the two terms come from the same root and seem to be patterned after the prophetic condition for the restoration of the messianic kingdom: "(re)turn to Me [with a restored heart], and I will return to you [with restored blessings]" (Zech. 1:3; Mal. 3:7; cf. Matt. 3:1–2; 4:17). If all of the messianic blessings for Israel were fulfilled in the cross-work of Christ, then why is Israel's repentance (Acts 3:19) so closely tied with the purpose of the second advent? The text reads "repent . . . *in order that* He may send the Christ appointed for you" (v. 20).[2] Nowhere in Scripture is it ever said to Gentiles that their repentance would result in God's sending the Messiah. On the contrary, 1 Thessalonians 1:9–10 says that Gentile repentance has simply put them in a position to "wait" for the Messiah's return. Also of significance in Acts 3:20 is the specificity of address "for you." That this addresses Jews alone, and especially Jews as "national Israel," is affirmed by Acts 3:1, 13–18. Therefore, this connection between Jewish repentance toward Messiah and the messianic advent for the Jews (cf. John 4:22; Rom. 11:23, 25–26) necessitates a period of postponement until fulfillment is realized.

The Pauline Interpretation of Postponement

In the Pauline apologetic for national Israel, the rejection of the promised Messiah by Israel is presented as having brought a suspension in the fulfillment of the messianic promises to Israel (Rom. 11:12, 15, 23, 25–28, 31). Paul argues that it is only because God has not failed (and will not fail) in His promise to *national Israel* (cf. 1 Kings 8:56; Zeph. 3:11–20), that *Gentiles,* who presently share in Israel's Messiah during the church age, can have assurance of God's promised blessings (Rom. 9:6; 10:1; 11:11, 29–32). Conversely, present Gentile reception of mercy is an assurance of Israel's future reception of mercy (Rom. 11:30–31). Yet, even the present mercy that has come to Gentiles is not complete but awaits a final fulfillment. In Romans 15:8–12 Paul cites from four Old Testament (LXX) passages that predicted Gentile salvation (Ps. 18:49; Deut. 32:43; Ps. 117:1; Isa. 11:10) in order to show that God is fulfilling His promise to bless the Gentiles through Israel's Messiah in His confirmation of the Abrahamic covenant (cf. Gen. 12:3; John 4:22). The Old Testament contexts depict an obeisance of the Gentile nations, a future accomplishment attending the Second Advent when Israel is restored as head of the nations and itself becomes the instrument of universal blessing, in complete fulfillment of the Abrahamic covenant (cf. Deut. 28:13; 30:1–10; Zech. 8:22–23). The argument would then run, If *individual* Gentiles are now being saved (Acts 15:14), it is a proof of the future fulfillment of the promise of *national* Gentile salvation. Therefore, like the proof offered in individual Jewish salvation for national Israel's salvation, individual Gentile salvation guarantees that national Israel must be restored to carry out her role with respect to national Gentile salvation (Isa. 19:23–25).

Consequently, dispensationalists have observed that in order for God to fulfill His stated purpose in sending the Messiah to Israel (Matt. 1:21; 4:17; 6:10; 26:29; Luke 12:32; Acts 1:6), He must restore Israel, first to spiritual faith in the Messiah as Redeemer and then to the spiritual and national blessings under Messiah as Ruler. Theologically, the phenomenon that has occurred as a result of national rejection has been a delay in the fulfillment of national restoration.

THE TERMINOLOGY OF POSTPONEMENT

The technical expression for this delay in the fulfillment of the messianic program for Israel is derived from the Greek verb *apotelō* meaning "to bring to completion, finish."[3] This *apotelesmatic* interpretation recognizes that in Old Testament texts that present the messianic program as a single event, a near and far historical fulfillment is intended, separated by an indeterminate period of time. Older dispensational writers referred to this as an "intercalation" or a "gap." However, we prefer the term "prophetic postponement." *Postponement,* because it retains the original idea of an interruption in fulfillment, while supplementing it with the notion that such a delay is only temporary, and *prophetic,* because we understand a purposeful, preordained act in the divine program.

Such a postponement was implied in Old Testament texts concerned with Israel's hardening (Isa. 6:9–13; Zech. 7:11–12) and judicial exile (Deut. 4:27–30; 28:36–37, 49–50, 64–68), yet not fully revealed until the New Testament revelation (John 12:37–40; Acts 28:25–28; Rom. 11:25–26). This postponement in Israelite history is not so much an interruption of redemption as an *extension* of predicted hardening (Rom. 11:7–10). The Exile, which was a punishment for national disobedience, has therefore been prolonged during the present age until the appointed time for Israel's national (and spiritual) restoration (Acts 1:7; 3:21; Rom. 11:25–27). So that none can question the infallibility of the divine promise to Israel (Rom. 9:6; 11:29), *individual* Israelite redemption is presently being fulfilled *within* the church (Rom. 11:1–5). This salvation of an individual Jewish remnant (a part of the "all Israel," Rom. 9:8b; 11:24, 27) during the present age testifies to the ultimate salvation of a national Remnant ("all Israel," Rom. 11:26) in the age to come. This previously unrevealed aspect of the messianic plan (Rom. 16:25–26; Eph. 3:3–6) reveals that the promise of national Israelite redemption (Rom. 11:23b) will be accomplished by Messiah in the future as certainly as individual Jewish and Gentile salvation has been effected in Messiah at present (Rom. 11:12, 15, 23, 31).

The Expression of Postponement

The expression of postponement is implied in Old Testament restoration texts that are cited or alluded to in the New Testament in terms of future fulfillment. For instance, the Old Testament promised that the city of Jerusalem would be delivered from Gentile domination by messianic intervention (Zech. 14:1–4). This is an event that has never seen fulfillment in Israelite history in terms of the prophetic expectation. The New Testament, however, records that the Messiah during His first advent promised this fulfillment at His second advent (Luke 21:24b–31). In this New Testament prediction of fulfillment, given in response to questions concerning the future (v. 7), Jesus teaches that the destruction of the Temple (vv. 20–23), the period of Jewish Diaspora (v. 24a), wars on an international scale (v. 10), natural disasters (v. 11), persecutions (vv. 12–19), and celestial and terrestrial phenomenon (vv. 25–26) will all *precede* the time of deliverance (national redemption) brought by the second advent (vv. 27–28). Therefore, the final redemption for Israel ("this generation," v. 32), has been postponed until these events (including national Israelite hardening) culminate with the conclusion of "the times of the Gentiles" (v. 24b; cf. Rom. 11:25).

When the Old Testament records that the Messiah will be born (Isa. 9:6) and will rule on the throne of David and over his kingdom (9:7), it is portrayed as *one* messianic advent. However, returning again to our text in Acts 3, we understand that the complete fulfillment of this advent has been postponed. Here it is explained that the Messiah was sent to Israel (from heaven to be born on earth), in fulfillment of Isaiah 9:6 (cf. Acts 3:18), and *will be* sent *again* to Israel (from heaven to rule on earth) to fulfill Isaiah 9:7 (Acts 3:20–21).

One must ask why a *second* coming would be necessary if all the prophetic promises (to Israel) were fulfilled (as preterists and historicists contend) at the first advent (i.e., at the Cross)? It should also be noted that the apotelesmatic approach is different from the "already/not yet" dialectic, in that the latter would see a *partial* fulfillment of the *complete* promise, while the former would see a *complete* fulfillment of *part* of the promise.[4] Therefore, rather than interpreting Jesus as partially fulfilling the promise to reign on David's throne by His present heavenly session as Lord over the church (Acts 2:34–36; Heb. 1:3; 12:2), this is seen as postponed for a *future* earthly enthronement, which completely fulfills the literal requirements of the Old Testament context with respect to national Israel (2 Sam. 7:16; Ps. 89:4; Matt. 19:28; 25:31).

Qualifications for Postponement

It is important to remember that the messianic promises were originally directed to national Israel (cf. Matt. 15:24), and as such they have their ultimate fulfillment *exclusively with Israel.* While the church occupies a parenthetical *period* in the fulfillment of Israel's destiny, it is clear from both the teaching and the tenor of the New Testament epistles that the church has not been relegated to a parenthetical *position* by this historical consequence (cf. Eph. 1:12; 2:6–7; 3:9–10; 5:25–27; Col. 1:26–27; etc.). Rather, the New Testament revelation concerning the church gives it a distinct purpose in the messianic plan, alongside that of Israel, in the consummation of the ages to the glory of God the Father (1 Cor. 15:23–28). It is in the church that the elect (Jew and Gentile) have an equal access to God (Eph. 2:11–22)—a new revelation of God's saving grace through Israel's Messiah, which has incorporated Gentiles as fellow heirs of the messianic blessings (Eph. 2:3–6), including the inheritance of the messianic kingdom (1 Cor. 6:10; Gal. 5:21; Eph. 5:5; 1 Thess. 2:12; 2 Thess. 1:5).

It must further be recognized that the restoration promises made to national Israel indicate a future fulfillment *in the same manner* as the redemptive promises have found past fulfillment. As the Messiah's first advent was originally directed to national Israel and was accomplished literally in terms of Israelite redemptive expectation (Isa. 53; Dan. 9:26), so the Messiah's second advent will fulfill the prophetic expectation of Israelite restoration (Acts 1:6; Rom. 11:26–27; 2 Thess. 1:5–10; 2:3–12; Rev. 19:11–20:9). If this was to be understood otherwise (e.g., in the first advent as in the historicist interpretation), then why did Jesus in the Olivet Discourse and Peter in Acts (3:19–21) project its fulfillment into a time attendant to the second advent? Or, if this text was intended to find its fulfillment in A.D. 70 (the preterist interpretation) with the greater domination of the Gentiles (Romans) over Israel, how are "the times of the Gentiles" thereby "fulfilled" (i.e., concluded) and Israel's fortunes restored? The only way to harmonize these discrepancies is to reinterpret historic fulfillment in terms different (e.g. nonliteral, nonfuture) from the Old Testament prophets.

We must further note that apotelesmatic passages, where intervals in the fulfillment of prophecies occur, are a common biblical phenomena, especially in the Prophets (where the messianic restoration of Israel is addressed). The length of an interval is inconsequential to the fulfillment of the prediction, as can be seen from past historical predictions that encompassed many centuries (e.g., the prophecy of the Exodus and establishment in the Land, Gen. 15:13–16). The final section in this chapter presents a survey of many such passages that represent examples of prophetic postponement.

POSTPONEMENT AND
CHRONOLOGICAL CONTINUITY

The apotelesmatic approach includes both an extension of Israel's exilic condition and a *postponement* of Israel's restoration, with a *parenthetical* period incorporated to fulfill the messianic redemptive promises for those (whether Jew or Gentile) who have accepted Israel's Messiah (John 1:11–12; 1 Cor. 1:24). Since Israel's hardening did not permit the promise of national repentance toward Messiah at the first advent (John 12:37–40), this will be fulfilled at the second advent (Rom. 11:25; cf. Ezek. 36:26–27). An objection to this concept of postponement, especially in prophetic passages where a definite measure of time or space is specified (e.g., Dan. 9:24–27), has been that in such cases the units of time or space must be understood to run *continuously* and *successively.*[5] However, postponement does not affect such fulfillment of measured events. The same chronological events are fulfilled in the same temporal order as if no interruption occurred. Dispensational writers have sought to illustrate this by the imagery of a "prophetic clock." If we reckon that this clock is keeping only "Israeli time," the hands on the clock presently have frozen in the "times of the Gentiles" position, to resume their continuous run and complete the appointed hour "when the times of the Gentiles is fulfilled." From the human perspective it would seem that the clock has stopped, and the perceived interval may appear as a failure in fulfillment. From the divine viewpoint, nothing has changed, and all is proceeding according to schedule (since the "times of the Gentiles" was always an intended part of the fulfillment). Therefore, despite the apparent delay in fulfillment, the promise to Israel has not been prevented but simply postponed.

POSTPONEMENT AND
THE PROPHETIC PERSPECTIVE

Another way to view postponement is that of "prophetic viewpoint." The rationale here is that biblical authors recorded prophetically the events concerning both advents of Christ, but had no need to describe an intervening history (particularly since that history related more to fulfillment for Gentiles than for national Israel). To illustrate, let us imagine the Old Testament prophets looking at "mountaintops of prophetic revelation" (the messianic advents). They could clearly see the mountaintops, but from their vantage point the two mountaintops appeared to converge as one peak (i.e., as *one* messianic advent). In between these mountains lay a valley (the church age), which, of course, was hidden from view. In 1 Peter 1:10–12 we seem to find a confirmation of this principle. In this text, addressed to predominately Gentile exiles (cf. 1:14; 2:9–10; 4:3–4), it is explained that the prophets of Israel had received revelation concerning God's intentions to bring Messiah's gracious salvation to the Gentiles (1 Peter 1:10a; e.g., Isa. 9:1–2; 19:21–25; 42:1–2; 56:1–8). These prophets had known that Israel's Messiah, "the Servant of the Lord," was to be a "light to the nations" (Isa. 42:6; 49:6) and had diligently sought to discover in their prophetic writings the appointed time for the messianic advent (1 Peter 1:10b–11a), which for them, according to 1 Peter 1:11b, combined both the first advent ("the sufferings of Messiah," cf. Isa. 53) and the second advent ("the glories to follow," cf. Isa. 11:1–5). These prophets could not clearly discern when the Gentiles would receive mercy (the church age, cf. Col. 1:26–27), for most of the promises to this effect were connected with the time of "the glories to follow" (the messianic Age, cf. Isa. 11:10; 42:6; 60:3; Mal. 1:11.)

This may have been the basis for James' argument in Acts 15:13–19, for he cited from Amos 9:11–12, which has as its context the future restoration of Israel: "In that day . . . I will restore the captivity of My people Israel." James may be grounding his plea for the present acceptance of Gentile believers on the principle of Gentile salvation in the restored Davidic (millennial) kingdom, which made no mention of proselyte requirements. In this case, James' interpretive words introducing the citation: "After these things I will *return*" (Acts 15:16), may imply the second advent.[6]

Therefore, it is evident from many prophetic texts that a postponement of messianic fulfillment *has occurred,* otherwise we are left to explain such fulfillment in terms other than that understood by the prophets, the apostles, and our Lord in their eschatological narratives.

POSTPONEMENT AND CHRISTOCENTRIC INTERPRETATION

Those who adopt alternate interpretive systems insist that the New Testament reinterprets the Old Testament in christological terms, so that complete fulfillment of the messianic program is now understood to take place within the church. Jesus, however, employing this hermeneutic in His commentary on Isaiah 61:1–2a (Luke 4:16–21), appears to have understood a postponement in the fulfillment of this text. In the Lukan narrative, Jesus, applying the Old Testament text to Himself in terms of fulfillment (Luke 4:21), abruptly ended His selected passage (Isa. 61:1–2) in midsentence with the words, "to proclaim the favorable year of the Lord" (Isa. 61:2a). The completion of this sentence in Isaiah 61:2b reads, "and the day of vengeance of our God; to comfort all who mourn." If the Lord's purpose at the first advent was to redeem rather than to reign, then we can understand why the second half of this verse, which focuses on the second advent (with its attendant judgment on the nations), was omitted. It will not do, as some claim, that it was omitted in order "to stress the grace of God,"[7] for the words in verse 2c—"to comfort all who mourn"—and especially those in verse 3, also stress the grace of God. It seems preferable to conclude that Jesus knew that the day of Gentile judgment was to be postponed and so read only that portion of the verse for which He could claim present fulfillment.

Opponents of this view claim that no gap was intended here, because even if the entire passage was not cited, "the day of God's wrath as well as the day of redemption were inaugurated by our Lord's ministry."[8] Historicists and preterists who make this argument would find this "day of wrath" fulfilled either at the Cross or in A.D. 70.[9] The problem with such an interpretation is that at these times wrath fell on the Jews, not on the Gentiles as predicted in the Isaiah text. By contrast, Isaiah 61 sees the nation of Israel revived and restored (vv. 2c–10) for a witness *to the Gentile nations* (v. 11), who in fact will *serve* the Jews (vv. 5–6), not *destroy* them. Again, we must ask why the Parousia was postponed if two of its primary goals—the day of vengeance (on the nations), and the restoration of Israel— were *already* fulfilled at the Cross (or in A.D. 70) and within the church? The above example of christocentric interpretation of the Old Testament, therefore, supports prophetic postponement. We now turn to one of the most contested examples of prophetic postponement, the seventy-weeks prophecy of Daniel 9:24–27.

DANIEL 9,
AN EXAMPLE OF PROPHETIC POSTPONEMENT

Daniel 9:24–27 is accepted by dispensationalists as an example of prophetic postponement. Conservative and critical scholars alike hold that Daniel's seventy weeks (v. 24) are to be interpreted as seventy weeks of *years.*[10] This resulting period of 490 years (70 x 7) is divided according to verses 25–27 as periods of seven weeks (49 years), sixty-two weeks (434 years), and one week (7 years). Dispensational scholarship has traditionally accepted the context of this passage as messianic, with the Messiah coming after the sixty-two weeks (i.e., after the 7 weeks + the 62 weeks = 483 years) to die. Some see the words "and have nothing" to mean "without inheriting the messianic kingdom" (v. 26a), leaving the fulfillment of this purpose to the final week (v. 27), which depicts the resumption of the messianic promise for Israel with the overthrow of the Antichrist (the apocalyptic prerequisite to the establishment of the messianic kingdom; see chart 1).

The significance of Daniel's prophecy was attested by the first-century Jewish historian Josephus: "He [Daniel] not only predicted the future, like the other prophets, but specified when the events would happen" (*Antiquities* x. 268). In this respect, Daniel 9:27 uniquely serves as the single Old Testament text cited by our Lord in the synoptics as a chronological indicator of eschatological events (Matt. 24:15; Mark 13:14). It is also thought to be the text underlying Paul's eschatological treatise in 2 Thessalonians 2:3–10 concerning "the son of destruction [Antichrist] and the Temple" (language that has no other literary referent but Dan. 9:27),[11] and also may have served as a literary paradigm for the structure of the book of Revelation.

Dispensationalists have been accused of theological bias in their apotelesmatic interpretation of Daniel 9:26–27; but it is rather the interpretation of Daniel 9:27 in light of the New Testament citations and allusions, along with an exegesis of the original text itself, that has convinced dispensationalists of the seventy-weeks prophecy as an example of prophetic postponement. For this reason it is important for both nondispensationalists as well as dispensationalists to understand the apotelesmatic argument with respect to this important text.

The Apotelesmatic Interpretation of Daniel's Seventy-Weeks Prophecy

Because of the nature of Daniel's terminology in the ninth chapter, the earliest attempts at commentary have revealed a diversity of interpretations.[12] The question that has most concerned commentators has been the identification of the *terminus a quo* (the commencement) and the *terminus ad quem* (the conclusion) of the prophecy. We will bypass discussion of the *terminus a quo* of the prophecy (Dan. 9:25a),[13] in order to focus on the *terminus ad quem*.

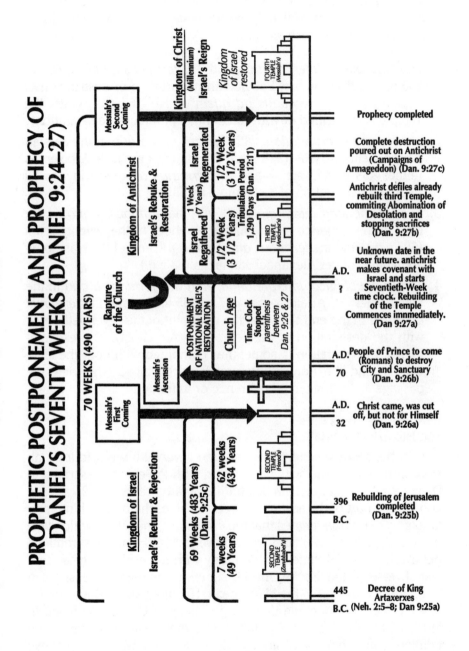

PROPHETIC POSTPONEMENT AND PROPHECY OF DANIEL'S SEVENTY WEEKS (DANIEL 9:24–27)

70 WEEKS (490 YEARS)

Kingdom of Christ
(Millennium)
Israel's Reign

Kingdom of Israel restored

FOURTH TEMPLE (*Messiah's*)

Prophecy completed

Messiah's Second Coming

Kingdom of Antichrist

Israel's Rebuke & Restoration

Israel Regathered 1 Week (7 Years) Israel Regenerated

1/2 Week (3 1/2 Years)

1/2 Week (3 1/2 Years)

Tribulation Period
1,290 Days (Dan. 12:11)

THIRD TEMPLE (*Antichrist's*)

Complete destruction poured out on Antichrist (Campaigns of Armageddon) (Dan. 9:27c)

Antichrist defiles already rebuilt third Temple, commiting Abomination of Desolation and stopping sacrifices (Dan. 9:27b)

Rapture of the Church

POSTPONEMENT OF NATIONAL ISRAEL'S RESTORATION

Church Age

Time Clock Stopped *parenthesis between Dan. 9:26 & 27*

A.D. ?

Unknown date in the near future. antichrist makes covenant with Israel and starts Seventieth-Week time clock. Rebuilding of the Temple Commences imnmediately. (Dan 9:27a)

Messiah's Ascension

A.D. 70

People of Prince to come (Romans) to destroy City and Sanctuary (Dan. 9:26b)

Messiah's First Coming

A.D. 32

Christ came, was cut off, but not for Himself (Dan. 9:26a)

Kingdom of Israel

Israel's Return & Rejection

69 Weeks (483 Years) (Dan. 9:25c)

62 weeks (434 Years)

SECOND TEMPLE (*Herod's*)

396 B.C.

Rebuilding of Jerusalem completed (Dan. 9:25b)

7 weeks (49 Years)

SECOND TEMPLE (*Zerubbabel's*)

445 B.C.

Decree of King Artaxerxes (Neh. 2:5–8; Dan 9:25a)

However, a brief summary of competing interpretations[14] of the seventy-weeks prophecy will help us understand the difficulties in attempting to resolve these termini:

1. *The Maccabean Interpretation,* with the *terminus a quo* in 605 or 586 B.C. (either the first Babylonian deportation or destruction of Temple) and the *terminus ad quem* in 167–165 B.C. (when the Temple was purified or with Antiochus Ephiphanes' desecration).

2. *The Roman Interpretation,* with the *terminus a quo* in the Persian period—either Cyrus (538 B.C.), Darius (519 B.C.), or Artaxerxes (either 458 or 445 B.C.)—and the *terminus ad quem* in A.D. 70 (with the destruction of the Temple by Titus).

3. *The Hasmonean Interpretation,*[15] with the *terminus a quo* as the time of the issuance of Jeremiah's prophecy of the seventy years (605 B.C.), and the *terminus ad quem* as the end of the Hasmonean dynasty under Alexander Jannaeus (88 B.C.).

4. *The Eschatological Interpretation,* with the *terminus a quo* in the Persian period (Artaxerxes in 457 or 445 B.C.),[16] and the *terminus ad quem* in the end times (at the midpoint of the seventieth week with the desecration of the Temple by Antichrist). The eschatological interpretation is sometimes combined with both the Maccabean and the Roman interpretations by those who view the passage as having a dual reference or fulfillment.

Interpretive Views and Historical Validation

In the first two interpretations, the seventieth week follows almost immediately the sixty-ninth week, with the events described in Daniel 9:27 having been already fulfilled (with events in v. 26 already considered part of the seventieth week). The eschatological interpretation, by definition, argues that the events in Daniel 9:27, which take place only in the seventieth week, have not yet been consummated but await literal fulfillment in harmony with the eschatological context of verses 2 and 24, the Olivet Discourse, and parallel passages in Revelation. If one takes the Maccabean, Hasmonean, or Roman view, one must either conclude that the prophecy of Daniel has failed in terms of precise historical fulfillment or that it was intended to be fulfilled other than in a strictly literal fashion. Because of these chronological difficulties, S. R. Driver declared at the turn of the century, "The prophecy admits no explanation, consistent with history, whatever."[17] Lester Grabbe has more recently written, "Much of

9:24–27 does not clearly and easily fit the known historical context. This is highlighted by practically all the major [critical] commentaries which resort to a great deal of emendation in order to make the statements correspond with history."[18]

In like manner, because the historical events do not fit with any known history, amillennial and postmillennial interpreters have sought to find a symbolical or spiritual fulfillment within the uninterrupted scope of the seventy weeks (i.e., the first-century). Employing a hermeneutic of replacement (of national Israel by the church), they argue for a christological fulfillment during the ministry of Christ or, at the latest, the time of the first preaching of the gospel to the Gentiles. However, John Collins[19] has observed in this regard that the book of Daniel is presented on two axes: the horizontal axis of chronology and the vertical spatial axis of imagery (contrasting heaven and earth). This latter axis figures prominently in every vision of the book *except* chapter 9, where the chronological axis, with a clearly *future* reference, is prominent. This indicates that the focus of Daniel 9 is not in relation to heavenly mysteries but is concerned with historically identifiable events that will transpire on earth. Therefore, any approach that seeks to deal with this text must do so on literal contextual-grammatical-historical terms.

The Basis for the Eschatological Interpretation

A difficulty with all noneschatological interpretations is the fact that in the conclusion to the prophecy in Daniel 9:27 no specific answer to the time of the end of captivity was given to Daniel. It was this very thing that Daniel was attempting to "understand" (v. 2a; cf. 8:17; 9:23) and the motivation behind his prayer (Dan. 9:19). Noneschatological views must find an end to exile in temporary Jewish revolts, all of which were unsuccessful and ultimately led to the destruction of the City, the Temple, and further exile. This, of course, offers no solution to Daniel's specific petition for his people's restoration (which concerned a return to Jerusalem and the rebuilding of the Temple, Dan. 9:16–19). However, what we do find in verse 27 are eschatological time markers, such as *qetz* ("end"), *yashbit* ("cause to cease"), and *kalah* ("end"), *'ad* ("until"), and *nech ratzah tittak* ("an appointed end"). These terms indicate that this section belongs to the eschatological period, qualified later in Daniel as "the end time" (cf. Dan. 12:4, 9, 13).[20] This identification is enhanced by the presence of parallel concepts between the two chapters (e.g., prayer for understanding, 9:2 // 12:8; desolation of Jewish people, 9:27 //

12:7; three-and-one-half-year period, 9:27 // 12:7, 11; the abolition of sacrifice, 9:27 // 12:11; and the abomination of desolation, 9:27 // 12:11). Thus, Daniel's prayer for an end to exile will be fulfilled in the eschatological age when all the elements of his petition will be realized.

The Eschatological Interpretation and Jewish Interpretation

The eschatological interpretation of Daniel 9:26–27 finds further corroboration in view of Jewish apocalyptic literature. In this literature, probably influenced in part by Daniel's seventy weeks, are found the themes of an end-time Jewish persecution and war on Israel, centered in Jerusalem (cf. 1 Enoch 56; 91–104), an Antichrist figure (Belial/Beliar) who serves as a portent of the imminent conclusion of the age and its cataclysmic end (cf. Sibylline Oracles 635–36; IV Esdras 13:31; Testament [T] of Joseph 20:2; T. Simeon 5:3; T. Naphtali 2:6; T. Issachar 6:1; 7:7; T. Reuben 2:1; T. Dan 5:10; T. Levi 18:12; T. Judah 25:3), and an avenging Messiah who is sent by God and fights for Israel (cf. T. Dan 5:10; cf. 5:3–7) and casts "the Antichrist" into eternal punishment (cf. T. Dan 5:10; T. Issachar 6:1; T. Levi 18:12; T. Judah 25:3).[21] At Qumran, many apocalyptic texts, and especially the Pseudo-Daniel texts, present an eschatological review of kingdoms and of a final conflict similar to that depicted in the biblical book of Daniel, particularly Daniel 9:27.[22] Of course, primary support is given by the New Testament eschatological texts already mentioned (Matt. 24:15; Mark 13:14; 2 Thess. 2:4–5), which interpret the events of the seventieth week as future to their time. Even if one considers that the events predicted in the Olivet Discourse were fulfilled in A.D. 70, the fact that Jesus viewed them as yet future in His time at least dismisses the Maccabean interpretation. The challenge to those who accept A.D. 70 as the *terminus ad quem* of the seventy weeks is to explain the details of the prophecy in the events of Roman history, a task of harmonization that will require as significant a degree of reworking the text as is required for the Maccabean interpretation.

The Eschatological Interpretation and Early Patristic Interpretation

In support of the dispensational eschatological interpretation, it should be noted that the earliest recorded church fathers' interpretations of Daniel 9:24–27 advocated an apotelesmatic approach.[23] Most of these interpreters maintained a futurist perspective that was consonant with Jewish apocalyptic and rabbinic interpretation (cf. the *Seder Olam Rabbah,* chap. 28, the oldest tradition for interpreting the seventy weeks). In order to understand the eschatological nature of the events presented by this prophecy and the hermeneutical precedent in the text for literal historical interpretation, let us consider the context of our passage.

The Context of Daniel 9:27

Daniel 9:27 concludes the prophecy of the seventy weeks (9:24–27), which is part of the division of the book that records visions of future earthly kingdoms, human and divine (chaps. 7–12).[24] The reference to the seventy weeks and their predicted fulfillment in this text points to the purpose for Daniel 9:24–27 in relation to the prayer of Daniel (9:3–19) following his observation of the seventy-*years* prophecy in Jeremiah 25:11–12; 29:10 (Dan. 9:2). The prophecy in Daniel 9:24–27 is declared to be the divine response to Daniel's prayer as communicated by the heavenly messenger Gabriel (9:20–23). Since the prophecy appears as an answer to Daniel's prayer, the following should be noted:

1. Daniel's primary petition is for divine clemency toward the desolated Temple (v. 17), the people, and the City (vv. 18–19)
2. Daniel uses a number of terms that will be later developed in the prophetic response in verses 24–27[25]
3. the prayer contains vocabulary similar to the desecration terminology of Jeremiah and Ezekiel: (a) the departure of Israel from covenant (vv. 5, 10–11, 13, 14–15), (b) the judgment of the curses written in the Law (vv. 11, 13), (c) the refusal to hear the prophets (vv. 6, 10), (d) the sins of the fathers (vv. 6, 8, 16), (e) identification with holy Name (v. 19), (f) exile due to cultic rebellion (v. 7), and (g) the reproach from the nations caused by Israel's exile (v. 16).

The stated similarities are significant in that the concern of Jeremiah and Ezekiel was idolatry and desecration—the very problems faced by Daniel as a captive in exile. Further, Jeremiah's prophecy concerned the judgment of the Gentile nations, beginning with Babylon (Jer. 25:12–14) and extending to all historical oppressors of national Israel (vv. 15–38). This judgment is also affirmed in Daniel 9:27. Being more specific, a survey of the desecration motif in these prophets reveals that desecration by foreign invaders (as a result of

Israelite defilement through violations of covenantal worship) forms the major focus of their discourses. Further support may be found in the association of the terms *shiqqutz* ("abomination") and *meshomen* ("desolation") in Jeremiah and Ezekiel, which most likely influenced Daniel's cryptic construction of *shiqqutzim meshomem* ("abomination of desolation") in Daniel 9:27. If this is so, then Daniel may be attempting to include a theological summation of desecration into this expression, that is, to convey in a single thought the entire corpus of prophetic doctrine touching on any future events earmarked by this phrase. This may be helpful in explaining why Jesus in the Olivet Discourse (Matt. 24:15; Mark 13:14a) used this expression to denote the signal event that would serve as warning of the arrival of apocalyptic fulfillment (Matt. 24:16–31; Mark 13:14b–27). The point here is that Daniel's prophecy must be interpreted within the context of his contemporaries, who envisioned fulfillment in eschatological terms (cf. Jer. 31:27–37; Ezek. 37:23–28).

The Relationship of Daniel 9 to Jeremiah

Daniel's prayer helps us to especially draw a link between the desecration/restoration context of Jeremiah's prophecy and that of Daniel's seventy weeks.[26] Just as Jeremiah's prophecy was a reaction to desecration, with the promise of resultant judgment on all foreign desecrators, so was Daniel's. Just as the consequence of this judgment of the nations was to result in Israel's restoration (spiritually and nationally), Jeremiah 30–33, so also in Daniel (cf. chaps. 11–12, which are prefaced by a declaration of their eschatological nature in Dan. 10:14). This answers to Daniel's petition for Israel's restoration based on divine election (9:17–19; cf. Ezek. 36:22–23). What is significant here is that Daniel 9:3–19 places the prophecy of 9:24–27 in a historical context as an *extension* of Jeremiah's historical prophecy.[27] Therefore, as Jacques Doukhan has pointed out, "The seventy-weeks' prophecy must be interpreted with regard to *history* in as realistic a way as Daniel did for the prophecy of Jeremiah."[28]

The Prophetic Goals
of the Seventy-Weeks Prophecy

Equally important to the contextual setting of Daniel 9:27 are the six goals (six infinitives) given in Daniel 9:24 that serve to establish the *terminus ad quem* of the prophecy. The interpretation of these goals is germane to the consideration of postponement in the seventy weeks; for if all of these goals can be proven to have been fulfilled historically, then it can be argued that the seventy weeks were meant to be interpreted as being fulfilled consecutively *without* interruption. These goals are (1) "to finish the transgression," (2) "to make an end of sins," (3) "to make atonement for iniquity," (4) "to bring in everlasting righteousness," (5) "to seal up vision and prophecy," and (6) "to anoint the most holy [place]."

First, it is crucial to observe those for whom this prophecy is to find fulfillment, namely "your people and your holy city" (v. 24). In other words, the fulfillment of the seventy-weeks prophecy relates to national Israel and the city of Jerusalem. Because such a Jewish remnant did return to Judah to nationally resettle the land, and to rebuild Jerusalem, this prophecy should not be interpreted other than in terms of literal, historical fulfillment for national Israel, even though that return was not the one destined to attain these eschatological goals. It nevertheless sets the precedent for all future fulfillment.

Setting aside the debate over the arrangement of these goals, it is important to consider their *nature* to determine whether they could have been fulfilled in past history or if they require an eschatological fulfillment. In verse 24a the first three goals relate to the sins of national Israel. The terms "finish" (transgression) and "end" (sin) both look at the culmination of a condition. A similar expression is found in an eschatological context in the Dead Sea document known as Psuedo-Daniel (4Q 243–45).[29] According to the Jewish commentator Abarbanel, the condition of Israelite punishment required the 490 years of this prophecy to complete the sins committed *in addition* to the violation of the sabbatical law (cf. 2 Chron. 36:21). Other Jewish commentators such as Rashi and Metzudos, held that this referred to a period following the 490 years (which they believed ended with the destruction of the Second Temple), "the last exile whose purpose it will be to terminate [i.e., *to atone for*] transgression."[30] Thus, according to rabbinic tradition, the return to Jerusalem, and the rebuilding of the City and Temple, did not historically fulfill this goal; rather, it awaits a consummation at the end of time. This final atonement, while based on the past work of the Messiah, will be effected for the national remnant of Israel only in the future (Zech. 12:10; 13:1; Ezek. 36:25–27; 37:23; Jer. 31:33–34; Isa. 59:20–21, etc.). It is significant that in the year that the seventy-weeks prophecy was given, Cyrus freed the Jews, ending their foreign captivity and their unavoidable contact with idolatry and desecration. Although a remnant returned to Judah, idolatry and transgression continued (cf. Ezra 9:1–2; Neh. 9:2) and in fact reached a climax in the time of Jesus by the nation's rejection of His messiahship (cf. Acts 7:51–52). This action alone revealed that this prophetic goal for Israel was yet unfulfilled.

The final three goals appear distinctly eschatological, as some noncanonical apocalyptic parallels suggest.[31] The phrase "everlasting *righteousness*" (or, better, "vindication") may have in view a theodicial "age of righteousness" (cf. Isa. 1:26; 11:2–5; 32:17; Jer. 23:5–6; 33:15–18) that resolves the theological scandal (note Dan. 9:15–16) of the former age characterized by "the rebellion" (i.e., Israel's rejection of the Messiah). Therefore, this age will be a vindication of God's promise to national Israel (Ezek. 36:17–23) and a reversal of her condition and fortunes with respect to Messiah, hence a "messianic age" or the messianic kingdom. This eschatological restoration may also be intended in the goal "to seal up the prophetic vision" (Dan. 9:24), which probably has the fulfillment (i.e., "confirmation,") of Jeremiah's prophecy in view.[32] However, the determining phrase is the final one: "to anoint the Holy [of Holies]" (Dan. 9:24). Rabbinic interpretation refers this to the Third Temple, since *Tosefta Sotah* 13:2 records that the Second Temple had not been anointed. This goal is specifically related to the consecration of the chamber that housed the ark of the covenant, whose presence sanctified the Temple by virtue of the *Shekinah* (the Divine Presence). Since neither of these was present in the Second Temple, according to *Yoma* 21b, rabbinic tradition held that the ark will be revealed by the messianic king, who will also build the Third Temple (cf. Jer. 3:16–17; Zech. 6:12). Since Daniel's primary concern in his prophecy is the restoration of the Temple, this eschatological goal, standing at the end of the series of goals, may well determine the focus of fulfillment for the whole.

PRINCIPAL INTERPRETIVE PROBLEMS

The major interpretive questions concern (1) the division of the "seven weeks and sixty-two weeks" of Daniel 9:25, (2) the placement of the events they describe (the building of the City, the appearance of the Messiah) as occurring prior to the conclusion of these weeks, and (3) the discernment of an interval in fulfillment between the sixty-ninth (v. 26) and seventieth week (v. 27). The first part of the problem concerns whether the division of the seven and sixty-two weeks should be understood as one unit of sixty-nine weeks or divided into two separate sections, and then whether the events should be placed in the first section of seven weeks or in the second section of sixty-two weeks. The second part of the problem concerns whether the seventieth week follows immediately after the sixty-ninth week or if it should be treated separately with respect to postponement and future chronological fulfillment.

The Question of the Division
of the Seven and Sixty-two Weeks

The resolution of the question of the division for the "seven weeks and sixty-two weeks" depends in part on the matter of the Masoretic accentuation.[33] The Masoretes placed a disjunctive accent (*athnach*) under the word "seven," which might indicate that they interpreted the two sections as separate divisions. If so, three distinct periods of time are marked off, and the punctuation would imply the appearance of an "anointed" (*mashiah*) at the end of both the seven and the sixty-two week periods (usually the former is identified as Cyrus and the latter a different ruler or Christ). There are, however, formidable reasons for rejecting the Masoretic accent at this point.

First, Masoretic accents are simply interpretive opinions concerning the text and should be weighed as one would any other commentary. In this regard, the opinions of the Masoretes are often questionable, as logical division sometimes is disregarded for other metrical concerns.[34] One such an objection concerning the use of the *athnach* (disjunctive accent) in this context appears nearby, in verse 24, where it appears beneath the word "everlasting" and seems to divide the six infinitives as three negatives plus one positive plus two positives. However, the structure of the goals is more symmetrical with a division of three negatives plus three positives.[35] In addition, the fact that this rabbinic commentary spans a period to a millennium after Christ, when the Jewish/Christian disputations were well advanced, invites the suspicion of an anti-Christian bias, especially in such a famous messianic apologetic text as Daniel 9.[36] Indeed, if one accepts the *athnach* as legitimate here, the christological interpretation of the passage is put in doubt.

Second, earlier textual traditions (Greek—LXX Theodotion, Latin Vulgate, Syriac Peshitta) testify to an ancient reading that combines the numerical elements seven and sixty-two to equal one unit (i.e., sixty-nine).[37] These versions may well preserve a pre-Masoretic reading of the text or an early Jewish or Christian oral tradition concerning the seventy weeks.

Third, if the *athnach* is retained, the logic of the passage is complicated. For instance, it would appear that the entire period of the sixty-two weeks (434 years) was required to build the plaza and the moat (v. 25), and that the "anointed one" (v. 26) appears after the seven weeks (49 years), but is not killed until after the sixty-two weeks (434 years later)! Of course, this later event could be possible if *two* different "anointed" were intended, however, the chiastic structure of the passage argues for only one "anointed."

Fourth, William Shea contends that his analysis of the poetic form of Daniel 9:24–27, on the basis of syllable and metrical count, demands that the units of seven weeks and sixty-two weeks be one epoch of time. Any other arrangement would disrupt the structural parallelism and poetic balance of the passage.[38]

Therefore, it seems preferable to accept the alternative to the Masoretic accentuation that divides the seven and the sixty-two weeks (i.e., grouping sixty-nine weeks) and to place the events as follows: the first unit of seven weeks (forty-nine years) comprises the period of the rebuilding of the Temple and the City (v. 25a); the second unit of sixty-two weeks (434 years) is the time period prior to the coming of the Messiah (v. 25b). After the sixty-two weeks He is killed and the Temple and the City are destroyed (v. 26). The final third unit of one week (seven years) comprises the period of the covenant (the first half of the seven years), its violation with the desecration of the Temple (the midpoint of the seven years), and the final destruction of the Desecrator (the last half of the seven years), verse 27.[39]

The Question of the Division Between the Sixty-Ninth and Seventieth Week

The second problem is whether there is justification for a temporal interval after the sixty-ninth week, constituting a prophetic postponement in fulfillment of the events of the seventieth week. It has been argued that if there was no division between the seven and sixty-two weeks that there should not be one between the sixty-ninth and seventieth week. We have noted, however, that the sixty-ninth week has already been set off as a distinct unit comprised of the seven and sixty-two weeks. This would imply in itself that the events of the seventieth week are to be treated separately. Further, the events in verse 26—"the cutting off of Messiah," and of the "people of the prince"—are stated to occur *after* the sixty-nine weeks. If this was intended to occur *in* the seventieth week, the text would have read here "during" or "in the midst of" (cf. Daniel's use of *hetzi,* "in the middle of," v. 27). This language implies that these events *precede* the seventieth week but do not *immediately* follow the sixty-ninth. Therefore, a temporal interval separates the two. It is also important to note that the opening word of verse 27 (*higbbir,* "confirm") is prefixed by the *waw* consecutive, a grammatical connective that indicates a close consequential relationship to a preceding verb. This use indicates that the events of verse 27 are *subsequent* to those of verse 26. Furthermore, the very language of these two verses, first speaking of "the prince [*nagid,* "leader"] who is to come" (v. 26), and then of that prince that later comes (the "he" of v. 27), implies that a separation of time exists between these events.

Jesus' Description
of the Parenthetical Period

Jesus' interpretation of the order of the events of the seventieth week in the context of prophetic history also appears to confirm this understanding. In Matthew 24:7–14 it is predicted that persecution, suffering, and wars would continue to the end of the age, climaxing in a time of unparalleled distress (vv. 21–22; i.e., "the time of Jacob's distress"; cf. Dan. 12:1; Jer. 30:7). Only *after* these events does Jesus make reference to Daniel 9:27 (Matt. 24:15) concerning the crucial event of this time of tribulation, the appearance of "the desolating abomination." If the seventy weeks were intended to progress sequentially, without interruption, why does Jesus place this intervening period *before* the fulfillment of the events of the seventieth week? The text of Matthew in particular reveals that Jesus' preview of the future was to answer His disciples' questions concerning His (second) coming and the end of the age (Matt. 24:3). Jesus here explains why His coming is necessary (for divine intervention and national repentance, vv. 27–31; cf. Zech. 12:9–10) and when it will occur ("*after* the tribulation of those days," Matt. 24:29). According to Matthew, the events described in this period prior to the messianic advent could not have been fulfilled in A.D. 70 with the destruction of Jerusalem, since these events usher in and terminate with the coming of Christ.[40] It is often asked what justification dispensationalists have for stretching out the seventy weeks to two thousand years. If we can appreciate the length of time required for the fulfillment of these events predicted by Jesus for this intervening period, we have the answer.

Temple Motifs in Daniel
as Eschatological Motifs

An analysis of the motifs of Temple desecration and restoration, especially in relation to the use of the phrase "abomination of desolation" (Dan. 9:27) in the synoptic gospels, leads to an eschatological interpretation of these events.[41] A number of interpreters have suggested that the Temple is the hinge on which Daniel's view of history turns.[42] The era of the four world kingdoms, as well as Daniel's career, begins in the time of the Babylonians, who destroyed the First Temple.

The restoration of the Second Temple in the Persian period (or even Herod's expansion in the Roman period) was not significant enough to be regarded as the fulfillment of Jeremiah's prophecy. Janssen argues that Daniel treats the Second Temple as insignificant and looks to an eschatological restoration of the Solomonic Temple as the culmination of history.[43] This would find support in intertestamental Judaism, which viewed the postexilic period as a temporary lapse in salvation history and held that its fulfillment would come in the eschatological age with an idealized restoration of preexilic Israel, in accordance with the covenantal promises. We would disagree with Janssen that Daniel thought of the Second Temple as insignificant, since his own anticipation and prayer was for its restoration and consecration; however, we would agree that Daniel does connect the Temple with the eschatological age in 9:27 (cf. 8:14), since its desecration and destruction (9:26) required a theological and historical resolution (i.e., reconsecration and restoration), which subsequent events of history, following the order of the sixty-nine weeks, also revealed. If during the seventieth week (v. 27) the Temple is desecrated by a cessation of the sacrificial system, and this follows the destruction of the Second Temple after the sixty-ninth week, logic necessitates that during an intervening period a Third Temple will be built.[44]

It is also possible to discern a causal relationship between Temple desecration and messianic advent based on the desecration/restoration pattern (see chart 2): the desecration of the First Temple brought a prediction of messianic advent (v. 24), and Messiah came during the time of the Second Temple to bring the promised restoration to the Temple (still desecrated at this time).[45] In the future, the desecration of the Tribulation Temple (v. 27) will bring back the Messiah to restore the Temple to its millennial design. This relationship may partially explain the reason why in the Olivet Discourse "the abomination of desolation" is the pivotal event from which events hasten toward the Second Advent.

Prophetic Postponement and the Chiastic Structure

Some object that the events in Daniel 9:27 are *parallel* to those in verse 26 because of the chiastic structure and that, therefore, only the Second Temple is in view. However, chiasm is simply a literary device recognizing the inversion of associated words or ideas and does not by itself govern the timing of the fulfillment of the events expressed. In literary terms there may be parallelism, but this does

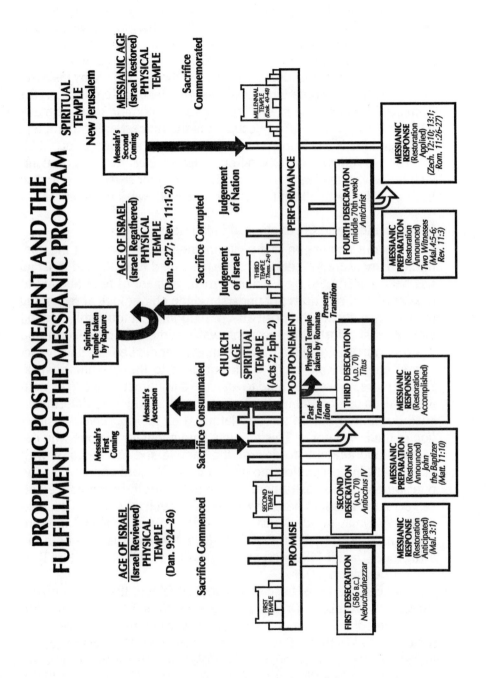

PROPHETIC POSTPONEMENT AND THE
FULFILLMENT OF THE MESSIANIC PROGRAM

not require that the historical events described be continuous without interruption. For instance, "the prince" (*nagid*) in verse 26 is qualified as one "who is to come," i.e., one who was previously introduced to Daniel's audience in 7:8, 23–24 as being from the fourth kingdom—Rome. This identification is confirmed in 9:26 by his association with the people who destroyed the Second Temple, i.e., the Romans. The reference to this "prince" at his coming must be made with the "he" of verse 27a because it is the nearest antecedent, and the basic idea is the same—he will desecrate the Temple (cf. 7:25). However, historically, no known Roman leader ever "made a covenant" with the Jewish leaders (*harabim*, "the many") for seven years, and so this awaits future fulfillment when the seventieth week commences.

Postponement and Chronological Fulfillment

It is our contention that postponement does *not* affect the continuity of measured events, since the measured time allotted to Israel has been interrupted by a different measurement of time allotted to the Gentiles. If one does not understand the chronological reckoning in this sense, those who posit an A.D. 70 fulfillment must still contend with at least a forty-three-year interval of time (the crucifixion and destruction of Jerusalem) that is directly indicated as having occurred after the sixty-ninth week but prior to the seventieth week. Furthermore, those who hold to an A.D. 70 fulfillment have to explain the final clause of Daniel 9:27, namely, "that which is determined shall be poured out on the desolator," (i.e., the *appointed destruction* of the Desolator).[46] This predicted judgment for the one who desecrates and attempts to destroy the Temple and City, accords with an element in desecration motifs that have the Lord announcing the punishment of His instruments of judgment for their arrogance and self-actuated intent to destroy what is holy. Such an end was decreed for the Assyrian invaders (Isa. 10:23–26) and was repeated in more detail in Daniel 11:36 (cf. Rev. 13:5–8), a text that displays both the arrogance (Daniel 11:36–38) and aggression (v. 39) of the future Desolator (the Antichrist).[47]

We could add to these chronological factors the critical observation that the six-fold restoration goal of Daniel 9:24 was not fulfilled immediately after the sixty-ninth week, but instead verse 26 indicated that both the City and the Temple would be destroyed, followed by a determined period of desolations. This was all to be accomplished *before* the seventieth week in verse 27. It is not until the completion of the seventieth week that we find complete fulfillment of the goals.

The Influence of Postponement
on New Testament Eschatology

Jesus' citations from Daniel in His prophetic discourse, along with those of Isaiah, Jeremiah, and Zechariah, suggest that He and His disciples understood their message as a continuation of the biblical prophets and that they were evaluating their generation and modeling their messages in accordance with these prophecies. This is especially noticeable in a comparison of their eschatological discourses. For instance, Jesus' "cleansing of the Temple" pericope has for its background Jeremiah's temple sermon, and it is in this context that Jesus makes His predictions about the destruction of the City and the Temple. The Olivet Discourse likewise contains a striking resemblance to the prophetic judgment passages of Jeremiah and Ezekiel. If these are then linked with the citation from Daniel, we see a pattern of dependence upon collections of prophetic texts that were themselves dependent upon one another. Indeed, the only way a first-century audience could have understood the meaning of Jesus' warning of "the abomination of desolation" of Daniel 9:27 (since it is left unexplained by Daniel and Jesus) was from a comparative study of the terms in the desecration motifs used by the other prophetic writers.

The Seventieth Week and the
Structure of the Olivet Discourse

The confirmation of the postponement of the seventieth week and of a parenthetical period of history involving further exile and persecution for the Jewish people is made by a comparison of the sequence of events presented in the synoptic eschatological discourses and the eschatological treatise on the Temple Desecrator in 2 Thessalonians 2:3–4. John McClean has demonstrated the structural impact of Daniel's seventy weeks and particularly the concept of the "abomination of desolation" on each of the synoptic gospels and the Johannine Apocalypse.[48] He found that eight literary motifs from Daniel correlated with the synoptics and that each gospel could be divided into three prophetic sections corresponding to Daniel 9:27. McClean's three divisions are as follows:

1. First half of the Seventieth Week: *Preliminary Signs of the Tribulation* (Matt. 24:5–14; Mark 13:5–13; Luke 21:8–19)

2. Midpoint of the Seventieth Week: *The Major Sign of the Abomination of Desolation and the Destruction of Jerusalem* (Matt. 24:15–28; Mark 13:14–23; Luke 21:20–24)

3. Second half of the Seventieth Week: *Eschatological Fulfillment with the Coming of the Son of Man* (Matt. 24:29–31; Mark 13:24–27; Luke 21:25–28)

The consideration of the order of these events in light of the Danielic prophetic structure suggested by the use of Daniel 9:27 in Matthew and Mark, show a marked influence, if not dependence, upon the seventy-weeks prophecy. Let us further consider the corroboration of events between Daniel 9, the Olivet Discourse, and the book of Revelation.

The Seventieth Week and the Structure of the Apocalypse

McClean's analysis of the book of Revelation[49] further reveals that the structure of the judgment section (chaps. 4–19) contains linguistic and thematic parallels with the synoptics that reflect an amplification of the synoptic eschatological discourses. Revelation 6:1–11 (the first five seals) was found to be the midpoint in the seventieth week and to correlate directly with the preliminary signs of the synoptics. Further, Revelation 7–19 was demonstrated to be an expansion of the synoptic gospels within the framework of Daniel 9:27. This is particularly evident in John's incorporation of the three-and-a-half years division of the seventieth week and the development of the abomination of desolation motif through the various beasts of chapters 12, 13, and 17. Finally, the third section (the Great Tribulation) of Revelation's six major sections[50] develops into four subsections (4:1–5:14; 6:1–17; 8:1–18:24; 19:1–21) shaped by the seal, trumpet, and bowl septet judgments. These septet judgments are structured according to the seventieth week:

1. The First half of the Week (Dan. 9:27a): *The Seal Judgments* (Rev. 4:1–6:17); Synoptic Correlation: *The Preliminary Signs* (Matt. 24:4–14; Mark 13:4–13; Luke 21:8–19)

2. The Second half of the Week (Dan. 9:27b): *The Trumpet Judgments* (Rev. 7:1–13:18); Synoptic Correlation: *The Abomination of Desolation* (Matt. 24:15–28; Mark 13:14–23; Luke 21:20–24)

3. The Final Days (Dan. 9:27c): *The Bowl Judgments* (Rev. 14:1–19:21); Synoptic Correlation: *The Parousia and Close of End Times* (Matt. 24:29–31; Mark 13:24–27; Luke 21:25–28)

It may be seen, therefore, that Daniel 9 has significantly informed the sequence and motif selection of the individual synoptic accounts of the Olivet Discourse and 2 Thessalonians 2. If one accepts McLean's structure of Revelation, it also could be argued that Daniel 9 has in part shaped the genre, motifs, language, and generally all of the structure of the book of Revelation.

ADDITIONAL EXAMPLES OF PROPHETIC POSTPONEMENT

Old Testament prophetic texts are replete with examples of statements in which a partial fulfillment can be discerned in history but complete (or ultimate) fulfillment awaits a future, ideal time, usually the eschaton. The following passages include a near historical fulfillment and a far Day of the Lord fulfillment in the same context:

Eschatological Day of the Lord Postponement Texts

Near Historical Fulfillment	Far Day of the Lord Fulfillment
Isaiah 2:5–9	Isaiah 2:10–22 (cf. Rev. 6:16–17)
Isaiah 10:20–23	Isaiah 11:11–16
Isaiah 13:1–8	Isaiah 13:9–16 (cf. Matt. 24:29; Rev. 6:12–13)
Obadiah 1–14	Obadiah 15–21
Joel 2:1–17	Joel 2:28–31 (cf. Matt. 24:37–41; 2 Thess. 1:9; Rev. 6:12)
Zephaniah 1:7–16	Zephaniah 1:17–18
Zechariah 1:4–13	Zechariah 1:14–18
Malachi 3:8	Malachi 3:9–10
2 Thessalonians 2:3a, 7a	2 Thessalonians 2:3b–4, 7b–8
2 Peter 2:9a	2 Peter 2:9b
2 Peter 3:2, 5–6, 9 (cf. 3:15)	2 Peter 3:3–4, 10–13

Old Testament messsianic texts also reveal (in the light of the NT revelation) a distinction between a historical (first) advent and eschatological (second) advent. We may refer to these as eschatological *messianic* postponement texts.

Eschatological Messianic Postponement Texts

Historical or First Advent	Eschatological or Second Advent
Isaiah 9:1–2	Isaiah 9:3–5
Isaiah 9:6 (cf. Matt. 4:16; Luke 1:79)	Isaiah 9:7
Isaiah 52:13–55:13	Isaiah 56:1–8
Isaiah 59:16–17b	Isaiah 59:17c–21
Isaiah 61:1–2a (in light of Luke 4:18–19; cf. 7:22)	Isaiah 61:2b–11 9cf. Rev. 21:2)
Zechariah 9:9	Zechariah 9:10
Isaiah 11:1–3	Isaiah 11:4–9
Jeremiah 23:5	Jeremiah 23:6–8
Psalm 22:1–21	Psalm 22:22–31
Malachi 3:1	Malachi 3:2–3
Malachi 4:2	Malachi 4:1, 3, 5–6
Genesis 49:10a	Genesis 49:10b
Deuteronomy 18:15a, 18	Deuteronomy 18:15b, 19
Zechariah 3:8	Zechariah 3:9–10
Psalm 2:7 (cf. Acts 13:33, Heb. 1:5, 5:5)	Psalm 2:8 (cf. Rev. 2:26–27)

It is probable that many of the desecration/restoration motif texts in the Prophets may also bear this distinction, with a partial (near) fulfillment in the return to the land and the rebuilding of the Temple and City, and an ultimate/eschatological (far) fulfillment in national Israel's regathering and rebuilding of the Temple at the end time (in the Tribulation and the Millennium).

CONCLUSIONS

Prophetic postponement is a distinct tenet of dispensational interpretation. It is not a *creation* of this system prompted by its view of separate programs for Israel and the church but the *observation* that such distinctions were made in New Testament eschatological texts employing Old Testament messianic and restoration passages.[51] Such observation then prompted the recognition of separate programs for Israel and the church and their development systematically. In this study we have sought to provide biblical and interpretive arguments in support of the apotelesmatic approach. The following summary represents some of our conclusions:

1. The present physical domination of Gentile powers and the present spiritual program of the church suggest that the literal historical fulfillment of Israel's national ascendancy and spiritual revival has been postponed until a future age.

2. The evidence for this prophetic postponement is not restricted to any one text as considered earlier in this chapter but is a characteristic of Day of the Lord and messianic prophetic texts. It may be further supported by the restoration motifs of the prophets that have not yet seen complete fulfillment.

3. Although prophetic postponement is not exclusive to Daniel 9:26–27, this text serves as a model text for this phenomenon in light of its use in the synoptic gospels, the Thessalonian epistles, and the book of Revelation.

4. Prophetic postponement is demonstrated in New Testament eschatological texts with the Olivet Discourse and the judgment section of the Apocalypse structured by Daniel 9:27.

5. The New Testament further demonstrates the acceptance of prophetic postponement through its continuation of the Old Testament restoration promises to national Israel (e.g. Acts 3:19–21; Rom. 11:25–31). The second advent of Christ is seen to be uniquely associated with the fulfillment of these promises (e.g., Matt. 24:30–31; Acts 1:6–7; 3:20; 2 Thess. 2:8).

NOTES

1. The term *anapsuxis* ("refreshing") is commonly used by Luke to refer to "the expectation of the time of salvation as *relief* following afflictions" (e.g., Luke 21:7–19, 28, 36; Acts 9:16; 14:22), and therefore this connection with *kairoi* ("times") and *apo prosopou tou kuriou* ("from the presence of the Lord") may refer to the deliverance of the Jewish remnant from Gentile domination and resultant persecution (ultimately effected at the end of the tribulation period) by the advent of Messiah. In this respect it is analogous to *anesis* ("relief") in 2 Thessalonians 1:7; cf. J. Kremer, "*anapsuxis*," in *EDNT*, Horst Balz and Gerhard Schneider, eds. (Grand Rapids: Eerdmans, 1990), 1:95. The term *apokatastasis* ("restoration") is derived from the verb *apokathistemi* ("to restore [to an earlier condition]"), used in Acts 1:6 for "*restoring* the kingdom to Israel," and in Matthew 17:11 and Mark 9:12 (cf. Malachi 4:5) of Elijah's coming to "*restore* all things."

2. Purpose (in order that) is here indicated by conjunctive *hopos* + *an* and the aorist subjunctive. This construction governs both purpose clause—"that your sins may be wiped away" and "that He may send the Christ."

3. The usual sense of *telos* as "end" or "goal" may here have the more technical idea of "the consummation that comes to prophecies when they are fulfilled" (Luke 22:37); cf. Arndt and Gingrich, *A Greek-English Lexicon of the New Testament* (Chicago: Univ. of Chicago Press, 1957), 819:1. Therefore, with the prefix *apo*, which basically has the connotation of "separation from something," the idea is of a delay or interruption in the completion of the prophetic program. The term "apotelesmatic" has been used by scholars writing about prophecy for at least one hundred years.

4. Don N. Howell, Jr., "Pauline Eschatological Dualism and Its Resulting Tensions," *Trinity Journal* 14, no. 1 (Spring 1993), 3, 7–8.

5. E.g., Philip Mauro, *The Seventy Weeks and the Great Tribulation: A Study of the Last Two Visions of Daniel, and of the Olivet Discourse of the Lord Jesus Christ* (Swengel: Bible Truth Depot, 1944), 97.

6. The verb *anastrepso* is used of an actual return. Luke used it previously in Acts 5:22 of officers who physically "went back." Thus, Luke most likely has in view a literal bodily return of the Lord.

7. E.g., Joachim Jeremias, *Jesus' Promise to the Nations* (London, SCM Press, 1958), 38.

8. Robert B. Sloan, *The Favorable Year of the Lord: A Study of Jubilary Theology in the Gospel of Luke* (Austin: Schola, 1977), 173.

9. E.g., David Chilton, *Days of Vengeance* (Tyler: Institute for Christian Economics, 1990).

10. Cf. John C. Whitcomb, "Daniel's Great Seventy-Weeks Prophecy: An Exegetical Insight," *Grace Theological Journal* 2, no. 2 (Fall 1981), 259–63; Robert C. Newman, "Daniel's Seventy Weeks and the Old Testament Sabbath-Year Cycle," *JETS* 16 (1973), 229–34.

11. Cf. Pasquale De Santo, "A Study of Jewish Eschatology with Special Reference to the Final Conflict" (Ph.D. diss., Duke Univ., 1957), 356; G. Henry Waterman, "The Sources of Paul's Teaching on the 2nd Coming of Christ in 1 and 2 Thessalonians," A Paper Presented to the Midwest Regional Meeting of the Evangelical Theological Society (Deerfield, Illinois: Trinity Evangelical Divinity School, 21 March 1975), 8.

12. E.g., the oldest Christian source for patristic interpretations on the seventy-weeks prophecy, lists nine exegetes with eleven interpretations; cf. Jay Braverman, *Jerome's Commentary On Daniel: A Study of Comparative Jewish and Christian Interpretations of the Hebrew Bible*, CBQMS 7 (Washington D.C.: The Catholic Biblical Association of America, 1978), 103–12.

13. Cf. Paul D. Feinberg, "An Exegetical and Theological Study of Daniel 9:24–27," in *Tradition and Testament: Essays in Honor of Charles Lee Feinberg*, John S. Feinberg and Paul D. Feinberg, ed. (Chicago: Moody, 1981).

14. Cf. Michael Kalafian, *The Prophecy of the Seventy Weeks of the Book of Daniel: A Critical Review of the Prophecy as Viewed by Three Major Theological Interpretations and the Impact of the Book of Daniel on Christology* (New York: University Press of America, 1991).

15. Cf. Ronald W. Pierce, "Spiritual Failure, Postponement, and Daniel 9," *Trinity Journal* 10 NS (1989), 211–22.

16. Cf. Harold W. Hoehner, *Chronological Aspects of the Life of Christ* (Grand Rapids: Zondervan, 1977), 116–28.

17. S. R. Driver, *Daniel,* The Cambridge Bible for Schools and Colleges (Cambridge: At the University Press, 1900), 8.

18. Lester L. Grabbe, "The End of the Desolations of Jerusalem: From Jeremiah's 70 Years to Daniel's 70 Weeks of Years," in *Early Jewish and Christian Exegesis: Studies in Memory of William Hugh Brownlee*, C. Evans and W. Stinespring, eds. (Montana: Scholars Press, 1987), 69.

19. John J. Collins, *The Apocalyptic Vision of the Book of Daniel*, Harvard Semitic Monographs 16, Frank Moore Cross, ed. (Montana: Scholars Press, 1977), 175–76.

20. For this reason the Jewish commentator Rashi says that "the end of the Romans who destroyed Jerusalem will be a total destruction through the promised Messiah" and that the "desolation decreed" for the City is "after the final wars waged by the Messianic king and the war of Gog and Magog."

21. Cf. Eugene E. Carpenter, "The Eschatology of Daniel Compared with the Eschatology of Selected Intertestamental Documents" (Ph.D. diss., Fuller Theological Seminary, 1978).

22. E.g., Second Ezekiel (4Q 385–89); Son of God (4Q 246); 1QS 1:22–24; 3:13–4:26; 9:16; 10:19; QH 5:36; 50:5; CD 6:10, 15; 13:14 1QpHab 5:7–8; 1QM 1:4–7; 3:21–22); and especially related to Daniel: 4Q ps Dan Aa/Dand 209; Pseudo-Daniel (4Q 243–45); The New Jerusalem (4Q 554); The Vision of the Four Kingdoms (4Q 547). For translations of the newer texts see, Robert Eisenman and Michael Wise, *The Dead Sea Scrolls Uncovered: The First Complete Translation and Interpretation of 50 Key Documents Withheld for Over 35 Years* (Massachusetts: Element, 1992), 4Q 458, 4Q 390.

23. Representing an apotelesmatic approach are Africanus, Hippolytus, Appollinarius of Laodicea, Eusebius, and Tertullian. The earliest recorded futurist teaching on this text is that by Irenaeus (ca. 180).

24. Cf. David W. Gooding, "The Literary Structure of the Book of Daniel and Its Implications," *Tyndale Bulletin* 32 (1981), 48–51.

25. E.g., *hashomem* ("desolations"), verses 17–18; *marad* ("transgression"), verse 9; *'avin* ("iniquity"), verses 5, 13, 16; *chata'* ("sin"), verses 5, 8, 11, 20; *miq^edash* ("Sanctuary"), verse 17 (cf. v. 20); *'ir* ("city"), verse 19; *'am* ("people"), verses 19–20; and *torat Moshe* ("law of Moses"), verses 11, 13.

26. Cf. B. W. Jones, "The Prayer in Daniel 9," *Vetus Testamentum* 18 (1968), 488.

27. The Jewish commentators Abarbanel and Malbim understood the reference of the seventy weeks as an additional interpretation of the seventy years of Jeremiah. The Malbim adds that Jeremiah's prophecy had a dual meaning: first, the seventy-year exile had satisfied the punishment for the desecration of the seventy sabbatical years (Lev. 26:34; 2 Chron. 36:21); but, second, other sins in addition to the violation of the sabbatical law (e.g., idolatry, bloodshed, licentiousness, cf. Yoma 96), would require the full period of 490 years for atonement as prescribed in Daniel 9:24.

28. Jacques Doukhan, "The Seventy Weeks of Dan. 9: An Exegetical Study," *AUSS* 17 (Spring 1979), 8.

29. In line 51 we read, *lmsf rs"* ("to bring Evil to an end"); cf. Robert Eisenman and Michael Wise, *The Dead Sea Scrolls Uncovered* (Massachusetts: Element, 1992), 67–68.

30. Abarbanel noted that the return to Jerusalem and even the rebuilding of the Second Temple did not bring the expected redemption nor atone for past sins, since it was itself a part of the Exile and atonement. He held that the real and complete redemption was still far off in history and thus not yet fulfilled according to Daniel's prophecy.

31. Cf. e.g., on *tzedeq 'olamim* ("everlasting righteousness") *11QPsa* col. xxii. Here, in an apocryphal psalm addressed to Zion (Jerusalem) concerning the anticipated deliverance from Gentile domination (as in Daniel 9), it is written, "May you attain *everlasting righteousness*" (line 16).

32. The "sealing of the prophetic vision" (a hendiadys), like the sealing of other documents in the ancient Near East, was for authentication or confirmation (cf. 1 Kings 21:8). The sense, then, is that of the fulfillment of prophecy, just as in goal number two the same infinitive (i.e., the *kethiv*) was used in relation to the fulfillment (or end) of sin (cf. the *keri*).

33. The Masoretic accents, called *ta'mim* ("meanings," lit. "taste"), are written signs designed to preserve the oral tradition of accentuation, which originally could not be introduced into the written text of the Bible itself (since it would be considered an addition to the sacred text), but later were incorporated into the text when it was transmitted in the form of a codex (a copy of the Bible not in scroll form), between the sixth to the ninth centuries A.D.

34. Cf. William Wickes, *Two Treaties on the Accentuation of the Old Testament,* The Library of Biblical Studies, Harry Orlinsky, ed. (New York: KTAV, 1970 reprint), 2:40.

35. Other examples include Genesis 7:13; 25:20; Exodus 35:23; Leviticus 16:2; Numbers 28:19; Isaiah 49:21; 66:19.

36. Cf. Thomas E. McComiskey, "The Seventy 'Weeks' of Daniel Against the Background of Ancient Near Eastern Literature," *Westminster Theological Journal* 47 (1958), 19; Risto Santala, *The Messiah in the Old Testament in the Light of Rabbinical Writings,* William Kinnaird, trans. (Jerusalem: Keren Ahvah Meshihit, 1992), 95–107.

37. Cf. Roger T. Beckwith, "Daniel 9 and the Date of Messiah's Coming in Essene, Hellenistic, Pharisaic, Zealot and Early Christian Computation," *Revue de Qumran* 10 (1981), 522.

38. Cf. William H. Shea, "Poetic Relations of the Time Periods in Daniel 9:25," *AUSS* 18, no. 1 (1980), 59–63.

39. Klaus Koch ("Die Weltreiche im Danielbuch," *Theologische Literaturzeitung* 85 [1960], 892–932; "Spätisraelitisches Geschichtsdenken am Beispiel des Buches Daniel," *Historische Zeitschrift* 193 [1961], 1–32) has argued cogently for these three divisions, and especially for the eschatological interpretation of the final one week in light of intertestamental Judaism and apocalyptic literature.

40. For this reason, consistent preterists must interpret Christ's coming as also having occurred in A.D. 70. To do so, however, requires the employment of a nonliteral hermeneutic, since the events cannot be reconciled with either the literal interpretation of the Old Testament citations and allusions in the Olivet Discourse or the actual events of the destruction.

41. Cf. J. Randall Price, "The Desecration and Restoration of the Temple as an Eschatological Motif in the Old Testament, Jewish Apocalyptic Literature, and the New Testament" (Ph.D. diss., Univ. of Texas at Austin, 1993).

42. Cf. Annie Jaubert, *La Notion d'Alliance dans le Judaisme.* Patristica Sorbonensia 6 (Paris: Seuil, 1963), 82–85; Robert Hanhart, "Kriterien Geschichtlicher Warheit in der Makkabäerzeit," in *Drei Studien zum Judentum,* Theologische Existenz Heute 140 (Müchen: Kaiser, 1967), 14.

43. Enno Janssen, *Das Gottesvolk und seine Geschichte* (Neukirchen-Vluyn: Erziehungsverein, 1971), 51–54.

44. See further, Thomas Ice and Randall Price, *Ready to Rebuild: The Imminent Plan to Rebuild the Last Days Temple* (Harvest House, 1992), 197–207, 228–36.

45. Cf. Kenneth A. Matthews, "John, Jesus and the Essenes: Trouble at the Temple," *Criswell Theological Review* 3, no. 1 (Fall 1988), 101–26.

46. The *waw* on *'ad* (usually "until") should be taken as pleonastic ("namely") and *kalah* ... *tittak* as a hendiadys, so that the idea is of a "decreed" or "appointed end" (Niphal of *charatz* = "things determined") for *shomem* ("[the] desolator") is understood.

47. Cf. George M. Harton, "An Interpretation of Daniel 11:36–45," *Grace Theological Journal* 4, no. 2 (Fall 1983), 205–31.

48. John A. McClean, "The Seventieth Week of Daniel 9:27 as a Literary Key for Understanding the Structure of the Apocalypse of John" (Ph.D. diss., Univ. of Michigan, 1990), 121–86.

49. Ibid, 187–258.

50. The six sections of the book of Revelation according to McClean are (1) Prologue (chap. 1), (2) Letters to the Seven Churches (chaps. 2–4), (3) God's Great Tribulation (chaps. 4–19), (4) Kingdom of God (chap. 20), (5) New Jerusalem (21:1–22:5), (6) Epilogue (22:6–21).

51. This was apparently the methodology employed by the early church fathers who had not systematized their observations and, therefore, could not be accused of interpretive bias.

The interpretation of the second chapter of Acts is crucial to a dispensational understanding of Scripture. Both Peter's speech and the conduct of the believers demonstrate that the early church did not yet self-consciously distinguish itself from Israel. Whether or not Christ would restore the kingdom to Israel and take His seat on David's throne at that time is left open in the early chapters of Acts. The answer only becomes obvious as the narrative of Acts unfolds. The kingdom was not restored, and it is quite wrong to identify the throne of David with God's extraterrestrial throne.

8

A DISPENSATIONAL
UNDERSTANDING OF ACTS 2

Zane C. Hodges

Acts 2 has long been a focal point for dispensational discussions. The way in which an expositor deals with this chapter can reveal much about his theology. In recent days, Acts 2 has once more come to the fore. It is a kind of centerpiece in the current debate about the nature of dispensationalism. This chapter seeks to revisit Acts 2 in light of the contemporary debate.

DISPENSATIONALISM IN ACTS 2

The role Acts 2 plays in dispensational thought is not surprising. Its contents make this role inevitable.

The Birth of the Church

So far as the New Testament record is concerned, the Christian church was born on the Day of Pentecost. This is described in Acts 2. The word *church* as an entity *already* in existence is first found in Acts 2:47 (according to all but a few manuscripts).[1] The reference to the church made by our Lord in Matthew 16:18 confirms this. In that text, Jesus refers to the church as if it were still future: "on this rock *I will build* My church."[2]

Classic dispensationalism[3] has usually insisted that Acts 2 is the record of the church's birth. It has normally denied that the church of Acts 2 stands in direct continuity with some kind of Old Testament

167

"church," that is, with the "people of God" in ages past. At the same time, it has rejected the ultradispensational concept that Acts 2 describes a Jewish "church" that is to be distinguished from the later, predominantly Gentile (and Pauline) church.

However, most dispensational teachers have not insisted on a total discontinuity between the church and Old Testament saints. Of course, there is not. In political and cultural terms one might speak of the Anglo-Saxon world, of which the United States and Great Britain are a part. But this would in no way nullify the obvious fact that Great Britain and the U.S. are separate countries.

So we may speak of the family of God as composed of all born-again people of all ages (Eph. 3:15). But we also speak of national Israel (when totally converted: Rom. 11:26) as an entity distinct from the church within the larger family of the redeemed.

On the other hand, the effort to distinguish more than one "church" within the book of Acts is a classic case of over refinement. In Acts 15, for example, it is unwarranted to suggest that Paul and Barnabas thought of themselves as members of a church to which Peter and James did not belong. The whole narrative underscores Paul's and Barnabas's concern for the unity of the church to which believers both in Jerusalem and also Antioch belonged.[4]

The Prophecy of Joel

Dispensationalists have not always spoken with one mind about the issues raised by Peter's quotation of Joel 2:28–32, recorded for us in Acts 2:17–21. At least two issues are important here.

1. "This is that" (Acts 2:16). Some dispensational thinkers have urged that the phrase "this is that" is not intended to announce the *fulfillment* of Joel's prophecy on this occasion. Rather, it signifies something analogous to the phenomenon described by Joel. According to this view, the phrase "this is that" means something similar to "this is like that," or "this is that sort of thing."

Such an interpretation is unlikely on linguistic grounds. The Qumran documents have alerted New Testament scholarship to the so-called Qumran pesher mode of interpretation.[5] In pesher exegesis, expressions resembling the one Peter employed were used regularly to refer to contemporary fulfillment. It would be surprising if Peter used this expression in some other way, of which we do not have other analogous examples.

We may conclude that Peter meant to say that the outpouring of the Spirit fulfilled Joel's prophecy. But this in no way clashes with fundamental dispensational convictions. Dispensationalists correctly recognize that the church is not directly prophesied in the Old Testament. And it should be noted that Joel 2 does not prophesy it!

What Joel 2 *does* prophesy is the outpouring of the Holy Spirit in "the last days" (cf. Acts 2:17). This outpouring is seen by Joel as fundamentally an endowment, widely spread among Israelites (cf. Acts 2:17–18),[6] which enables men and women, young and old, and bondslaves of both sexes to engage in prophecy. But the prophecy of Joel does not intimate that this same outpouring of the Holy Spirit was also a spiritual "baptism" by which all those so baptized would be brought into the church, the Body of Christ (1 Cor. 12:13). And neither does it disclose that such a body would be characterized by an absolute equality between Jews and Gentiles (Eph. 3:6). It is faulty exegesis to conclude that Joel's prophecy even implied these things. The hidden reality of the church remains hidden reality even when Joel's prophecy is seen to be fulfilled at Pentecost.

2. Signs and wonders (Acts 2:19–20). A fulfillment of Joel's words about the outpouring of the Spirit is one feature of this passage (see chapter 3). However, it appears that Joel's prophecy about signs and wonders is not fulfilled here (or anywhere else in Acts either). For that matter, this prophecy has *never* yet been fulfilled.

Sometimes efforts are made to find a fulfillment. F. F. Bruce was inclined to refer these statements (partially?) to the eclipse that occurred at the crucifixion, and he conjectures that "on the same afternoon the paschal full moon *may well* have appeared blood-red in the sky in consequence of that preternatural gloom" (italics added).[7] But most students correctly recognize such speculation as grasping at straws.

The simple fact is that the signs and wonders forecast by Joel are the well-known signs that immediately precede the end of this age and the manifestation of our Lord Jesus Christ in power and glory (see Matt. 24:29–30; Mark 13:24–26; Luke 21:25–27; Rev. 6:12–17). No interpretation of the prophecy of Joel can possibly be right if it ignores the fact that Joel's signs and wonders are a "set piece" in the eschatological drama presented in the New Testament.

This leads to an inevitable conclusion: some kind of hiatus exists between the fulfilled and unfulfilled portions of Joel's prophecy. Yet Peter quotes both parts together as if both could have been fulfilled in the present situation. Could they have been?

The answer is yes, which is made quite plain in Acts 1. There the disciples ask the crucial question, "Lord, will You *at this time* restore the kingdom to Israel?" (v. 6). It should be noted that the question follows immediately on a statement by the Lord Jesus about the impending baptism of the Holy Spirit (v. 5).

Our Lord's response is genuinely noncommittal: "It is not for you to know times or seasons which the Father has put in His own authority" (v. 7). This means, of course, that the answer was not theirs to have. But equally it means that, from their viewpoint, the answer *might have been* yes. Thus, so far as Peter knew on the Day of Pentecost, the kingdom might have been given to Israel *at that time.* And if it had been fulfilled, then the "signs and wonders" of Joel's prophecy would have been fulfilled too.

When the events of Acts 2 occurred, Peter possessed only limited knowledge of the program of God. He understood that the outpouring of the Spirit was a fulfillment of Joel's words, and he so announced this fact. What he did not comprehend was whether or not the rest of the quoted prophecy would be fulfilled "at that time" (cf. 1:6). Only if the kingdom were restored to Israel would Joel's signs and wonders take place, since this array of signs is the immediate precursor of the returning King.

But, once again, Peter had no inkling that the outpoured Spirit would create a body in which Jews and Gentiles stand on an equal footing. As late as Acts 10, in the household of Cornelius, he was caught by surprise when the Spirit was poured out on his Gentile audience (10:44–48; 11:15–17). What this means is that the true scope of the baptism of the Holy Spirit—its total effects—were not comprehended by Peter at Pentecost. His quotation of Joel as being partially fulfilled on that day does not mean that he saw more in the baptism than Joel's own words can be taken to imply.

In fact, Peter's words in the following chapter (3:19–21) lead some to conclude that if Israel would have repented then, God would have sent Jesus back to them.[8] Had this transpired, it would have meant the restoration of the kingdom "at that time."

Of course, it did not happen. But as far as God's messenger knew at Pentecost, it could have. Thus, the Joel quotation fits this suspenseful theme most admirably. Part of Joel's prophecy had just taken place. Would the rest very shortly be fulfilled as well? Neither Peter nor any of the other apostles knew. That knowledge was the Father's prerogative (1:7). But what we now can see is the nearly 2,000-year hiatus between the words of Joel's prophecy given in Acts 2:17–18, and those given in verses 19–20. Thus, the era of the Christian church remains fundamentally a parenthesis in the on-going program of God. The Joel text, by its very nature, implies a genuine measure of discontinuity in God's accomplishment of His purposes for Israel.

The Church Within Israel
(Acts 2:46–47)

What has been said so far indicates that, in its earliest experience as recounted in Acts 2, the church was not self-consciously separate from Israel. The key term here is "self-consciously." Even the leaders of the infant church, like Peter, were by no means anticipating that in the near future great numbers of Gentiles would be a part of this new organism created at Pentecost. When that realization did sink in for some, it was strongly resisted by others (cf. Acts 15). Fortunately, leaders like Peter and James knew how to take the necessary steps while maintaining real sensitivity to the feelings of believing fellow-Jews.

So we see, at the conclusion of Acts 2, that the distinctively Christian observance of the Lord's supper was practiced concurrently (although in separate locations) with worship in the Jewish Temple in Jerusalem (2:46–47). But this was entirely appropriate. For the issue of whether the kingdom would, or would not, *at that time* be restored to Israel was as yet unresolved. So long as the message of repentance to the nation carried with it this possibility, God did not reveal to the church or to its leaders the distinctive nature and character of the church as we now know it.

In fact, the record of the early chapters in Acts shows a rapid increase in conversions among Israelites. Three thousand were won on the Day of Pentecost itself (2:41), but by Acts 4 the number of males had reached five thousand (v. 4). This suggests that if women and children were counted, the church probably had no fewer than ten to fifteen thousand converts. Acts 6:7 reports continued multiplication, as well as the conversion of "a great many of the priests." Clearly, by this time the church was a significant movement in Israel.

Nevertheless, the rapidly increasing numbers were far from comprising a majority of the Jewish residents of Jerusalem,[9] to say nothing of Israelites throughout Palestine. A national repentance was still far from being achieved, however impressive the number of converts. With chapter 7, however, the progress of the church among Israelites was dealt a blow through the martyrdom of Stephen and subsequent persecution (8:1). Only gradually does Acts unfold the truth that the church was to become a predominantly Gentile entity with national Israel largely blinded to the claims of Christ.

Indication that this was a major concern to Luke is demonstrated unmistakably in the final chapter of Acts. There, the final scene in the book shows Paul presenting his message to a body of Jewish leaders in Rome (28:23), which results in a divided house (v. 24), just as Israel has been portrayed as divided throughout the book. Luke climaxes this scene with Paul's quotation from Isaiah forecasting the divinely ordained blinding of the nation (vv. 25–27).

Following this quotation from the prophet, Luke's "hero" (Paul) makes his last statement in this book. It is a definitive declaration that, obviously, Luke wishes every reader to note with care: "therefore let it be known to you that the salvation of God has been sent to the Gentiles, and they will hear it!" (v. 28).

This, then, is Luke's definitive answer to the question of Acts 1:6: "Lord, will you *at this time* restore the kingdom to Israel?" And the answer, which has long been obvious from the Lucan narrative, is, "No, not at this time." A period of Gentile mission—undetermined in length—is the real program of God at the present time. The restoration of the kingdom to Israel has been deferred until a future day. And immediately before that day, the signs and wonders spoken of by the prophet Joel will be fulfilled. That is to say, they will occur "before the coming of the great and awesome day of the Lord" (2:20).

Thus, the book of Acts serves as a historical demonstration of a fundamental theme of Pauline theology: "For I do not desire, brethren, that you should be ignorant of this mystery, lest you should be wise in your own opinion, that hardening in part has happened to Israel until the fullness of the Gentiles has come in. And so all Israel will be saved, as it is written" (Rom. 11:25–26a). According to the book of Acts, the kingdom is not *now* going to be restored to Israel precisely because the nation is partially ("in part," v. 25) hardened. Israel is a divided house (Acts 28:24, 29). Only at the return of Christ will there be a truly national repentance by Israel. For "all Israel will be saved" only when "the Deliverer will come out of Zion, and He will turn away ungodliness from Jacob" (Rom. 11:26). We get a glimpse of this national repentance from Zechariah 12:10–14. The restoration of the kingdom to Israel awaits that momentous day.

PROGRESSIVE DISPENSATIONALISM AND ACTS 2

A contemporary movement within dispensationalism that calls itself "progressive dispensationalism" has taken a novel tack in regard to Israel's kingdom. Their analysis, however, remains inchoate, their efforts to elucidate notwithstanding.

The Throne of David

All should acknowledge that the throne of David is inseparably wed to Israel's kingdom, which we have just been discussing. From the very beginning of his two-volume work, Luke makes this concept plain. Thus, when the angel Gabriel made his thrilling declaration to Mary, he states of Jesus,

> Do not be afraid, Mary, for you have found favor with God. And behold, you will conceive in your womb and bring forth a Son, and shall call His name Jesus. He will be great, and will be called the Son of the Highest; and the Lord God will give Him the throne of His father David. And He will reign over the *house of Jacob* forever, and of His kingdom there will be no end (Luke 1:30–33).

This is the only explicit reference to David's throne in Luke or Acts until we reach Acts 2:30. Together, the two texts constitute Luke's only direct mention of a "throne" associated with King David.

One should specifically note here that in recording what Gabriel said Luke cites words that completely ignore any suggestion of universality of dominion of that throne. Gabriel does not say that Jesus will rule *all mankind* from David's throne but simply "the house of Jacob." Luke does not make the slightest intimation that by sitting on this throne Mary's Son will gain universal dominion. Of course, He will have such dominion from David's throne, as various Old Testament passages make clear. But obviously, this fact is *not a part* of Luke's theme here. Gabriel's announcement focuses very narrowly on the *Jewish* nature of David's throne.

Nor is such an emphasis accidental in this context. One may observe, for example, that even Mary's *Magnificat* relates God's mercy to her with His mercy to Israel (Luke 1:46–55; see esp. vv. 54–55). Similarly, Zacharias's *Benedictus* is totally focused on what God is doing for Israel through the advent of His Son (vv. 67–79).

Accordingly, when we read Luke 1 we are inhaling the very atmosphere of Old Testament Jewish expectation. We hear from the lips of Mary and Zacharias those grand hopes for national deliverance that were so inextricably bound up with the expectation of the divine King who would rule "Jacob" from David's throne.

This is what we have here—and nothing more. Despite this fact, progressive dispensationalists assert that the Lord Jesus even now is reigning from David's throne, although national Israel has experienced none of the deliverance of which Mary and Zacharias spoke so glowingly in this context.

Were it not for the fact that serious men have proposed this view, it might well be dismissed out of hand. According to the understanding of Old Testament saints, whom Mary and Zacharias represent so effectively, the throne of David could mean only one thing—the earthly throne that began with the reign of David himself and was passed down to his physical descendants who also sat on it. No one was entitled to sit on that throne unless he was, in fact, of Davidic lineage. Thus, Luke tells us carefully that Gabriel was sent to "a virgin betrothed to a man whose name was Joseph, *of the house of David*" (v. 27). So also Zacharias affirms that God "has raised up a horn of salvation for us *in the house of . . . David*" (v. 69). It was common Jewish belief that is expressed in the question of John 7:42: "Has not the Scripture said that the Christ comes from the seed of David and from the town of Bethlehem, where David was?"

There is not the slightest shred of evidence that the throne of David ever was conceived as anything other than the earthly seat of authority where David reigned and where only his physical descendants could legitimately reign. The term "throne of David" simply refers to this—nothing else.

The Throne of God

However, progressive dispensationalists, in spite of consistent usage of the Bible, are not deterred from declaring that, even today, Christ is reigning from the throne of David. But this means that they must apply the term *throne of David* to what is actually the throne of God! And they feel the freedom to do this even in the absence of a single text that explicitly makes this identification. The result is a view that would have shocked any biblically literate Old Testament Jew—and should shock New Testament exegetes today.

The progressive dispensational case for this view has been argued from Acts 2. We must now consider the way in which this concept has been derived from Luke's second reference to David's throne found in verse 30.

1. The argument from Acts 2:30. In an article in a recent symposium volume entitled *Dispensationalism, Israel and the Church*, Darrell Bock, professor of New Testament studies at Dallas Theological Seminary, has sought to identify the throne of David with the throne of God, where the Lord Jesus Christ now sits.[10] Rather than survey the entire article, it should suffice to analyze the core of Bock's argument as presented on page 49.

We can begin with Bock's treatment of the quotation from Psalm 16 found in Acts 2:25–28 and interpreted by Peter in verses 29–31:

Having mentioned the need to call on the Lord, Peter turns to recent events. He recounts Jesus' ministry and death but notes that death is not able to hold him (vv. 22–24). Peter goes on to note that *such impotency* for death was predicted in Psalm 16, the second Old Testament citation in Acts 2 (vv. 25–28). (italics added)[11]

It is of interest to observe that Bock does not say, in so many words, that Psalm 16 predicted *the resurrection of Christ.* Bock has Old Testament colleagues (and perhaps he agrees) who believe that there are few, if any, direct messianic prophecies in the Old Testament. They suggest that the "fulfillments" pointed out by New Testament writers are mostly to be understood in terms of typology.[12]

The words that immediately follow do not clear this up: "The text is clearly presented as having been fulfilled in Jesus' resurrection. The Psalm 16 citation leads into the mention of David and a defense of the fact that *a resurrection understanding* of the text cannot refer to David, since he is buried (v. 29)" (Italics added).[13] Unfortunately we are not enlightened by these words on just how Bock feels that the prophecy has been "fulfilled," since this could refer to a typological fulfillment too. Very strange indeed is the statement that "a resurrection understanding of the text cannot refer to David." This leaves open the possibility that some other "understanding" could refer to David.

But Peter's point is plain. The text could not refer to David *at all,* since David experienced no resurrection prior to his body experiencing corruption. The same argument is used by Paul in Acts 13:35–37. Bock's imprecise expressing of his position makes understanding difficult. Bock proceeds:

> The crucial linking allusion appears at this point. Peter notes that David was a prophet. Not only was David a prophet, he was the conscious beneficiary of an oath God had made to him that one "of the fruit of his [David's] loins" (KJV) would sit on his throne (Acts 2:30). The key term is kathisai (to sit), which is reintroduced in the citation of Psalm 110 (note kathou, "sit," in v. 34). The allusion in verse 30 is to Psalm 132:11, a psalm which is *strongly Israelitish and national in tone.* (italics added)[14]

But unless Bock is reading the Greek text in the form found in the Majority Text (not likely, to be sure),[15] there appears to be a translational gaffe here that slightly overstates the similarity between verses 30 and 34. As read by the standard modern editions of the Greek New Testament, the verb *kathisai* in verse 30 is not to be read as intransitive ("to sit") but as transitive ("to seat"; cf. the NIV here).[16]

In verse 34, however, the intransitive sense "to sit" is correct, even though a slightly different Greek verb is involved. But, in view of the difference in verbs, Bock is not technically accurate when he states that the former verb is "reintroduced" in the quotation from Psalm 110.

Clearly this would be quibbling were it not for the fact that Bock is trying to make the verses parallel by appealing to the use of a single verb in the same sense in both verses. Technical considerations aside, the use of a verb for sitting proves nothing about whether or not the two thrones are to be identified. What else does one do on a throne?

Suppose that ones states, "Mr. Smith is destined to sit in the governor's chair in Austin and currently is sitting in the chair of the chief justice of the Texas supreme court." Would anyone ever conclude from this that the words "sit" and "sitting" intimate that the two chairs in question are identical? Obviously not.

It is perfectly safe to say that no one in Peter's day could have been expected to glean from his words that somehow the throne of David and God's extraterrestrial throne were to be identified. For that idea to be clear, it would have to be stated directly. But Peter does not do that here, nor does any writer anywhere else in the New Testament. What is truly relevant is Bock's observation that the quotation found in verse 30 comes from a Psalm (132) "which is strongly Israelitish and national in tone." This, of course, is precisely what we saw in connection with Luke's first reference to the throne of David in Luke 1:28–33. The true character of the Davidic throne is that it is indeed Israelitish and national, and hence "earthly." Nothing indicates that such characteristics can be applied to the celestial throne of God.

Bock's argument continues:

> The Psalm in turn is a reflection of the promise made to David in 2 Samuel 7, especially verse 12. This 2 Samuel passage is better known as the Davidic covenant. What is crucial is that David's awareness of this covenant promise is immediately linked to his understanding of the resurrection promise in Psalm 16, which in turn is immediately tied to the resurrection proof text of Psalm 110 (vv. 31–35). *Being seated on David's throne is linked to being seated at God's right hand.*[17]

But is it? And even if it is, "linking" is not equivalent to "identification." Bock's argument contains a logical fallacy. Bock has rested much on the idea of "linking" without acknowledging that two things can be linked without any necessity that they be equated. Certainly there are various senses in which the throne of David can be linked with God's celestial one. After all (as Paul teaches us in Romans 13) all earthly power proceeds from God in heaven. If anyone is entitled to occupy David's throne in a future day, it would certainly be David's descendant who now occupies the right hand of the throne of God. Indeed, the writer of Hebrews presents our Lord as seated "at the right hand of the majesty on high" (Heb. 1:3) where He is "waiting till His enemies are made His footstool" (Heb. 10:12–13).

It is most certainly not while He is on this heavenly throne that He achieves the victories associated with the Davidic throne in Luke 1 (see earlier discussion). On the heavenly throne He simply waits for that. But His presence on God's throne is a guarantee that someday He also will sit on David's throne as Victor over all of Israel's enemies. This is the true link between the heavenly and earthly sessions of Christ.

But the idea that the two thrones can in any sense be equated is illusory. It is not supported by any hard data at all. Yet even apart from this consideration, Bock has missed the point of the quotation from Psalm 110 in Acts 2. As verse 33 makes clear, the real link is with the outpouring of the Holy Spirit. It is a well-confirmed New Testament teaching that the gift of the Holy Spirit is the *direct consequence* of our Lord's ascension to the Father.

According to John's gospel, the Lord informed the disciples, "It is to your advantage that I go away; for if I do not go away, the Helper will not come to you; but if I depart, I will send Him to you" (16:7). Earlier He had also said, "And I will pray the Father, and He will give you another Helper, that He may abide with you forever" (14:16).

Our Lord's return to the Father and His intercession there are necessary to the outpouring of the Holy Spirit. Thus, in Luke-Acts the gift of the Spirit is termed "the Promise of the Father" for which the disciples must wait until after Jesus' ascension to heaven (Luke 24:49; Acts 1:4).

Bock labels Psalm 110 a "resurrection proof text." However, it is not an explicit statement of the resurrection since the resurrection is not mentioned in the Psalm. It does prophesy enthronement at God's right hand.[18] The point of Peter's quoting Psalm 110 is simply this: the seated Christ is the Source of the Spirit's outpouring. By His intercession He has secured what God the Father had promised. This is precisely what Acts 2:33 states: "Therefore being exalted to the right hand of God, and having received from the Father the promise of the Holy Spirit, He poured out this which you see and hear."

This precise point—the ascension—is in view in Acts 2:34: "For David did not ascend into the heavens, but he says himself . . ." It is simply incorrect to treat Psalm 16 as linked with Psalm 110 by asserting that both are resurrection proof texts. Psalm 16 is, but Psalm 110 is not. Rather, Peter quoted each Psalm with its own quite distinct emphasis in support of two different elements in his presentation.

We conclude, then, that Bock's linkage between the two quotations breaks down under scrutiny. And his next statement is an enormous leap into thin air: "In other words, Jesus' resurrection-ascension to God's right hand is put forward by Peter as a fulfillment of the Davidic covenant, just as the allusion to Joel fulfills the new covenant."[19]fn The argumentation that has led up to this conclusion proves (as we have seen) absolutely nothing that even impinges on the identification Bock wishes to make.

2. Joel and the new covenant. The final statement quoted above asserts that somehow Joel's prophecy relates to the fulfillment of the new covenant. Elsewhere in his article Bock states, "In fact, 'the promise of the Father' alludes not only to Joel but to a key promise of the new covenant in Jeremiah 31, an important eschatological text that promised a bestowal of the Spirit to God's people."[20]

But equating the prophecy of Joel with the new covenant is just as invalid as equating the throne of David with the throne of God. As a matter of fact, the new covenant promise (whether in Jeremiah 31:31–34 or in Hebrews 8:7–12) does not even mention the Holy Spirit. Much less does it promise the widespread prophetic enablement that Joel revealed.

Jeremiah's prophecy and Joel's must be carefully distinguished. Jeremiah predicts the regeneration/sanctification of the entire nation of Israel ("for they all shall know Me, from the least of them to the greatest of them," Jer. 31:34). This has never been fulfilled and will not be until the Second Advent, when "all Israel will be saved" (Rom. 11:26; notice v. 27). Joel's revelation, however, predicts a prophetic endowment brought to pass by the outpoured Spirit of God. According to Peter, this prophetic endowment was fulfilled at Pentecost.

CONCLUSION

Acts 2 will always remain a focal point in dispensational discussion, as well it should. But classic dispensationalism can treat this text straightforwardly and with a minimum of complexity. Progressive dispensationalism, on the other hand, is forced to rely on intricate, subtle, and ultimately invalid, arguments.

Notes

1. Contemporary textual critics generally prefer the more lightly attested reading on the alleged grounds that the support includes the best manuscripts. However, Nestle-Aland cites only P74^{vid}, Aleph, A, B, C, 095, 81, 1175, and *pc* (a few) in support of the reading that omits the words "the church." Thus, these words are found in by far the largest number of surviving manuscripts. But even if they are rejected, it is clear that the entity formed in Acts 2 is to be so identified (see Acts 5:11; 8:1, 3; etc.). See the introduction to *The Greek New Testament According to the Majority Text*, 2d ed., Zane C. Hodges and Arthur L. Farstad, eds. (Nashville: Nelson, 1985), ix–xliv.

2. All italics within Scripture quotations in this chapter have been added.

3. This is my term for the basic dispensational grid shared by men like J. N. Darby, Lewis Sperry Chafer, John F. Walvoord, and Charles C. Ryrie. Differing opinion on various points does not annul the essential unity of thought. The survey by Craig Blaising seems overdrawn; see his introductory article, "Dispensationalism: The Search for Definition," in *Dispensationalism, Israel and the Church: The Search for Definition*, Craig A. Blaising and Darrell L. Bock, eds. (Grand Rapids: Zondervan, 1992), 13–34.

4. In a similar way the clash between Paul, on the one hand, and Peter and Barnabas, on the other, in Galatians 2:11–21 clearly indicates the controlling principle conception that there is but one church in which all those present ought to conduct themselves according to the guidelines enunciated by Paul.

5. For a discussion of pesher interpretation, see Richard N. Longenecker, *Biblical Exegesis in the Apostolic Period* (Grand Rapids: Eerdmans, 1975), 38–45, 200–204. See also Donald Juel, *Messianic Exegesis: Christological Interpretation of the Old Testament in Early Christianity* (Philadelphia: Fortress, 1988), 49–56.

6. The expression "all flesh" does not contradict what is stated above. Ernst Haenchen (*The Acts of the Apostles: A Commentary* [Philadelphia: Westminster, 1971], 179) is correct when he says, "In the original text *pasan sarka* does not mean man in general, but Luke also does not yet intend Peter to proclaim the gift of the Spirit to all men, for that would be anticipating the decisive turning-point of the Cornelius episode." In context, "all flesh" will mean all kinds of Israelite flesh: young and old, male and female, slave and free.

7. F. F. Bruce, *Commentary on the Book of the Acts*, NICNT (Grand Rapids: Eerdmans, 1954), 69.

8. Haenchen (*Acts*, 208), speaking as a nonevangelical, seems to infer a similar conclusion; "If the Jews turn from their old ways, there will come 'seasons of refreshing from the presence of the Lord' (i.e. God), and God will send the Messiah Jesus forechosen for the Jews. Thus the conversion will also hasten the Parousia—cf. 2 Peter 3.12."

9. Joachim Jeremias (*Jerusalem in the Time of Jesus* [Philadelphia: Fortress, 1975], 83) estimates the population of Jerusalem at about 55,000, swelled at Passover by perhaps as many as 125,000 pilgrims. But he cites one source (Pseudo-Hecataeus) as giving the pre-lOO A.D. population of Jerusalem at 120,000.

10. Darrell L. Bock, "The Reign of the Lord Christ," in *Dispensationalism*, Blaising and Bock, eds., 37–67.

11. Ibid., 49.

12. Examples of this unfortunate trend include the following articles, one by a professor (Glenn) and the other by a graduate writing in *Bibliotheca Sacra* (Bateman): Donald R. Glenn, "Psalm 8 and Hebrews 2: A Case Study in Biblical Hermeneutics and Biblical Theology," *Walvoord: A Tribute*, Donald K. Campbell, ed. (Chicago: Moody, 1982), 39–51; and Herbert W. Bateman III, "Psalm 110:1 and the New Testament," *Bibliotheca Sacra* 149 (October-December 1992), 438–53. Historically, liberal exegetes have denied direct Old Testament prophecy about the Lord Jesus Christ and have sought the meaning of such prophecies in the immediate historical context (i.e., the so-called *sitz im leben*) of the Old Testament. The wholesale abandonment of direct messianic prophecy by many evangelicals is a capitulation to this view, for which "typology" is a fig leaf.

13. Bock, "The Reign of the Lord Christ," 49.

14. Ibid.

15. See n. 1.

16. See also BGD (Bauer-Gingrich-Danker) Greek lexicon, 389, under *kathizo* (1).

17. Bock, "The Reign of the Lord Christ," 49.

18. The ascension of Christ is a conclusion drawn by Peter based on the combination of the messages in Psalm 16 (a prophecy of Christ's resurrection) and Psalm 110 (a prophecy of Christ's enthronement at God's right hand).

19. Bock, "The Reign of the Lord Christ," 49.

20. Ibid., 48.

The phrase "already/not yet" has been widely adopted in biblical studies to refer to inaugurated eschatology. Though the phrase is used to differentiate present fulfillment in distinction to future fulfillment, it is insufficient to specify what that fulfillment might be. Different individuals use the phrase, sharing only verbal agreement but not understood meanings. The interpretations of Anthony Hoekema, George Ladd, and Darrell Bock all are questioned on the basis of the interpretation of either the Old Testament or the New Testament texts. When an application of inaugurated eschatology is introduced into dispensational studies, the difference between Israel and the church is reduced from two peoples with different roles in God's purposes for history to two peoples saved at different times in history. This revision results from abandoning the meaning expressed in the Old Testament promises and replacing it with the meaning of the promise as supposedly expressed in the New Testament. This often disregards the literal interpretation of Old Testament passages. Finally, the focus of the system is reduced from a theological focus on the glory of God to a Christological focus on Christ, the Lord of redemption.

9

PROPHETIC FULFILLMENT:
THE ALREADY AND NOT YET

Elliott E. Johnson

F or many, the publication of *Dispensationalism, Israel and the Church* has given new direction to dispensational studies, positioning it in the center of evangelical scholarship and discussions. One contributing factor has been the adoption of the phrase "already and not yet" to describe progressive fulfillment in the present and future dispensations. Walter Kaiser comments, "One of the most commonly shared advances was the advocacy of a carefully defined inaugurated eschatology wherein both the 'already' and the 'not yet' fulfilled were provided for."[1] This phrase, introduced into evangelical scholarship by George Eldon Ladd, refers to the fulfillment of the kingdom of God already present in Jesus Christ and in the yet future of His second coming. This chapter is written to assess the consequences of adopting the concept into dispensational studies. Three questions will provide direction to the assessment:

1. What does the phrase mean as it has been used?

2. Is the phrase sufficient to represent agreement in inauguration eschatology among evangelicals?

3. Is the phrase helpful to dispensational theology and interpretation?

THE HISTORY OF THE PHRASE

The concept of "the already and not yet" has appeared in the tradition that Amos Wilder called the "historical-critical exegesis" of Jesus' teaching.[2] In method, this tradition focused on the synoptic gospels primarily and treated the textual record critically in attempting to comprehend the historical substance of Jesus' teaching and ministry. The concept first appeared in 1926 in the early writings of C. H. Dodd.[3] He "anticipated the majority of late Anglo-Saxon scholars who maintained that for Jesus the kingdom of God was both present and, in some (usually only unimportant) way, future."[4] In time, however, Dodd settled on a "realized eschatology" in which Jesus saw in His own ministry the realization of Old Testament hope and the coming of the kingdom of God.[5]

It is interesting that Anthony A. Hoekema quotes approvingly the phrase "realized millennialism" to describe Christ's present reign.[6] Yet at the same time he prefers the term "inaugurated eschatology" in which the phrase "already and not yet" contrasts the present reign of Christ with a yet future new heavens and new earth in which Christ reigns.

In an attempt to correct the emphasis of Dodd, W. G. Kümmel (1943) employed the phrase of "already and not yet." Göstra Lundström described Kümmel's perspective as

> Biblical realism. . . . It was felt to be useless to try to deny that Jesus did not see the Kingdom of God only futuristically, but also preached the presence of this Kingdom in word and deed. The question arose, how sayings of the present and future fit together in Jesus, and furthermore, how the presence of the Kingdom of God is to be understood.[7]

Kümmel's attempt to address all of the passages and to find a harmony among them is a commendable goal.

Kümmel begins with the decisive text of Dodd—Matthew 12:28. He understood "that the future Kingdom of God had already begun in his (Jesus') activity."[8] He takes the image of a house with a strong man to be a portrayal of Satan and his dominion. Jesus as the stronger One took away from Satan some of those in whose lives he then ruled. Kümmel concludes that "this fight has already been won, because Satan must *be* bound if he can be robbed. . . . And as it is a definite Jewish expectation that in the last day Satan will be bound, this pronouncement too means that the Kingdom of God has begun its operations."[9]

Kümmel thus concludes that the meaning of the mission of Jesus is to announce the approach of the kingdom of God and to make this future, at the same time, already a present reality. George E. Ladd (1964) at this juncture raises a question: How can a future eschaton (realm) be a present reality in the activity of Jesus?[10] So Ladd introduces his contribution to the critical discussion by emphasizing a new meaning of the kingdom of God: "We have seen that both in the Old Testament and in rabbinic Judaism, God's kingdom—his reign—can have more than one meaning. . . . This is the key to the solution of the problem in the Gospels."[11] Thus, in discussion of the crux passage (Matt. 12:28), he concludes, "Instead of waiting until the end of the age to reveal his kingly power and destroy satanic evil, Jesus declares that God has acted in his kingly power to curb the power of Satan. In other words, God's kingdom in Jesus' teaching has a twofold manifestation: at the end of the age to destroy Satan, and in Jesus' mission to bind Satan."[12] Thus, Ladd posits that the concept of kingdom is now defined dynamically as "kingship" or "kingly power" or even "royal rank." Whereas a kingdom is commonly defined to consist in a king exercising kingly power in a domain or realm of rule, he all but eliminates the issue of realm.[13] Even his former student, Eldon Jay Epp recognizes the reductive error in this definition:

> Jesus' teaching takes a surprising turn, for under "The Kingdom Present as the New Age of Salvation" he argues that, while the dynamic meaning of "kingdom" is "the truly distinctive element in Jesus' teaching," a number of uses of "kingdom" portray "an eschatological realm into which men enter" and also "a realm of salvation which is present." (*The Presence of the Future: The Eschatology of Biblical Realism*, 195, 196).[14]

Thus, Ladd finds himself indicted by the same criticism he posits against Kümmel: What is the common realm that is both present (already) and future (not yet)?

Darrell Bock (1992) proposes a solution to the problem of realm in the already Davidic kingdom in the church and the not yet Davidic kingdom in the Millennium as he adapts the discussion into dispensationalism. He too recognizes the difficulty of the argument for fulfillment since the term "kingdom of God"[15] does not appear in the Old Testament, so he bases his argument on "clear allusions."[16]

In addition to the question of realm, Bock also addresses the question of inauguration of the kingdom that is already. Dodd had introduced the idea that the kingdom had broken into history in the mission of Jesus, but it remained vague when the kingdom would arrive. Was it in Jesus' rejection of Satan's temptation (Matt. 4:1–11) or in the casting out of demons (12:28ff.) or in Jesus' authority expressed through His followers in casting out demons (Luke 10:9) or in Satan's defeat at the Cross (John 12:31–32)? In addition to these exegetical questions, a theological question must be faced: Can God's kingdom actually appear on earth without Christ's death on the cross already having been accomplished? Bock's answer to these questions appears in the concept of transition—the appearance of the new work of God while the former works of God disappear: "The kingdom begins to arrive with Jesus' ministry. But this beginning is not complete until the bestowal of the Father's promise of the Spirit in Acts 2, an act that inaugurates the new covenant, which in turn finds its basis in the death of Christ (Luke 22:20)."[17]

This historical reconstruction of the inauguration of the kingdom then becomes the basis for the development of "realm" found in Acts 2 and 3. His argument begins with an examination of Peter's explanation of the resurrection and exaltation of Jesus. David spoke of Jesus' resurrection (Ps. 16) based on God's oath that one of his descendants would sit on his (David's) throne (Acts 2:30 alludes to Ps. 132:11 in the wording of the oath and promise). Then Peter argues that Christ was exalted to the right hand of God because David never ascended to heaven but rather spoke of his (David's) Lord seated at God's right hand (Ps. 110:1). Bock then draws the conclusion, "Being seated on David's throne is linked to being seated at God's right hand. In other words, Jesus' resurrection-ascension to God's right hand is put forward by Peter as a fulfillment of the Davidic Covenant."[18] That enthronement of Christ then sets the stage for defining the realm of Jesus' rule as Davidic king over the remnant of Jewish believers who were later joined by Gentile believers. He summarizes: "This invisible kingdom, lacking a visible king, is a 'sneak preview' kingdom in that this new community is to show God's active power in the transformation of sinners from sin to righteousness."[19]

In summary, we see in Dodd that the *already* is Jesus' mission and the *not yet* is a transcendent order beyond time and space that is not history. In Kümmel the *already* is the person and activity of Jesus, but not in rule over his disciples, and the *not yet* is the new age analogous to the Jewish apocalypse. In Ladd the *already* is Christ's dynamic reign in salvation and the *not yet* is the reign of Christ for a thousand years over the earth before the final consummation of God's redemptive purpose in the new heaven and earth in the age to come. Finally, in Bock the *already* is the partial and inaugurated fulfillment of David's reign in that salvation can only be found in Christ and the *not yet* is the ultimate consummation of David's reign to come over Israel and the whole earth in the Millennium.

THE SUFFICIENCY OF THE PHRASE

As we turn to assess the use of the phrase "already and not yet," we must ask whether it is sufficient. As the phrase has emerged to describe the progress made in the realization of the kingdom of God, we will seek to question its sufficiency in describing progress in this fulfillment. An important concept in this consideration is the principle of progressive revelation. "Progressive revelation is the recognition that God's message to man was not given in one single act but was unfolded in a long series of successive acts and through the minds and hands of many men of varying backgrounds."[20] In addition, progressive revelation is often associated with stages of fulfillment. So the question confronts us: "Is the phrase sufficient?" The answer must be, "Yes, but not completely."

It is sufficient because it affirms a clear continuity between the revelation of the Old Testament and the person, actions, and words of Jesus Christ, which fulfill that revelation. Matthew carefully documents the birth and the early experiences of Jesus as fulfillments of Old Testament prophecies (e.g., Matt. 1:22–23 cp. Isa. 7:14; Matt. 2:4–6 cp. Micah 5:2). Matthew does not merely allude to Old Testament words but introduces each quotation by indicating the relationship in which the prophets spoke of Jesus and his experiences (see chapter 4). Luke, with equal forthrightness, quotes Jesus' sermon at Nazareth in which Jesus affirms that the words from Isaiah 61:1–2a are being fulfilled in His ministry (Luke 4:18–19). Beasley-Murray summarizes the point: "Luke was able to emphasize the element of fulfillment contained in Mark 1:15 and to make plain without ambiguity the presence of the divine sovereignty in the proclamation and deeds of Jesus. Only instead of using the symbol of 'sovereignty of God,' Luke set forth the reality under the symbol of the jubilee release that brings salvation."[21] He argues persuasively that "the good news of liberty to the captives" probably does not refer to return from exile but to full emancipation for those who have known the bitterness of captivity to evil and sin. This is due to the imagery of the release proclaimed at the opening of the year of Jubilee on the day of atonement (Lev. 25:8ff.). That scope of release from evil fits with other general terms, such as "poor" or "brokenhearted," in the passage. In addition, those who mourn are in Zion, which would not fit the image of captivity (Isa. 61:3).[22]

Thus, the gospel accounts view Jesus in His person as a fulfillment of the promise of a descendant to Abraham and to David. In
addition, His birth experiences and His ministry are seen as involving fulfillments of promises to Israel. Those matching events in His
life enabled Peter to identify Him as Messiah (Matt. 16:16 and parallel passages). Further, the gospel accounts treat His death, burial,
and resurrection as fulfillments of what the Old Testament prophesied. These are all first-advent related promises as the partial quotation of Isaiah 61:2 indicates.

But several questions remain unanswered that pose a challenge
to the use of the phrase "already and not yet." Though there is present fulfillment in Christ's first advent, what does that fulfillment include? Was the kingdom of God, ruling through Christ, established
on earth before the Cross? In Luke's account Jesus stopped short in
His quote of Isaiah 61:2. Whereas Jesus proclaimed the year of God's
favor, He did not quote the phrase "the day of vengeance of our
God." The Old Testament prophets repeatedly said that God's judgment is necessary to establish God's rule over the earth's rebellious
population. In other words, did the kingdom of God arrive on earth
before the day of God's vengeance appeared?

A related question concerns the extent of what is fulfilled in
Christ's first advent. If Jesus is recognized as Messiah by God, as He
was, is God's recognition sufficient for the kingdom of God to appear
on earth? If a remnant also did accept His claims, would that acceptance be sufficient for the kingdom to appear even though the nation's leaders (the Sanhedrin) rejected Him and His claims? Or could
there be a spiritual fulfillment among the remnant without a political
and national fulfillment in Jerusalem? And would such a fulfillment
be a Davidic kingdom?

In view of these questions, the phrase "already and not yet" is
not completely sufficient because it fails to clarify and delineate the
discontinuity between what was anticipated in the Old Testament,
what was present in Christ, and what will yet come to fulfillment in
Christ. The phrase merely affirms the tension that something is fulfilled and something is yet to be fulfilled. Thus, our assessment will
focus on these ambiguities.

First, the phrase is not sufficient because it fails to provide a
basis for agreement on what is fulfilled and what is yet to be fulfilled.
There undoubtedly will be objection to this assessment by the claim
that the gospel records' use of Old Testament prophecies and promises provides the basis for agreement. Ladd has recognized a problem with this basis when he asserts that "the idiom 'the kingdom of

God' does not occur in the Old Testament."[23] So the Gospels' use of the Old Testament promises cannot be an examination of the direct use of kingdom-of-God promises. Bock correctly states that to see how God accomplished His kingdom program one 'must "look at associated concepts as well as individual terms."[24] And it is at this point of "associated concepts" that the problem appears. In Bock's argument for a Davidic kingdom now, fulfilled after Christ's ascension, is the alleged association of Psalm 110 and the Davidic throne (Acts 2:29–35). Although Psalm 110 is authored by David, it is by no means necessarily referring to the Davidic throne.[25] Even Peter's use of the Psalm (Acts 2:34–35) only argues for proof of Jesus' ascension and exaltation to God's right hand. The presence of the same word *sit* (Acts 2:34 and 30; see also chapter 8) does not provide a sufficient link to demonstrate that David's throne is God's right hand. So that argument from associated concepts is by no means a necessary or convincing basis for agreement.[26]

However, the more common support for agreement rests in how Jesus treats His ministry as a fulfillment of kingdom promises. But this discussion is also a contested one involving a number of statements by Jesus (Luke 4:21; Matt. 11:2–6; Luke 7:28; Matt. 12:28; Luke 10:9, 18; 11:20; and 17:20). Suffice it for our purposes to demonstrate that the "strongest statement"[27] (Matt. 12:28) remains contested and thus fails to provide a basis for agreement upon what is fulfilled.

In Matthew 12:28, Jesus asserts, "But if it is by the Spirit of God [finger of God, Luke 11:20] that I cast out demons, then the kingdom of God *has come upon you.*" Ladd summarizes his view of the verb, *has come upon*: "A vigorous debate has been waged over the precise meaning of the Greek word *ephthasen*, 'has come.' Many have interpreted the word to designate proximity, not actual presence. But other uses make clear that the verb connotes actual presence, not merely proximity."[28]

The fact of the vigorous debate indicates that the word may mean either and that the context must settle the issue. The context includes Jesus' discussion of the strong man who is bound by the stronger one so that his possessions may be taken. The issue concerns the sense of "bound." Bock comments on the theology: "In Judaism, the coming of Messiah and the demonstration of his authority were seen as marking the end for Satan. . . . Satan's defeat in the New Testament is often expressed in relation to the cross or the return of Jesus (John 12:31–32; Col. 2:14–15; Rev. 12:10–12; 20:1–3)."[29] What Bock recognizes in New Testament revelation is anticipated in the conflict of Genesis 3:15, where a fatal blow is struck against the serpent. If this is the case, then the sense of the "binding" during Jesus' life could hardly imply a true or real arrival of the kingdom of God. Rather, it was so very near that its power could already be felt "as the dawn precedes the sunrise,"[30] or else as "signs of the kingdom were present but not the kingdom itself."[31]

Adolf Schlatter provides a helpful and realistic summary interpretation of Jesus' life and ministry in the historical context of Jewish expectation. In general, Jesus bore the messianic office God had given Him at His baptism. Jesus' ministry revealed God in word and deed and carried out God's royal will.

> Jesus based His statement that God now revealed Himself as king on His mission. He who listened had part in the kingdom and therewith the grace of God and eternal life. He had reached the goal. But this by no means excluded hope, for the office of Christ which Jesus bore did not embrace fulfillment. Fulfillment was something to be hoped for and awaited, so long as the mission of Jesus consisted in preaching repentance, and He therefore Himself was the unknown and rejected.[32]

In spite of the fact that the phrase "already and not yet" provides no general basis for agreement on what is fulfilled and what is not fulfilled, many evangelicals continue to use the phrase to describe inaugurated kingdom eschatology. In so doing, they have arrived at their conclusions on *different bases*. And these differences lead to a second assessment of the "already and not yet." It is not sufficient because it fails to clarify the extent of what is fulfilled in the presence of the kingdom after the First Advent.

Anthony Hoekema speaks of Christ's present reign as a "realized millennialism," which is His heavenly reign on earth. It will continue until Christ returns. "The binding of Satan . . . means that throughout the gospel age in which we now live the influence of Satan, though certainly not annihilated, is so curtailed that he cannot prevent the spread of the gospel to the nations of the world"[33] This would lead to the conclusion that the reign of Christ is present in a spiritual sense in which the influence of Satan is curtailed in a general display and the redemption of the elect translates them from Satan's domain into a spiritual reign of Christ. The "not yet" in Hoekema's model is then seen to be the new heavens and the new earth.[34]

George Ladd regards the present reign of Christ at the Father's right hand as a fulfillment of the Davidic reign. "It is difficult to avoid the conclusion that Peter means that in Jesus' exaltation and session at the right hand of God, God has fulfilled the promise of Psalm 110.

Peter, under inspiration, has *transferred* the throne of David *from Jerusalem*—Zion (Ps. 110:2)—*to heaven*" (italics added).[35] Thus, the present reign of Christ is the result of a *reinterpretation* of the Old Testament because "the Old Testament did not clearly foresee how its own prophecies were to be fulfilled."[36] Consequently, Old Testament hope is *changed* due to New Testament interpretation, and the basis for a "not yet" rests only on Revelation 20:1–6 interpreted in a literal sense.[37] Ladd misconstrues this inaugurated eschatology as historic premillennialism.

Darrell Bock also interprets a Davidic fulfillment, but (as he argues) not because of change in Old Testament expectation based on reinterpretation in the New Testament. Rather, he will interpret a partial Davidic fulfillment in the *already* and a completed Davidic fulfillment in the *not yet* future millennial reign. "What emerges is a picture of a career that comes in stages as different aspects of what the Old Testament promised are brought to fulfillment at different phases of Jesus' work."[38] He then adds concerning the naming of these stages. "One might characterize these phases as the 'already' and 'not yet'. . . . terminology, since all Bible students accept its presence in soteriology: 'I am saved (i.e., justified) already—but I am not yet saved (i.e., glorified).'"[39] The question arises, can the same analogical construct as illustrated by justification/glorification be formulated with kingdom already/kingdom not yet, as Bock wishes to do? The answer is, "not clearly."

The lack of clarity arises from the term *kingdom*, which may emphasize "reign" or "realm." Justification is the legal and positional basis of salvation. If *kingdom* means "reign," then the legal basis of a future kingdom was not Christ's historic ministry but rather David's historic reign (2 Sam. 7). If, on the other hand, *kingdom* means "realm," then the present right to kingdom citizenship is available in Jesus' historic ministry (Matt. 5:3, 10), but that does not necessarily argue for the presence of the kingdom on earth as a legal basis for the future kingdom. In either case, an argument for the presence of the kingdom does entail an *expanded* kingdom when compared to the Old Testament expectation. But it seems difficult not to conclude that this *expanded* kingdom is not a *changed* kingdom, as Ladd argued. This interpretation includes a change in *throne* (God's personal throne rather than God's delegated throne to David), a change in *realm* (the church with Jews and Gentiles incorporated equally rather than Israel in the land with proselyte Gentiles), and a change in *reign* (spiritual authority only rather than spiritual and political authority).

In conclusion, it appears that the phrase "already and not yet" has garnered a widespread agreement among many evangelicals that exists at a verbal level but not at a level of shared meanings. The phrase "already/not yet" that some describe as not completely sufficient, actually is quite insufficient to describe a common understanding of an inaugurated eschatology.

THE PHRASE IN DISPENSATIONALISM

Although the phrase is insufficient to identify *kind* or *extent* of present fulfillment, yet it does affirm the fact of some fulfillment already. The kind and extent of fulfillment are thus in need of being defined. Would this limited contribution warrant its adoption into dispensationalism? Darrell Bock would view it as a necessary corrective in emphasis. It affirms that "different aspects of what the Old Testament promised" can be distinguished and these can be correlated to different phases of Jesus' work.

As a corrective he writes, "Dispensationalists have tended to underemphasize the 'already,' minimizing what is presently fulfilled in God's program in an attempt to maintain distinctions."[40] While not stated, this distinction is between Israel and the church and between God's present and future program. The question becomes, Does some of what was promised for Israel find fulfillment in the church? Is the church properly described as "spiritual Israel" or "true Israel," or is it more properly described as a new and distinct work of God? Is there continuity or discontinuity or an appropriate combination of the two in the relationship between Israel and the church?

The discussion within dispensationalism would be clarified if a clear definition of dispensationalism could be shared. Ryrie's description is clear: "Dispensationalism views the world as a household run by God . . . administering its affairs according to His own will and in various stages of revelation in the process of time."[41] It thus has elements of unity (His own will) and elements of discontinuity (various stages). Ryrie highlights this in regard to progressive revelation: "Only dispensationalism can maintain the unity [in purpose] and diversity [in administration] at the same time and offer a consistent, cohesive and complementary system of interpretation."[42] Thus, Ryrie regards dispensationalism as a system of theological conclusions that becomes a system of interpretation of the Bible.

Blaising and Bock propose a definition of dispensationalism that emphasizes historical description more than biblical description of progressive revelation. Progressive dispensationalism is "a futurist premillennialism that has strongly maintained the imminent return of Christ and a national and political future for Israel in the divine plan for history. It is characterized by a canonical approach to Scripture that interprets discontinuities of the Old and New Testaments as historical changes in divine-human dispensations reflecting different purposes in the divine plan."[43]

This definition highlights theological doctrines and hermeneutical method. In a number of respects, it defines dispensations in response to the issues of Ryrie's threefold *sine qua non*: (1) the distinction between Israel and the church; (2) the literal interpretation of the Bible; (3) the goal of the glory of God.

Rather than using one definition or the other, this author's assessment of the contribution of the phrase "already and not yet" will be made in relation to the influence upon these *sine qua non*. But remember, Ryrie treats them as *"sine qua non* of the system"[44] so that individual elements cannot be evaluated alone but must be considered as components of one system. Other traditions may agree on individual elements but do not adhere to the mutual influence of the three *sine qua non* as a system. So the question to be addressed is what does the "already and not yet" statement on the Old Testament fulfillment contribute to the *sine qua non* of the dispensational system?

1. The Distinction Between Israel and the Church

Blaising and Bock indicate the need for "revision in the dispensational view" of the relationship between Israel and the church. In summary, "There are important distinctions between Israel and the church in biblical theology, but there are also real theological connections that link them together in ways not expressed previously in dispensational thought."[45] It is here that the phrase "already and not yet" contributes, for it highlights connections between what was promised for Israel and what was partly fulfilled in the church.

The first contribution is a change in focus: "Instead of being anthropologically centered on two peoples, it is Christologically centered."[46] No one would deny the Christological unity of the canon in the progressive revelation of His person and work. The question turns on the focus or center within the system. The rationale for this new focus is that "Christ the King is seen as the agent, director and fulfillment of dispensational change."[47] Such a theological focus may be appropriate for a theological system but misses the essence of the dispensational system of interpretation. As a preacher approaches an Old Testament passage, that person asks what God says to the church in words originally addressed to Israel. In other words, how do we apply God's messages to Israel to believers in the church to-day. This model of the system with the new focus on Christ the king provides little help as a hermeneutic in these questions.

These common connections to Christ proposed by Blaising and Bock are then worked out in distinctions between Israel and the church as seen in the following summary of comments.[48] They begin by rejecting "two peoples in the sense of two different humanities with parallel destinies." Instead, the distinction is "primarily of two dispensational groupings of humanity." As their definitions implied, the distinction is primarily soteriological—a people before Christ under the Mosaic covenant and a people after Christ under the new covenant, rather than being distinct administrations of peoples who accomplish different purposes in God's will. Then they distinguish three dispensations: (1) *Israel*—the grouping in which divine blessings were poured out upon Israel while Gentiles were alienated or subordinated; (2) *Church*—the grouping in which divine blessings of the Spirit are going to Jews and Gentiles equally while national blessings are in abeyance; (3) *Kingdom*—the progressive relationship of Israel and the church suggests that the equality of Jew and Gentile in the regenerating, renewing, Christ-uniting ministry of the Holy Spirit both be carried forward and enhanced in glorification. This unity of blessing rests in one new covenant. In the future, the new covenant blessing is expressed on a "national, political scale . . . oriented to Zion, the new Jerusalem from which the Son of David, the Christ of Israel and the nations, rules."[49]

This new focus and the new distinctions between Israel and the church are clearly "revisions." The revisions are such that they raise important theological and exegetical questions. These questions feature the great covenants (Abrahamic, Davidic, and new), which are all alleged to experience "already" fulfillment and "not yet" fulfillment. In view of our present discussion on Israel and the church, we will only consider conclusions drawn from the fulfillment of the new covenant.

It seems strange that the new covenant is seen to be the basis of the Spirit's blessing, with the "already" fulfillment coming from a covenant completely established in Christ's death, and yet the Holy Spirit is described as merely the "firstfruits" (Rom. 8:23) and "seal" (Eph. 1:13) of a relationship. Blaising and Bock propose further that the "not yet" phase will be "enhanced" in glorification. It seems strange that a covenant needing only Christ's death to establish it (Heb. 9:12) would have only partial fulfillment.

What appears strange is clarified when passages referring to glorification are related to the climax in redemption (Rom. 8:23 and Eph. 1:14). The point is illustrated in the Exodus. Under Moses, redemption from Egypt preceded the institution of the old covenant contract. The Mosaic covenant was added to implement the relationship introduced in the redemption from Egypt (Ex. 19:5–6). So it would naturally follow that redemption from Satan's dominion would precede the new covenant relationship. Redemption involves the purchase of one enslaved to be introduced into a new relationship. And that new relationship would be implemented in a covenant contract. So the New Testament revelation does not disclose stages of new covenant fulfillment but rather stages of redemption. There are at least three stages of redemption: as Satan is defeated at the Cross, believers are translated into the kingdom of God's Son (Col. 1:13–14); as Satan is bound (Rev. 20:1–3), believers are resurrected or transformed into glorified bodies (1 Cor. 15:42–44); and as Satan is judged (Rev. 20:7–10), the whole of creation will be new in glory (Rom. 8:23; Rev. 21–22). So the stages involve the progressive revelation of redemption rather than stages of new covenant fulfillment.

A second question arises due to the supposed equality between Jew and Gentile that will be carried forward into the next age. With that spiritual equality "a national and political future for Israel" will involve no distinct spiritual privilege. Indeed, a question would be raised whether the promise to Abraham that "through his descendants all nations of the earth shall be blessed" (Gen. 12:3) had been forgotten. Further, the question would be raised whether God's design for these descendants of Abraham to be "a kingdom of priests" (Ex. 19:6) would ever be satisfied. In fact, it seems impossible to have both a spiritually equal people as is in the church and a future for Israel as envisioned in the Old Testament. So there seem to be forced interpretations of the biblical data when the "already and not yet" model of progressive fulfillment is pressed to extend the biblical understanding of Israel and the church.

There are legitimate concerns for further clarification raised by Blaising and Bock, but these can be readily addressed within the traditional model of the system. That model preserves both the hermeneutical and theological features involving "two purposes of God expressed in the formation of two peoples,"[50] Israel and the church. This model of the system can combine traditional distinctions while at the same time hearing the concerns of new issues.

In the *unity* of God's will within the whole canon, the focus is upon Christ in relation to both Israel and the church:

1. There is one Savior and Lord who is Christ, who was available in promise to Israel and who is available in the gospel to the church. The gospel concerns fulfillment of promise about Christ in the First Advent.

2. There is one people of God present in the whole Bible in the sense that all are saved through Christ. Israel's faith rested in God, who promised blessing through the Seed of Abraham (Gen. 12:3), and the church's faith rests in God, who provides Abraham's blessing through Jesus Christ (Rom. 4).

3. Jesus Christ is the ultimate heir of Old Testament promise as the Seed of Abraham (Gal. 3:16) and as the Son of David (Matt. 1:1).

In the diversity in the administration of God's will, the distinctions between Israel and the church reflect distinct revelations and purposes in God's plan:

1. There is a distinction in relationship to the election and promised blessing given to Abraham. Israel is the natural heir of the election and blessing given to Abraham. The church is without any natural claim to Abraham's blessing except as the promised blessing was to extend to all nations through Abraham (Eph. 2:11–13).

2. There are two people of God in the sense of accomplishing distinct purposes of God in His plan. Israel experiences in her history the *mercy of God* in spite of the people's repeated rebellion against their national election so that in mercy they will be transformed to accomplish God's will in the kingdom (Ex. 19:5–6). The church experiences the *grace of God* in spite of its having no claim or right to inherit God's blessing. And each member, Jew and Gentile, is included as an equal participant in Christ (Eph. 2:14–3:6).

In the kingdom, Israel, through God's mercy, will rule under Christ and fulfill the Abrahamic and Davidic covenant promises. The church, through God's grace, participates in the kingdom in its relationship to Christ (bride) and as joint-heirs of Christ.

Thus, this traditional model recognizes the church as a new work of God in Christ, yet related to the Old Testament through the promises fulfilled in Christ. The church is distinct in relation to Old Testament revelation but not disassociated from the covenants because of her relationship with Christ. In other words, Christ is related in fulfillment of Old Testament prophecy, and the church in her relationship to Christ experiences some of the blessing of this prophecy.

2. The Literal Interpretation of the Bible

Blaising and Bock again refocused the issue of hermeneutics from an interpretive strategy to "biblical authority."[51] This new focus is, of course, more important than method or strategy. However, a commitment to biblical authority entails an interpretive strategy that respects this authority. The literal principle was a strategy designed to allow the biblical text to speak for itself and thus speak authoritatively. Blaising's proposal to follow the "normal function of literary language"[52] is certainly consistent with the literal principle.

But more to the point of this assessment is the influence of the "already and not yet" view of the interpretation of progressive revelation. Waltke has recognized the impact: "This already—not yet model of dispensationalism, entailing a less than one-for-one correspondence between Old Testament covenants and prophecies and their partial fulfillment in the church, shakes the very foundations of dispensational hermeneutics, which includes a *consistent* literalistic interpretation of the Old Testament."[53] The crucial element that Waltke recognizes is the abandonment of the biblical authority of the Old Testament message as it was expressed in the original context when one uses only parts of the message in the partial fulfillment in the church.

Waltke is not alone in recognizing this influence. Ladd, who introduced the "already and not yet" model into progressive revelation concluded that "'the literal hermeneutic' does not work." A similar conclusion was recognized by Russell Bowers in the theology of Eric Sauer. Sauer does not use the phrase "already and not yet" but reaches similar conclusions about Old Testament covenants like the Davidic covenant. Bowers evaluates: "In holding to literal interpretation, Sauer does not eliminate the use of spiritualization. He himself 'spiritualizes' perhaps more than many other dispensationalists. But he clearly warns that mere spiritualizing is a dangerous circumventing of the simplest meaning of Scripture."[54]

Some may object to the assessment that Old Testament authority is being rejected because the partial fulfillment rests on the New Testament use of the Old Testament passage. Thus, the interpreter still works under biblical authority as found in the New Testament. Two problems are present in this claim.

The first is that objections remain as to whether New Testament usage, in fact, supports a partial fulfillment. Is the Davidic covenant or the new covenant partially fulfilled in the church (see chapter 5)? Again this would require more thorough exegesis than this chapter can pursue, but some of the problems were introduced.

The second problem was identified by John Feinberg:

Dispensational and nondispensational thinkers agree that the New Testament fulfills the Old Testament and is a more complete revelation of God; but there is disagreement as to what that means for the priority of one Testament over the other. Nondispensationalists begin with New Testament teaching as having priority and then go back to the Old Testament. Dispensationalists often begin with the Old Testament, but wherever they begin they demand that the Old Testament be taken on its own terms rather than reinterpreted in light of the New Testament.[55]

At issue is that the immediate context be allowed to express the message before the canonical context can expand the message in a sense unrelated to the original expressed message. The New Testament can allude to Old Testament passages in senses other than claiming a sense of fulfillment, but the "already/not yet" model tends to read some fulfillment as present and necessary in all such allusions.

3. The Goal of the Glory of God

In Ryrie's construct of the *sine qua non,* this is the ultimate unifying theme of the system. The emphasis is on the broadest unifying theme within the system ultimately informing all that God said and did. This goal (the glory of God) has been chosen in distinction to the goal of redemption common in the Reformed system. It is not that the Reformed tradition ignores the glory of God but simply does not identify the theme as an interpretive key in canonical interpretation.

Thus, the traditional focus in a dispensational system is theological, not merely Christological. God speaks and acts within the history of this earth to accomplish all that He purposed in the creation of the earth. That clearly involves redemption of a fallen mankind, but it also involves the reestablishment of man in position and rule on earth over evil. God's glory is displayed in His accomplishment of these purposes, including His mercy in establishing the rule of Israel and His grace in including the church in Christ's rule. These purposes are realized in the history of this earth before God would create a new heavens and earth. This is what Feinberg called a distinct "philosophy of history."[56] The phrase of "already and not yet" is Christocentric[57] and as such is less comprehensive than this glory of God goal.

CONCLUSION

There is a widespread judgment among evangelicals that an emphasis on inaugurated eschatology is imperative to a correct understanding of New Testament writings. The phrase chosen to express this judgment—"already and not yet"—has been assessed in this chapter. This assessment discovered that the phrase has been understood in different senses, such that the use of the phrase does *not* represent agreement on what is inaugurated. Among evangelicals, "inauguration" generally means that some promises concerning Jesus expressed in the Old Testament were fulfilled so that the kingdom was proclaimed.

A literal reading of the gospels and the epistles would naturally lead to an understanding of "first-advent fulfillment" of Old Testament promises. Many dispensationalists included these themes in their teaching. They stressed the consequences of first advent fulfillment in the formation of the church. A key distinctive of the dispensational system is the contrast between the church (newly created) and Israel (to whom the Old Testament had spoken directly). The church does not directly fulfill any of the promises addressed to Israel.

On the other hand, Christ as an Israelite does find Himself as one potentially addressed in these promises. That which is addressed is fulfilled in His Person, and many of the promises are fulfilled in the First Advent. He brings "the year of the Lord's favor" (Luke 4:18–21; Isa. 61:1–2a), which favor extends to the Gentiles in the ministry of Christ after the national leaders rejected the "Lord's favor" (Luke 4:28–30). But that favor need not be identified as the kingdom of David, nor is it the favor of completed redemption that follows the judgment of God's vengeance (Isa. 61:2b). This basic distinction within the system is vital in order that the church may discern its relationship to God's message to Israel and may identify what is yet to be fulfilled in Israel in Christ's second advent.

NOTES

1. Walter C. Kaiser, Jr., "An Epangelical Response," in *Dispensationalism, Israel and the Church: The Search for Definition,* Craig A. Blaising and Darrell L. Bock, eds. (Grand Rapids: Zondervan, 1992), 370.
2. Amos N. Wilder, *Eschatology and Ethics in the Teaching of Jesus,* rev. ed. (1939; New York: Harper & Row, 1950), 47–48.
3. C. H. Dodd, *The Gospel in the New Testament* (London: National Sunday School Union, 1926), 17–19, 38–39.

4. Richard H. Hiers, Jr., "Pivotal Reactions to the Eschatological Interpretations: Rudolf Bultmann and C. H. Dodd," in *The Kingdom of God in 20th Century Interpretation*, Wendell Willis, ed. (Peabody, Mass: Hendrickson, 1987), 18.

5. The kingdom was thus defined by God reigning in the hearts of men and was based on the decisive text of Matthew 12:28 (Luke 11:20), *ephthasen eph humas hē basileia tou theou*, in which Jesus' exorcisms mean the effective operation of the kingdom. That sense was then taken to influence *engiken* in Mark 1:14–15 and Luke 10:9–11, which means "has arrived."

6. Anthony A. Hoekema, *The Bible and the Future* (Grand Rapids: Eerdmans, 1979), 173–74.

7. Göstra Lundström, *The Kingdom of God in the Teaching of Jesus* (Richmond: John Knox, 1963), 201.

8. W. G. Kümmel, *Promise and Fulfillment* (Naperville, Ill.: Allenson, 1957), 107–8.

9. Ibid., 109.

10. George Eldon Ladd, *A Theology of the New Testament* (Grand Rapids: Eerdmans, 1974), 59.

11. Ibid., 63.

12. Ibid., 66.

13. "Kingdom . . . , a major territorial unit (realm) subject to a monarchial form of government (throne) usu. headed by a king or queen (ruler)" (*Webster Third New International Dictionary* [Chicago: Encyclopedia Britannica, Inc. 1966], 17:1244). "Basilea, usually translated 'kingdom,' it is to be noted first that it signifies the 'being,' 'nature,' and 'state' of the king. . . . The dignity of the king is expressed in the territory ruled by him, i.e., his kingdom" (*TDNT*, George Bromiley, ed. [Grand Rapids: Eerdmans, 1964], 1:579).

14. Eldon Jay Epp, "Mediating Approaches to the Kingdom: Werner Georg Kümmel and George Eldon Ladd," in *The Kingdom of God in 20th Century Interpretation*, Wendell Willis, ed., 49.

15. See Ladd, *A Theology of the New Testament*, 61ff., and Darrell Bock, "The Reign of the Lord Christ," in *Dispensationalism*, Blaising and Bock, eds., 37ff.

16. Bock, "The Reign of the Lord Christ," 37. The combination of "clear" with "allusion" seems enigmatic.

17. Ibid., 42.

18. Ibid., 49.

19. Ibid., 53.

20. Charles C. Ryrie, *Dispensationalism Today* (Chicago: Moody, 1965), 33.

21. G. R. Beasley-Murray, *Jesus and the Kingdom of God* (Grand Rapids: Eerdmans, 1986), 89.

22. The Sabbath rest of the year of Jubilee is argued as available to church age believers (Heb. 3:1–4:13) without denying a future expression of rest that depends upon a more complete stage of redemption and the Davidic kingdom.

23. Ladd, *A Theology of the New Testament*, 61.

24. Bock, "The Reign of the Lord Christ," 37.

25. Elliott E. Johnson, "Hermeneutical Principles and Psalm 110," *Bibliotheca Sacra* 149 (October-December 1992), 428–37, and Herbert W. Bateman, "Psalm 110:1 and the New Testament," *Bibliotheca Sacra* 149 (October-December 1992), 438–53. Bateman argues for such an identification, whereas Johnson argues that the textual evidence is incomplete for that conclusion.

26. David Dean, "A Study of the Enthronement in Acts 2 and 3," unpublished Dallas Theological Seminary thesis, 1993.

27. Ladd, *A Theology of the New Testament,* 65.
28. Ibid., 66.
29. Bock, "The Reign of the Lord Christ," 41.
30. C. T. Craig, *The Beginning of Christianity* (New York: Abingdon-Cokesbury, 1943), 87.
31. M. Dibelius, *Jesus,* Charles B. Hedrick and Frederick C. Grant, trans. (Philadelphia: Westminster, 1949), 68–88.
32. Göstra Lundström, *The Kingdom of God in the Teaching of Jesus* (Richmond: John Knox, 1963), 129.
33. Hoekema, *The Bible and the Future,* 229.
34. Ibid., 274ff.
35. George Eldon Ladd, "Historic Premillennialism" in *The Meaning of the Millennium: Four Views,* Robert G. Clouse, ed. (Downers Grove, Ill.: InterVarsity, 1977), 31.
36. Ibid., 27.
37. Ibid., 35–37.
38. Bock, "The Reign of the Lord Christ," 46.
39. Ibid.
40. Ibid.
41. Ryrie, *Dispensationalism Today,* 31.
42. Ibid., 36 (clarifications added).
43. Craig A. Blaising and Darrell L. Bock, "Dispensationalism, Israel and the Church: Assessment and Dialogue," in *Dispensationalism,* Blaising and Bock, eds., 379.
44. Ryrie, *Dispensationalism Today,* 43.
45. Blaising and Bock, "Dispensationalism, Israel and the Church," 377.
46. Ibid., 383.
47. Ibid., 382.
48. Ibid., 383–84.
49. Ibid., 384.
50. Ryrie, *Dispensationalism Today,* 44–45.
51. Blaising and Bock, "Dispensationalism, Israel and the Church," 378.
52. Craig A. Blaising, "Dispensationalism: The Search for Definition," in *Dispensationalism,* Blaising and Bock, eds., 31.
53. Bruce K. Waltke, "A Response," in ibid., 348.
54. Russell H. Bowers, Jr., "Dispensational Motifs in the Writings of Eric Sauer," *Bibliotheca Sacra* 148 (July-September 1991), 263.
55. John S. Feinberg, "Systems of Discontinuity," in *Continuity and Discontinuity,* John S. Feinberg, ed. (Westchester, Ill.: Crossway, 1988), 75.
56. Ibid., 84–85.
57. Blaising and Bock, "Dispensationalism, Israel and the Church," 382–83.

K ey Rapture passages are investigated to determine the relationship of the Rapture to the Tribulation. John 14:1–3; 1 Corinthians 15:50–57; and 1 Thessalonians 4:13–18 are discussed briefly. First Thessalonians 5:1–11 explicitly refers to the Rapture as well as to the Day of the Lord. The Christian is not appointed to the sudden destruction and to the wrath but instead to the Rapture. The implication is pretribulational. Second Thessalonians 2:1–12 clarifies that the Day of the Lord is more than Armageddon; it includes at least three-and-one-half, possibly seven, years of the Tribulation. This passage also shows that the apostle Paul and the Thessalonians were pretribulational in outlook. An extended discussion of Revelation 3:10 shows that this promise can only be an assurance that the church will not be present in the hour of trial, the Tribulation. Finally, a comparison of the epistles and the Olivet Discourse shows a different perspective and different addressees, and raises some logical questions for posttribulationism.

10

AN EXEGESIS
OF RAPTURE PASSAGES

Thomas R. Edgar

The passages usually associated with the Rapture are John 14:1–3; 1 Corinthians 15:50–57; 1 Thessalonians 4:13–18; 5:1–11; 2 Thessalonians 2:1–12; and, for many, Matthew 24:3–51. The basic issue for premillennialists is the timing of the Rapture relative to the Tribulation. Is it pre-, post-, or midtribulational? The Tribulation, due to established usage, is by definition the seven-year period known as Daniel's "seventieth week." We will focus on pre- versus posttribulational arguments. Once the Rapture and the Appearing are acknowledged as two separate events, as with both the pre- and midtribulationalists, the main difference is the length of the intervening period. Nevertheless, we must not overlook the fact that mid- as well as posttribulationalism denies an "any moment" Rapture, and both blur the distinction between Israel and the church.

There definitely is an appeal of simplicity to the idea that the Lord's future "coming" is only a single event, such that the Rapture and the Appearing are one event after the Tribulation. After all, Jesus did not say that He is coming twice. Why read two separate events into the prophecies of His future coming? On the other hand, neither did He say that His coming for the church is the same as His coming in glory. Why make one event out of two separate events? The posttribulational concept that the Rapture and the Appearing are one event is only an assumption. It requires just as much exegetical proof as the concept that they are two separate events.

We now know that the Old Testament prophecies of the Messiah's coming actually referred to two separate advents occurring more than 1,900 years apart. The prophets were bothered by the seemingly contradictory details describing the Messiah's suffering and His reign and victory. But they, as well as the biblical scholars of that day, would have scoffed at anyone interpreting them as two separate advents. The truth of a First and Second Advent was not recognized until after the fact. Now we have the biblical precedent that what may appear to refer to one future event may actually refer to two separate events. Consequently, we should not rely on the generalization that the many prophecies of the Lord's "coming" can only refer to one event.

Some passages describe the Rapture without indicating when it occurs. In the Upper Room Discourse, the Lord promises "His own" that He will go and prepare a place for them in His "Father's house" and that He will come again and take them along with Him so that they will be where He is (John 14:1–3). There is no implication that this refers to the glorious Appearing. A "yo-yo" rapture (as Gleason Archer describes the Posttribulational rapture),[1] where the raptured believers on the way to the "Father's house" are intercepted and carried back to the earth by the Lord as He comes in glory, does not harmonize well with the concept that He will come and take the believers to His Father's house.

The apostle Paul states that all believers will not die, but all will be changed into a glorified body fit for heaven in a moment, in the blinking of an eye, and at the last trumpet (1 Cor. 15:50–53). The only indication of time is the statement "at the last trumpet." This is the last trumpet for the church. It cannot, with any certainty, be equated with the "last trumpet" in the book of Revelation, which is itself only the "last" in a series of trumpets. This same chapter does connect the resurrection of believers with Christ's coming, or *parousia* (1 Cor. 15:23). But, until the issue is settled whether the Lord's "coming" (*parousia*) is in two phases or one, an interpreter should avoid assuming that which first must be proven.

The most specific description of the Rapture is in 1 Thessalonians 4:13–18. It is primarily a message of hope and encouragement to believers, in contrast to those who "have no hope" (1 Thess. 4:13, 18). Paul's central point is that Christians who have died are in no way behind those who are alive at the Lord's coming, since the dead will actually rise first; then, we will all go together to meet the Lord in the air. Verse 17 states that we shall be "snatched up in clouds to a meeting with the Lord in the air, and, thus, we shall always be together with the Lord."

The word "meeting," *apantsis,* does not imply that the meeting is to escort the Lord back to earth, as Douglas Moo claims.[2] It is used for a variety of meetings, such as meeting in war (Judges 6:35). Even as a technical term for a public welcome, it does not imply any necessity to escort the one welcomed back to the welcomer's domain.[3] Moo also contends that this passage shows a "suggestive" parallel with Jesus' *parousia* in the Olivet Discourse, since both passages "refer to a heavenly event with angels (archangel in 1 Thess. 4), clouds, a trumpet, and the gathering of believers."[4]

Even so, any future coming of the Lord will probably be a "heavenly event," and clouds, angels, and trumpets are to be expected. Since believers are gathered at the Rapture and believers are also gathered to enter the kingdom, the gathering of believers is not a significant parallel. On the contrary, specific signs of the Lord's appearing, such as judgment, signs in heaven, and turmoil on earth, are lacking in 1 Thessalonians 4:13–18. Nothing directly links this passage with the Lord's appearing.

THE RAPTURE AND THE DAY OF THE LORD:
1 THESSALONIANS 5:1–11

The apostle Paul continues his discussion of future events in 1 Thessalonians 5:1–11. The Thessalonians do not need to know "the times and the seasons," since the Day of the Lord will come like a thief in the night and bring sudden destruction upon the unbelievers (vv. 1–3). Only two out of the eleven verses concern unbelievers. These are only to emphasize, by contrast, the blessed hope for the believer as compared to destruction for the unbeliever. The believer is appointed to salvation and will live together with the Lord (v. 10).

Most interpreters, lexicons, and theological dictionaries conclude that *sleep* in the phrase "whether we watch or sleep, we shall live together with Him" (v. 10), refers to the sleep of death; i.e., "whether we are alive or dead." However, as Alford admits, this interpretation is "at the sacrifice of perspicuity."[5] All of the exegetical evidence supports the contrary view: that *sleep* means "not watching."[6] A different verb, often used for death, occurs in 1 Thessalonians 4:13 in a context discussing dead believers. The verb in this verse (5:10) is seldom used for death in biblical Greek. Out of twenty-two occurrences there is not one unequivocal case in the New Testament.[7] In this same context the verb is used to mean "not watching" (5:6) and "to sleep" (5:7). This context is an exhortation to watch. It concerns living believers, not dead ones. Finally, the accompanying verb translated "watch" does not occur with the meaning to "be alive," which the word must be given to contrast with "to be dead"; i.e., "whether alive or dead."

The almost universal argument for the meaning "sleep of death" is that it seems inconceivable that Paul would say that it makes little difference whether believers are watching or not.[8] But Paul does not imply that it makes little difference. He has urged the Thessalonians to watch, but he also gives them assurance that the Rapture is certain and does not depend on their watchfulness. All of the church will be raptured; there is no partial Rapture. The perspective is similar to 1 Corinthians 3:15 where Paul says, "If any man's work shall be burned up, he shall suffer loss but he himself shall be saved." Paul is not implying that it makes little difference if someone's works are burned up. He is giving assurance that one's salvation is certain and does not depend on his works. It is strange that interpreters who believe that all will be raptured, ready or not, find it inconceivable that this same concept would be found in 1 Thessalonians 5:10. Rather than being a general reference to the resurrection, this passage refers to a particular facet of the resurrection that is oriented to the time of the context. The stress on "watching or not watching" establishes that it refers to the resurrection as an explicit prophetical event—the Rapture.

The believer is not appointed to "wrath" but to "salvation" (1 Thess. 5:9). This is a precise aspect of salvation. It is oriented to the time of the context—to the time of the Day of the Lord. This orientation is confirmed by the comments in verse 10 linking the salvation with watching or sleeping. This is salvation as a definite prophetic event, the Rapture. Likewise, the "wrath" is an explicit prophetic event oriented to the time of the context. This is confirmed by its juxtaposition to the salvation mentioned in this verse; wrath is expressly opposed to the Rapture. The "wrath" (*orgē*) in this passage is the destruction of the Day of the Lord. This usage should not be surprising since this exact term occurs six times in Revelation 6–19 to describe God's wrath poured out at that time.

First Thessalonians 5:9 is not a "both/and" statement. The believer is not appointed to wrath and to salvation—to the Day of the Lord and the Rapture (the posttribulational view). The verse states "not one, but the other." The believer is appointed not to wrath, but to salvation; not to the Day of the Lord, but to the Rapture (pretribulationalism). The believer's hope is the Rapture. We are not watching

for wrath, but for the Lord. The passage indicates a distinct differentiation and certainly implies that the Rapture is prior to the Day of the
Lord.

The announcement that the sudden destruction occurs "when
they say peace and security" (v. 3) is not, as Gundry claims, to show
that they are already in turmoil and hope for peace.[9] Such an interpretation is contrary to the context. The context emphasizes the surprise. The sudden destruction comes just when they experience or
anticipate the opposite—peace and security. In the severe conditions
of the Tribulation (wars, rumors of wars, etc.) or at the end of the
Tribulation at Christ's appearing, will unbelieving men experience or
anticipate peace and security? This reference to peace and security
seems to place the arrival of the Day of the Lord sometime earlier
than the severe turmoil of the Great Tribulation.

Some, rather than defining the Day of the Lord as the Tribulation
or the last half of the Tribulation, have interpreted it as a dispensing
of "divine wrath," which occurs at the Lord's appearing or near the
end of the Tribulation. Such an interpretation assumes that this "divine wrath" differs from other wrath. As a result, they can allow for
the Rapture to be pre-Day of the Lord, or pre-divine wrath, and at the
same time still posttribulational. To clarify these issues, the Day of
the Lord must be biblically defined. Second Thessalonians will provide this information.

THE PROPER PERSPECTIVE:
2 THESSALONIANS 2:1–12

In his second epistle, Paul beseeches the Thessalonians "concerning [in behalf of] the coming of our Lord Jesus and our gathering
together to Him" (2:1). His express concern is the "Lord's coming
and our gathering to Him." He writes to quell any alarm and consternation they have as a result of thinking that they are in the Day of the
Lord. The Thessalonians had been led to believe through information
allegedly from Paul that the Day of the Lord was present (v. 2). The
resulting consternation and alarm must have related to their concept
of the Rapture, since this is Paul's explicit area of concern. The idea
that they were in the Day of the Lord conflicted in some way with
their understanding of future events, particularly in regard to the Rapture. They did not expect to be in the Day of the Lord.

Paul does not correct but accepts the Thessalonians' understanding of the Rapture and the Day of the Lord. He had already
taught them thoroughly regarding these events (v. 5). He reminds
them that the Day of the Lord cannot be present until the apostasy

comes and the "Lawless One" is revealed (v. 3). The rest of the paragraph (vv. 6–12) merely amplifies his answer. Thus, Paul finds no fault with the Thessalonians' understanding but rather relies on it to show that they are not already in the Day of the Lord. Only the false information needed to be corrected. The Thessalonians' perspective on the Rapture and the Day of the Lord is accurate.

The Thessalonian Perspective on the Day of the Lord

The Thessalonians, undergoing persecution, had accepted the idea that the Day of the Lord was present. It is unlikely they could have believed that the entire Tribulation, followed by the heavenly signs (Matt. 24:29), had already occurred and that now, in the Day of the Lord, they are face to face with the Lord's appearing. Yet, if Gundry's posttribulational view of that Day as Armageddon is correct, they would need to believe all this.[10] Nor could they have believed that they were in the events of the seventh seal of the book of Revelation as Rosenthal's interpretation would require.[11] They must not have believed that these events were either prior to, or the only events in, the Day of the Lord.

The Thessalonians' understanding (informed by Paul) of the Day of the Lord, will give us further insight. For instance, the Day of the Lord cannot begin with or be equated with the Lord's appearing, nor can it consist only of a period dominated by heavenly signs, since the Thessalonians could in nowise have believed that these were in progress or had occurred. Yet, they believed they were in the Day. They must have understood that initially the Day of the Lord would occur in the midst of relatively normal, if extreme, natural events such as persecution and wars. Otherwise, they could not have accepted that it was present. Also, since they already had believed for some time that they were in the Day of the Lord, they must not have considered the Day of the Lord to be a momentary event. They also must have understood the Day of the Lord to be a time of wrath imposed by human agents rather than some separate category stipulated as "divine wrath."

Someone may object that the Thessalonians knew that the apostasy and Lawless One were to begin the Day of the Lord, yet they still thought they were in it even though these events had not occurred. Since some form of apostasy is always at work and the first years of the Lawless One's career are quiet, they may not have put much stress on these events. In any case, it is far different to overlook two such introductory signs than to overlook worldwide cataclysmic events, such as the heavenly signs and the Lord's appearing. If the Thessalonians had believed that these cataclysmic events were the essential features of the Day of the Lord, they would specifically look for, not ignore, them. The fact that they could forget or overlook two such signs—the apostasy and the revelation of the Lawless One— emphasizes their expectation that the Day of the Lord would be relatively calm and not characterized by astounding signs at its beginning.

Paul's Perspective on the Day of the Lord

Paul's perspective is revealed not only through the Thessalonians' outlook and Paul's acceptance of it, but also directly by Paul's answer. Paul argues that the Day of the Lord cannot be present until "the apostasy comes first and the Lawless One is revealed" (2 Thess. 2:3). "First" does not mean "before" in the sense of a long interval.[12] If the Day of the Lord cannot be present until these events happen first, then as soon as they happen it can be present. These events initiate the Day of the Lord.

If the Day of the Lord, as Paul understands it, were to begin with the glorious Appearing at the end of the Tribulation, or with the seventh seal (Rev. 8:1), it seems odd that Paul does not mention the same heavenly signs given by the Lord as evidence for His appearing (Matt. 24:26–31) or some of the obvious signs of the latter part of the Tribulation. Instead, he mentions two signs that are, at the latest, mid-Seventieth Week. And one of these signs, if it refers to the "abomination of desolation" in God's sanctuary, is the same sign that Jesus gave for the *beginning* of "Great Tribulation" (v. 15). For Paul, the Day of the Lord must include the Great Tribulation of the Olivet Discourse. In answering the Thessalonians, Paul uses the signs of the apostasy and the Lawless One because, until these occur, one cannot be in the Day of the Lord; and he ignores the other signs because one can be in the Day of the Lord before they occur.

Interpreters usually assume that the Lawless One is revealed at the middle of the Seventieth Week, when he occupies the Temple of God (v. 15). But this is not a certainty. The passage does not detail what the "revelation" is. The statement, "who resists . . . so that he sits in God's sanctuary" (2 Thess. 2:4), may be merely descriptive of the man, as is the title "son of perdition" and the similar description "whom the Lord Jesus shall destroy" (v. 8). The Lawless One's "coming" (*parousia*, v. 9) is with signs and lying wonders. If his "coming" equates with his "revelation," this would occur at the beginning of the "Seventieth Week." Also, if the revelation of the Lawless One is spectacular and launches the Great Tribulation, it is more difficult to see how the Thessalonians overlooked it. Regardless, the revelation of the Lawless One, and hence the beginning of the Day of the Lord, occur, at the latest, by the middle of the Seventieth Week. The above observations open the possibility that it may be earlier.

The Perspective on the Rapture

The clearest insight from this passage is that Paul could not have taught the Thessalonians that the Rapture was posttribulational. He taught that the Rapture would be their joy and hope. This stands in marked contrast to their being shaken and alarmed regarding the Rapture, by the belief that they were already in the Day of the Lord. Otherwise, to be in the Day of the Lord would have caused them no problem concerning the Rapture since this would be expected if the Rapture were following the Tribulation. This is so evident a problem for posttribulationalism that Gundry tries to completely change the perspective by interpreting "shaken and alarmed" to mean "excited with anticipation."[13] He assumes that certain Thessalonians' failure to work (2 Thess. 3:6–13) is due to their anticipation. However, their failure to work has no certain connection to their prophetical outlook; and, if it did, it could just as easily be due to alarm. To interpret the terms "shaken and alarmed" as "excited with anticipation" is not only contrary to almost every translation and commentary but also is contrary to the usual meanings of the words involved. The word shaken (saleuō) means either to be physically shaken or shaken with apprehension. It occurs in Acts 17:13 accompanied by the word troubling. The word alarmed (throeō) occurs in Matthew 24:6 and Mark 13:7 in connection with wars and rumors of war, not an appropriate context for "excited anticipation." These words are negative in connotation. These two used together even more conclusively denote stress and alarm.

It is unlikely that the Thessalonians believed they had missed the Rapture since Paul had informed them that "living or dead" (1 Thess. 4:13–18), "watching or not" (5:10), every Christian will be raptured. He would have corrected this as an error in their thinking. They certainly could not have believed that God had forgotten an entire church or that the entire Thessalonian church was so unspiritual that God had left them behind. Neither is Archer's idea plausible that Paul was rebuking an "any moment Rapture" teaching.[14] Such an assumption depends on selecting the unlikely meaning "to be imminent" for the verb "to be present." In addition, had the Thessalonians believed that the Rapture was imminent, they would have been joyful, not alarmed.

How can their belief that they were in the Day of the Lord cause consternation about the Rapture to these Christians? Only if they expected never to be in the Day of the Lord and if that expectation was related to their concept of the Rapture. They expected to be raptured sometime prior to the Day of the Lord. Thus, if they thought they were in that Day, they would be alarmed regarding the Rapture. We see that Paul taught the Thessalonians a pretribulational perspective. In his answer to them, he assumes their perception's accuracy.

Hence, from this passage we conclude that the Day of the Lord is an extended period of at least three-and-one-half, possibly seven, years, culminating in the Lord's appearing and ensuing kingdom. The Rapture occurs before the Day of the Lord. This interpretation of the Day of the Lord also demonstrates that 1 Thessalonians 5:1–11 not only allows pretribulationalism but is based on it.

KEPT FROM THE HOUR:
REVELATION 3:10

The Lord Jesus Christ promised the church at Philadelphia, "I will keep you out of the hour of trial which is going to come upon the entire inhabited earth, to try those settled down upon the earth" (Rev. 3:10). This passage seems to promise that these believers will not be in the hour of trial (the Tribulation). For that very reason, it is probably "the most debated verse in the whole discussion."[15] Moo states, "It is probable that the reference is to the Great Tribulation, and all agree that the Philadelphian church is promised protection from it. The question is how?"[16] Is it by the Rapture or by divine protection through it? The amount of difficulty one view has in explaining a verse is often an indication of how strongly that verse supports an opposing view. If this is any indication, then the obvious difficulty and grammatically awkward arguments of posttribulational interpreters suggest that this verse strongly supports pretribulationalism. In stark contrast to posttribulational interpreters, pretribulational interpreters merely take the words and verse in their natural sense. Much of the posttribulational explanation depends on interpreting "keep out" to actually mean "keep in."

The Meaning of "Keep Out"

The expression "keep out" (*tēreō ek*) apparently means that the church has been removed (raptured) and is being kept out of, or away from, the "hour of trial." The meaning of the words and the grammatical constructions in this verse are similar to English. New Testament Greek, just as other languages, followed regular and logical grammatical principles. In reference to this verse, if the arguments (allegedly "from the Greek") seem strange or bizarre from an English perspective, they are, in all probability, equally strange or bizarre from the Greek perspective. One of the most recent and widely promulgated posttribulational discussions of Revelation 3:10 is by Robert H. Gundry. Other posttribulational interpretations will be discussed as appropriate.

"Keep" (tēreō). The verb *tēreō*, translated "keep," means "to guard, preserve, hold fast to, keep, and follow."[17] It is used seventy times in the New Testament, most often in John's writings. Some examples of its uses are "to keep the commandments" (Matt. 19:17), "to keep his own virgin" (1 Cor. 7:37), "to keep the good wine until now" (John 2:10), and to refer to the inheritance "kept" in heaven for the believer (1 Peter 1:4). Gundry argues that this verb always means to keep in, or to protect in a sphere of danger; therefore, the church will be in (kept in) the "hour of trial."[18] However, neither the believer's inheritance in heaven (1 Peter. 1:4), the virgin daughter (1 Cor. 7:37), nor the good wine (John 2:10) seem to be in a sphere of danger, nor does a study of the verb's many occurrences support the meaning "keep in." Any more specific meaning than "keep" is derived from the context, not from the verb itself.[19]

"Out" (ek). The preposition *ek* is very much like the English preposition "out." Although it can mean "out of, since, from the time of, because of, and by means of,"[20] its common meaning is "out." Some posttribulational interpreters have interpreted *ek* in this verse to allow for presence in the hour of trial, but Gundry's approach differs somewhat from others. He argues, "If *ek* ever occurs without the thought of emergence, it does so very exceptionally."[21] He concludes that to "emerge from out of" the hour of trial means that the believers must have been in the hour of trial. But a study of the 916 occurrences of *ek* in the New Testament[22] reveals that it has various meanings, of which approximately 186 clearly imply emergence and about fifty-two imply separation ("out of," "away from").[23] The stone did not emerge from within the tomb (John 20:1), nor did the chains emerge from within Peter's hands (Acts 12:7). Gundry's definition of *ek* is contrary to the evidence. *Ek* means "out," and frequently implies emergence. However, the idea of emergence is not in the preposition itself but comes from its combination with a verb of motion, such as "come (out)" or "go (out)." *Ek* often occurs with verbs of motion,[24] but it is the verb that gives the idea of motion in "emer-

gence." *Ek* cannot combine with a verb of nonmotion such as "stay" or "remain" and result in the meaning "to emerge." It cannot turn a verb of nonmotion such as *tēreō* ("keep" or "protect") into a verb of motion. Therefore, *ek* cannot mean "emerge" in Revelation 3:10, and it does not indicate presence "in" the hour of trial.

The expression "keep out." Neither Gundry's argument that "keep" means "keep in," nor that "out" means "emerge, go out" is a grammatical or a logical possibility in the expression "keep out" (*tēreō ek*). The combination "keeping in going out" does not make sense. Neither can the verb *tēreō* possibly mean "keep in" in combination with *ek* ("out"). Perhaps we may be excused for wondering how anyone could fail to see that "keep in going out" is impossible. Gundry tries to avoid this obvious contradiction by interpreting the words "to keep in and eventually emerge." He describes it as "protection issuing in emission."[25] He interprets *tēreō* to mean "keep or protect in" the hour of trial and *ek* to mean emergence or emission at the last moment, at or near the end of the hour of trial. He has merely added the two self-contradictory meanings he has assigned to the words as if they are numbers in an arithmetic problem, producing the grammatically impossible result that "keep out" becomes "keep and eventually out." This combination is not plausible. Gundry argues that this is necessary for *tēreō* to be meaningful and for *ek* to lay all the emphasis on emergence.[26] But in this case "keep" only functions until "out" takes over. How can a word receive proper emphasis in a construction when each word is only functioning part of the time? The pretribulational interpretation does give full meaning to both "keep" and "out," with the meaning "keep out." Does "stay out of the hospital" mean "stay in the hospital for several years and eventually emerge"? Obviously it does not; nor can "keep out" mean "keep in and eventually emerge."

Tēreō ek in John 17:15. Both Gundry and Moo attempt to derive a posttribulational sense from *tēreō ek* by an appeal to John 17:15, the only other occurrence of *tēreō ek* in biblical Greek.[27] John 17:15 states, "I do not ask that you take [*arēs*] them out of [*ek*] the world, but that you keep [*tērēsēs*] them out of [*ek*] the evil (one)." Gundry argues that the words "take out" (*arēs . . . ek*) are an "exact description of what the rapture will be." Then he concludes that since in this, its only other occurrence, "keep out" (*tēreō ek*) "opposes an expression which would perfectly describe the rapture,"[28] it cannot refer to the Rapture or the result of the Rapture in Revelation 3:10.

But *tērēsēs ek* ("keep out") is not in full contrast and opposition to "take out" in John 17:15. Instead, the entire expression "take out of the world" contrasts with the entire expression "keep out of the evil one." The difference is not due to the preposition *ek* but to the two different verbs "take" and "keep" and to the two different nouns, "the world" and "the evil one." The two expressions may contrast in their totality, but that does not require a different meaning for *ek* in each expression. For instance, if a father tells his son, "I am not asking you to take your friend out of town but that you keep him out of trouble," the two ideas contrast, but "out" does not have contrasting meanings such that one occurrence becomes "in." The father is certainly not saying "keep your friend in trouble." In John 17:15 the first *ek* definitely means "out of." There is no reason to think that the second *ek* has any other meaning, particularly "in."

Another scholar, George Ladd, also uses John 17:15 to argue that *tēreō ek* does not indicate bodily removal but "preserving from the power of evil even when in its very presence."[29] However, he has added the words "from the power of," which are not in the verse. Without these added words, Ladd's interpretation would have the Lord praying that the disciples be "kept or preserved in evil, or in the evil one." Moo similarly states that this verse is a prayer "for the disciples' preservation from the power of Satan."[30] Moo has added, as Ladd, the words "the power of." But the object of *ek* in this verse is "evil, the evil one (Satan)," not "the power of Satan." These unwarranted additions give no insight into the meaning of *ek* as it actually occurs. They do show the difficulty posttribulationalists face in avoiding the normal meaning of *ek* in Revelation 3:10.

In another effort to nullify *ek*, Moo argues that there are only three verses (John 17:11, 12, 15) other than Revelation 3:10 where *tēreō* has God or Christ as the subject and believers as the object. "In each case, *spiritual preservation* is clearly intended."[31] The first two verses (John 17:11, 12) use *tēreō* with the preposition "in" and provide no basis for interpreting "keep" (*tēreō*) with a preposition meaning exactly the opposite of "in" as also meaning "keep in." Neither can the fact that a verb has the same subject and object determine its meaning when it occurs in a different verse with a different preposition and in an entirely different context. Does "John kept his dog in the kennel," mean the same as "John kept his dog out of the trash," merely because the verb "kept" has the same subject and object in both? This entire approach is quite invalid in Greek even as it is in English.

"Out" means "in": one more try. Galatians 1:4 is also used by Ladd to argue that *ek* in Revelation 3:10 does not refer to physical removal from this age but to deliverance from its power and control.[32] However, since the verb accompanying *ek* in Galatians 1:4 does not

mean "kept," but very specifically means "take out," or "take away," the verse can hardly be understood as "to preserve, or protect" either "in, or through." Galatians 1:4 may well refer to the future event when believers are "taken out" of this age, the Rapture. If so, it directly supports the pretribulational view of Revelation 3:10. Another possibility is that it is a figurative expression describing believers as those "rescued out of this age." The figure is not of protection in but of "taking out"; thus, in the figure, *ek* still has its normal meaning.

Other prepositions. Gundry argues that John would have used the preposition *apo* ("from") rather than *ek* if he referred to a pretribulational rapture.[33] In New Testament times, the meaning of these two prepositions overlapped; consequently, *ek* would be as clear as *apo*. John uses *ek* four times as often as *apo*, showing a decided preference for *ek*. The claim that John would have used *apo* is without any basis in fact. Gundry also suggests several other prepositions,[34] none of which occur with *tēreō* in biblical literature. Most occur rarely in John's writings, and some do not occur with expressions of time. Of the seventeen standard prepositions used in the New Testament,[35] only two, *ek* and *apo*, could be used in Revelation 3:10 to indicate a pretribulational Rapture. Of these, *ek* is definitely John's preference. In contrast, there are three very common prepositions, two of which, *en* ("in") and *eis* ("into"), occur with *tēreō*, that would favor a posttribulational interpretation but are not used in Revelation 3:10. There is no justification for interpreting Revelation 3:10 as "keep, or protect in" the hour of trial.

The Effect of "Hour"

When Jesus promised the church, "I will keep you out of the hour of the trial which is going to come upon all the inhabited earth" (Rev. 3:10), He was referring to a specific, future, worldwide period of trial, i.e., "the Trial." Pretribulationalists have often pointed out that this means to keep out of the period when the trial occurs, not, as some posttribulationalists say, merely from some of the events in "the time." As we have shown, *ek* does not mean "in." The word "trial" is singular and definite. It must be interpreted together with "the hour," as a unit. The promise is to keep the church from the worldwide period known as "the Trial." This seems to require removal of the church from the earth.

Gundry argues that time still goes on in heaven, so the church cannot be removed from that "time."[36] He fails to notice that the "period of the trial" is to try those on earth. The promise is not to remove believers from "chronological time" but from the period on earth known as "the Trial." If someone says, "I am glad that I was not in the recent time of turmoil in the Soviet Union," he is not saying that he was not in "time" but that he was not in the Soviet Union during that time. To be kept out of a worldwide period of trial on earth indicates removal *from earth* during that time, not removal from time.

Gundry also contends that when Jesus said, "Father, save Me from this hour" (John 12:27) He was not asking for deliverance from the period of time, but from the events of the period.[37] But Jesus is asking that certain scheduled events, such as the Cross, not occur. He is not asking for protection in the events. If we applied this principle to Revelation 3:10, it would not be a promise to protect in but to cancel the events of the hour of trial. The only natural way to interpret Jesus' promise is in a pretribulational sense.

The Meaning of "the Trial"

The trial has the specific purpose to try "the earthdwellers." The expression "those dwelling on earth" occurs eleven times in the book of Revelation, but not elsewhere in the New Testament. It refers explicitly to those who are unbelievers on earth during the period described in Revelation 4–19. For example, they are tormented by the two prophets (11:10), worship the Beast, and are not in the Lamb's book of life (13:8, 12). They are described in the fifth seal (6:10) as having already killed believers, indicating that they are busy persecuting believers prior to the fifth seal. They experience all of the natural disturbances under God's control, the direct divine actions, and the turmoil caused by the Beast. Although Satan and the Beast do not have the intention of "trying" these "earthdwellers," their actions under God's control contribute to the trial. The "hour of trial" referred to in Revelation 3:10 not only is in the same context, but fits perfectly with the situation described in Revelation 4–19.

The word *trial* also occurs in 2 Peter 2:9 and apparently refers to God's actions. The other twenty occurrences in the New Testament are negative in character. Neither the Flood nor the destruction of Sodom and Gomorrah (2 Peter 2:5–9) are a direct "appearing" of God in judgment. God used a long, heavy rain in one case and fire or "burning sulphur" in the other. Both may be the miraculous use of natural means. In any case, both are similar to the events in Revelation, both are from God, and both are divine wrath poured out on earth.

There is no basis upon which to separate the events of Revelation 4–19 from, or into, "divine wrath" contrasted with some other "wrath" or "trial" in Revelation. Christ opens "the seals" (5:5–13), indicating that they are under His control. There are numerous statements by angels and the heavenly witnesses showing that God is in charge of these events. The destruction of Babylon the Great is by the ten kings allied with the Beast (17:7, 16), yet it is described as God's "wrath" (orgē, 16:19 and 19:15), and it is stated that God judged her (19:2).

Those "dwelling on earth" are clearly "tried" in the events of Revelation 4–19. The trials are worldwide. In accord with the normal use of *peirasmos* ("trial"), they are judgments and wrath from God. They are the main subject of the same book and context as Revelation 3:10. The correspondence fits perfectly. The "hour of trial" cannot be restricted to Christ's appearing in contrast to the totality of events in Revelation 4–19. The posttribulational concept that Jesus promises protection in these events is also contrary to several statements in Revelation indicating that many believers are slaughtered during this time.

A COMPARISON:
THE OLIVET DISCOURSE

There are certain differences in perspective in the Gospels' statements about the Lord's coming and the statements in the epistles regarding the Rapture. Out of many, some are selected from the Olivet Discourse (Matt. 24:1–25:46).

Not the Rapture

The Rapture is not referred to in Matthew 24:36–41 as some assume. The Lord makes a comparison between Noah's day, when the Flood "took away" the unrighteous, and His future coming, when one "will be taken" and the other left. Many fail to notice that the comparison is not with Noah but only with the unbelievers of his day. The context is judgment. Admittedly, in each part of the comparison a different verb for "take" is used. Yet, it would be unreasonable to ignore the parallel in both instances between "take away" and instead regard the comparison as "take away" compared with "left behind." Thus, the one taken away (vv. 40–41) is compared to those unbelievers taken away by the Flood. This is not the Rapture; the ones taken are unbelievers.

Different addressees

In the Olivet Discourse there are several parables exhorting the hearers to watch for the Lord's coming. All of them admonish the hearers to watch and be ready. If they are not, they will be punished eternally. One such parable is Matthew 24:45–51. By way of contrast, in the epistles to the churches the instruction is that whether "watching or not watching" we will live with the Lord (1 Thess. 5:10). The parables, and thus the Olivet Discourse, cannot be referring to Christians but to a mixed multitude.

Logical Questions

Days "cut off" versus Rapture. The Tribulation will be so severe that it will be terminated ("cut off") at the end of seven years rather than be allowed to continue and destroy all mankind (Matt. 24:21–22). The days are not "shortened" as if God changed His original plans,[38] but in accordance with prophecy the days are "cut off" after seven years "for the elect's sake." Why would the Tribulation be "cut off" for the elect's sake if the Rapture delivers the elect at this time? Once the Rapture occurs why not allow the Tribulation to go on since it makes no difference for the "elect's sake"? If the Tribulation is stopped by the Lord for the elect's sake, there seems to be no need for a Rapture. The believers could go into the Millennium. If it is inappropriate for Christians to enter the kingdom, then it must be due to some dispensational distinction between the church and those in the kingdom.

Why a Rapture after the Tribulation? Jesus describes the Tribulation as so severe that it is worse than anything before or after (Matt. 24:21). The verse does not refer to the destruction of Jerusalem in A.D. 70—it was not the worst time in history, nor was the destruction "cut off" for the elect's sake. The posttribulational view requires believers to go through the worst trial in history, in which many are slaughtered. Why, after allowing Christians to go through this, would the Lord rapture them right before the long-promised, glorious messianic kingdom? Will the Lord "cut off" the Tribulation for the elect's sake and then at His appearing destroy people indiscriminately so that they must be raptured to be safe? Why, after allowing the church to suffer terrible slaughter for years, would He now deliver them (rapture) when there is no danger, just before the glorious kingdom? There is no apparent reason unless for some cause it is not appropriate for Christians (the church) to enter the kingdom. But, if this is so, then there must be some dispensational distinction between Israel and the church. It certainly seems reasonable to remove the church (Christians) before, rather than after, the slaughter of the Tribulation. If there is no dispensational distinction precluding the church from the kingdom and if the Rapture is not to deliver from the Tribulation, there seems to be no reason for the Rapture, particularly a posttribulational Rapture.

Who Populates the Millennium?

If the Rapture occurs so that all the believers are taken away at the end of the Tribulation, then where are the believers who are necessary to enter and populate the Millennium? If the believers are all raptured and as the Scripture says all the unbelievers are sent to everlasting punishment, where is anyone to enter the kingdom? The difficulty this presents to the posttribulational interpreter is admitted by Moo.[39] It is made even more obvious by the examples of exegetical dexterity used to avoid this problem. Many other posttribulationalists merely ignore it.

Last-minute conversions? One posttribulational solution explains that after the Rapture, when the Lord appears many are converted and enter the millennial kingdom. This specifically disagrees with all of the parables of readiness for the Lord's coming. These parables discuss readiness based on extended action such as treatment of others, not on momentary action; and they stress that it is too late to change when the Lord comes. The most obvious is the parable of the ten virgins (Matt. 25:1–13). There is no question that this parable refers to the Second Advent. The most explicit point in this parable is that one must be ready *before* the Lord appears. Once He appears, it is too late and the door is shut (v. 10). All of these readiness parables preclude last-minute conversions to enter the kingdom.

Unbelievers will enter? Another defense is to claim that all the believers are raptured but unbelievers populate the Millennium. This actually requires two interpretational twists. The first, contrary to the opinion of most premillennialists, attempts to prove that unbelievers enter the Millennium. Second, this defense requires a nullifying of every passage that indicates that all living unbelievers are sent to punishment at the Second Advent.

Gundry and Moo solve this problem by deciding that the judgment of "the sheep and the goats," where it is explicitly stated that all unbelievers are sent to eternal punishment (Matt. 25:31–46), is not at the Second Advent after all but is at the end of the Millennium. Thus, having eliminated such a judgment at the beginning of the kingdom, they have made room for unbelievers to enter.[40] Moo argues that Scripture often blends prophetic events and that this account is a merging of a premillennial and postmillennial judgment, not requiring the "all" to be judged at the same time.[41] This is a single, unbroken discourse (the Olivet Discourse) discussing the Lord's coming in glory with His angels in order to render judgment before entering His kingdom. Yet, we are asked to believe that this parable in the discourse, indicating no difference in time, discussing exactly the same things, and specifically mentioning entrance into His kingdom, is actually talking about an entirely different event 1,000 years later. The argument is given that the unbelievers go to "eternal punishment,"[42] as if the end of the Millennium is the only time such an expression could be used. We are reminded, as an argument, that prophecy often blends two events separated by intervals of time. Does it seem unreasonable to wonder how the same interpreters who refuse to allow an interval of seven years between the Rapture and the Appearing can, in order to prove there is no such interval, now invent an interval of 1,000 years between judgments where there is no apparent gap? In this case they even see 1,000 year intervals in the same statement so that when it says all are judged this means some one time and some 1,000 years later.[43]

The entire tenor of Scripture is that the kingdom is for believers. Is it realistic to see the "earth dwellers" who slaughtered the believers, who obstinately rejected God over several years despite massive displays of His power, who were beast worshipers and God haters, while the remnant of believers who survived are raptured at the end of the Tribulation, walking happily in to enjoy the promised messianic kingdom? This is directly contrary to Paul's statement that those who cause tribulation for believers will be punished at the Lord's appearing (2 Thess. 1:6–10) and contrary to the statement of judgment referring specifically to all those who followed the "Man of Sin" (2 Thess. 2:9–12). It is contrary to John the Baptist's preaching and the Lord's teaching in the Sermon on the Mount that only the righteous will enter the kingdom. Are these interpreters also unaware that moving the parable of the "sheep and goats" is not sufficient? In order to maintain the idea that unbelievers escape judgment at the Second Advent, they must shift all of the readiness parables and other accounts of His coming to the end of the Millennium.

CONCLUSION

The descriptive passages (John 14:1–3; 1 Cor. 15:50–57; and 1 Thess. 4:13–18) make no explicit connection between the Rapture and the glorious appearing of Christ. First Thessalonians 5:1–11 delineates the believer's hope as salvation (the Rapture), not wrath, not the Day of the Lord. The two are plainly differentiated. Second Thessalonians 2:1–12 adds two distinct clarifications to the discussion. First, the Day of the Lord begins at least by the middle, possibly at the beginning, of the Tribulation, the "Seventieth Week" of Daniel. Second, the Rapture occurs before the Day of the Lord. Revelation 3:10 confirms this even more explicitly. The church has been promised not that it will be protected in but that it will be kept out of the worldwide time of trial described in Revelation 4–19. The exegesis of the Rapture passages definitely supports a pretribulational analysis of this event.

Finally, a comparison with the description of the Lord's appearing in the Olivet Discourse makes it apparent that the Rapture is not mentioned, nor does it fit in the perspective of the Olivet Discourse. A posttribulational Rapture will not fit in the biblical description of the Lord's appearing and resulting messianic kingdom.

The church's hope is the Lord. She should be looking for Him to come for her; she is not watching for the Tribulation.

The biblical evidence for a pretribulational Rapture is clear. It also presents the most reasonable hope. Why do posttribulationalists go to such extremes to deny an interval between the Rapture and the Appearing? They seem to have no problem with intervals. An interval, even 1,000 years, is no problem. Nor is the idea of two prophetic events blended into one. The antipathy toward pretribulationalism, it seems, is not due to the concept that the church is raptured seven years prior to the Appearing. Some postribulationists seem more inclined to move in the direction of amillennial interpreters than to be open to pretribulationism. There is an overreaching perspective encompassing amillennialists and nondispensational posttribulationalists. The basic opposition is not to a Rapture at a seven-year interval before the Appearing but to what this implies. It implies a specific and clear distinction between the church and Israel, between the church and the elect in general. The antipathy seems to be directed toward dispensationalism.

Notes

1. Gleason L. Archer, Jr., et al., *The Rapture: Pre-, Mid-, or Post-Tribulational?* (Grand Rapids: Zondervan, 1984), 215.
2. Archer et al., *The Rapture,* 181.
3. Erik Peterson, *"apantēsis," TDNT,* Gerhard Kittel, ed. (Grand Rapids: Eerdmans, 1964–74), 1:380–81.; Henry George Liddell, Robert Scott, and Henry Stuart Jones, *A Greek-English Lexicon,* 9th ed. (Oxford: Clarendon, 1940), 178.

4. Archer et al., *The Rapture,* 181.
5. Henry Alford, *The Greek New Testament* (Chicago: Moody, 1958), 3:279.
6. Thomas R. Edgar, "The Meaning of 'Sleep' in 1 Thessalonians 5:10," *JETS* 22, no. 4 (December 1979), 345–49.
7. The few New Testament examples cited by F. F. Bruce (*1 & 2 Thessalonians,* Word Biblical Commentary, no. 45 [Waco: Word, 1982], 114–15), such as "she is not dead but sleeping" (Mark 5:39) are certainly not unequivocal and actually seem to contrast with death.
8. D. Edmond Hiebert, *The Thessalonian Epistles* (Chicago: Moody, 1971), 225; Bruce, 1 & 2 Thessalonians, 114.
9. Robert H. Gundry, *The Church and the Tribulation* (Grand Rapids: Zondervan, 1973), 92.
10. Ibid., 98.
11. Marvin Rosenthal, *The Pre-Wrath Rapture of the Church* (Nashville: Nelson, 1990), 117.
12. Gundry, *The Church and the Tribulation,* 119–21.
13. Ibid., 121.
14. Archer et al., *The Rapture,* 126.
15. Gundry, *The Church and the Tribulation,* 54.
16. Archer et al., *The Rapture,* 197.
17. Reinhard Kratz, *"tēreō,"* *EDNT,* Horst Balz and Gerhard Schneider, eds. (Grand Rapids: Eerdmans, 1990–93) 3:354–55.
18. Gundry, *The Church and the Tribulation,* 58.
19. Thomas R. Edgar, "Robert H. Gundry and Revelation 3:10," *Grace Theological Journal* 3, no. 1 (Spring 1982), 19–49. This provides a detailed refutation of Gundry's arguments.
20. Gerd L. Ldemann, *"ek," EDNT,* 1:402–3.
21. Gundry, *The Church and the Tribulation,* 56.
22. W. F. Moulton, and A. S. Geden, ed., *A Concordance to the Greek Testament,* 5th ed. (Edinburgh: T. & T. Clark, 1978), 1058–67.
23. Edgar, "Robert H. Gundry and Revelation 3:10," 27.
24. Lüdemann, *"ek,"* 403.
25. Gundry, *The Church and the Tribulation,* 57–59.
26. Ibid., 57.
27. Ibid., 58–59; Archer et al., *The Rapture,* 197–98.
28. Gundry, *The Church and the Tribulation,* 59.
29. George E. Ladd, *The Blessed Hope* (Grand Rapids: Eerdmans, 1956), 85.
30. Archer et al., *The Rapture,* 197.
31. Ibid., 197–98.
32. Ladd, *The Blessed Hope,* 85.
33. Gundry, *The Church and the Tribulation,* 57–58.
34. Ibid.
35. H. E. Dana, and Julius R. Mantey, *A Manual Grammar of the Greek New Testament* (New York: MacMillan, 1927), 99–114.
36. Gundry, *The Church and the Tribulation,* 59.
37. Ibid., 59–60.

38. Rosenthal, *The Pre-Wrath Rapture of the Church,* 108–12. Rosenthal's position hinges on an improper understanding of the English translation of the verb *kolobo,* "to cut off." In Matthew 24:22 it means to terminate, not to make shorter.

39. Archer et al., *The Rapture,* 161.

40. Gundry, *The Church and the Tribulation,* 163–67; Archer et al., *The Rapture,* 162–63.

41. Archer et al., *The Rapture,* 162–63.

42. Ibid.

43. Ibid.

Within the theological system of dispensationalism, premillennialism has been a classic tenet. Historically, most dispensational premillennialists have held a pretribulational view of the Rapture as well. As a system, the pretribulational rapture view provides a more coherent and biblical understanding of the text within the framework of dispensational theology than does post- or midtribulationism. Recent arguments for posttribulationism fail to deal adequately with the biblical text. The distinction between the church and Israel supports the pretribulational understanding, and the biblical/exegetical arguments for pretribulationism demonstrate it to be the position most compatible with the premillennial view.

11

DISPENSATIONAL THEOLOGY
AND THE RAPTURE

Paul D. Feinberg

I t is appropriate to include chapters on the Rapture in a book on dispensationalism because dispensationalists have been predominantly pretribulationists. Dispensationalists by and large have been interested in eschatology and have made the coming of our Lord an important focus in their theology and ministry. In this chapter we will examine three theological concerns related to the Rapture: dispensational ecclesiology and the Rapture; the incompatibility of premillennialism and a posttribulational Rapture; the Olivet Discourse and the Rapture.

The purpose of this chapter, unlike the chapter by Thomas Edgar, is not to give a detailed exegesis of selected passages in order to consider their implications for dispensationalism and pretribulationism. At the same time, however, a theological analysis does not exclude or ignore sound exegesis. Rather, the concerns to be examined are broad, overarching, and structural issues, systematizing and harmonizing information or data from a variety of sources and texts.

DISPENSATIONAL ECCLESIOLOGY
AND THE RAPTURE

As mentioned, dispensationalists have commonly been pretribulationists. For many, a belief in the former was taken as determinative in favor of the latter. However, more recently the relationship between dispensationalism and pretribulationism has been challenged most thoroughly by Robert H. Gundry.[1] It is appropriate that we examine and evaluate his arguments.

He begins with the thesis that, if there is an absolute silence in the Old Testament about the church, a complete discontinuity between God's program for Israel and the church, and sharp breaks between dispensations, this would favor pretribulationism. On the other hand, if there is a partial revelation of this present age in the Old Testament with some relationship between Israel and the church, and dispensations that changed gradually, having transitional periods, then the door would be open to the presence of the church in the Tribulation.[2]

Gundry argues for the latter group of relationships. First, he points out that the dispensational argument that the church is a mystery in the Old Testament is used to set it sharply apart from Israel. However, he cautions those who take this argument as decisive against the church's presence in the Tribulation. All agree that there are a large number of Gentile saints who will be alive on the earth during the Tribulation period (e.g., Rev. 7:9–17). Though no Old Testament passages mention these saints, the Old Testament silence does not preclude their presence in the Tribulation.[3] What is true of Gentiles might be true of the church as well.

Second, Gundry affirms that there are Old Testament prophecies that specifically mention or imply the present church age. Our Lord's present session at the right hand of the Father in heaven is predicted in Psalm 110:1 and is presently being fulfilled (Acts 2:34–35). The church occupies a period of time foretold and related to Israel, namely the nation's worldwide dispersion (Deut. 28:25, 64, 65; 30:1–4). From this it follows that if the church can be present during the time of Israel's dispersion, she can also be present during the time of her trial. Furthermore, most dispensationalists see an interval between weeks sixty-nine and seventy in Daniel 9:24–27. The church exists during this period though it is not mentioned, and the destruction of Jerusalem is predicted even though it occurs in the church age. Gundry concludes that this demonstrates that this present age is not unforeseen in the Old Testament and is not unrelated to the future of Israel as predicted in the Old Testament.[4]

Gundry claims that the Old Testament not only predicts the present age but that the New Testament applies Old Testament prophecies to the church. He cites the following examples: Acts 2:16–21 is a fulfillment of Joel 2:28–32; Galatians 3:16 quotes Genesis 13:15 and 17:8, applying the promise of the land of Palestine to Abraham's spiritual seed; Paul's mission to the Gentiles in Acts 13:46–47 is based on Isaiah's Old Testament prediction that salvation would come to them (Isa. 49:6); Paul's statement in Romans 15:7–13 that Jewish and Gentile Christians have a duty to receive one another is based on what he finds in four different Old Testament prophecies (2 Sam. 22:50 [cf. Ps. 18:49]; Deut. 32:43; Ps. 117:1; Isa. 11:10); Peter teaches that the prophets predicted that grace would come to the Gentiles (1 Peter 1:10–12); and the new covenant of Jeremiah 31:31–34 is applied to the church in Hebrews 8:8–13; 10:15–17.[5]

Third, Gundry argues that the dispensational change from Israel to the church took place over a period of time beginning early in Jesus' ministry and ending sometime after Pentecost. For instance, Jesus defended His disciples against the Pharisaic charge that they do not fast by saying that the old dispensation is passing away and that a new one is coming in (Mark 2:21–22). Jesus taught that the "prophets and the Law" ceased with John the Baptist (Matt. 11:13; cf. Luke 16:16), and that "grace and truth were realized through Jesus Christ" (John 1:17). This last statement is a reference to the whole public ministry of Jesus, so grace and truth began before Pentecost. Jesus made all foods clean (Mark 7:18–19) before His crucifixion, resurrection, ascension, and giving of the Spirit. He gave instructions to His disciples about the future church, its establishment (Matt. 16:18), and its discipline (vv. 15–18). The teachings of Jesus, obviously given before Pentecost, are cited in the New Testament as the foundation of the church (1 Cor. 7:10, 12, 25; 1 Tim. 6:3; Heb. 2:3). Even with the church's existence after the Day of Pentecost, the baptism of the Spirit moves to the Gentiles over a period of time, and the preaching of the gospel goes first to a predominantly Jewish audience (Acts 3:12), then finally throughout the Gentile world in Paul's mission. The destruction of the Temple in A.D. 70 forcibly brings an end to animal sacrifices. Thus, Gundry argues, if there is a transitional period at the beginning of the church age, it is not unreasonable to think that there will be one at the end.[6]

Fourth, whereas the church is unique in many ways, Gundry points to the essential unity of all saints and the things they have in common. The latter are more fundamental and lasting. Abraham is the father of all who believe, although he is an Old Testament saint (Rom. 4:11; cf. 4:12, 16), and those who believe are called the seed of Abraham (Gal. 3:16). All believers receive Christ's imputed righteousness. Gentile believers are grafted into the wild olive tree of

Israel (Rom. 11:16ff.). Gentiles, who were far from God, are now brought near by the blood of Christ (Eph. 2:11–13). The perfection and completion of Old Testament saints requires New Testament saints (Heb. 11:40). In the New Jerusalem the gates bear the names of the twelve tribes of Israel, and the foundations have the names of the twelve apostles inscribed on them (Rev. 21:12, 14).[7]

The overlap in God's programs for Israel and the church at the outset of the church age argues for similar concurrent programs at the end of the church age. Some dispensationalists who also are premillennial hold that during the Millennium the church will rule the earth with Christ (1 Cor. 6:2; Rev. 5:10) and all other saints—Old Testament and Tribulation—thus suggesting overlapping programs in the plan of God. In addition to the different groups of saints who will reign in the Millennium, some believe that there will be those who still have their natural bodies as well as those who have received their glorified bodies. Furthermore, with the return of the Jews to Palestine from dispersion, we have a hint of God's simultaneous dealings with the church and Israel, as was the case during the era of the church's beginning. Thus, Gundry argues for God working through two covenant people at the same time.

Gundry realizes that the issue is not merely that God is dealing with various groups of people at the same time but that there are two groups of *redeemed people* and *witnesses*. They will coexist, possibly live by different regulations and conceivably preach variations of the gospel. According to Gundry, these problems do not "preclude the possibility of the presence of the church in the Tribulation."[8] One way in which perceived problems might be resolved is that there would be only one group of redeemed people in the Tribulation—the church. Jews who had accepted Jesus as Messiah would be part of the church as presently is the case (Rom. 11:5) and would be raptured at the posttribulational coming of Christ. Jews who are not converted and survive to the end of the Tribulation (Rev. 7:1–4) will repent, believe, and be saved as they look on their descending Messiah. They will have missed the Rapture but will enter the millennial kingdom in their natural bodies as subjects of the restored Davidic kingdom.[9]

Moreover, the Jewish cast to Daniel's seventieth week does not, according to Gundry, preclude the possibility of the church's presence any more than does a large host of Gentile saints. Though the church did not figure in the first sixty-nine weeks, neither did a large group of Gentile saints such as will be part of the seventieth week. Thus, the seventieth week is considerably different in this respect from the first sixty-nine.

In a posttribulational understanding of the Tribulation, God's sole witnessing body will be the church, which consists of saved Jews and Gentiles. Only at the Millennium will Israel be reinstituted as God's witness. According to Gundry, this is more reasonable than the pretribulational position, since Israel is experiencing final and bitter chastisement.[10]

Gundry is to be commended for his helpful and thorough treatment of the relationship between dispensationalism and a pretribulational Rapture. There are a number of areas where we can agree with him. He is correct in showing that dispensationalism is not a monolithic theological position. There are some who would see the discontinuities between Israel and the church in more radical terms and others who would recognize the differences with less contrast. He is right that the more one emphasizes the distinctions between Israel and the church, the more that distinction favors a pretribulational Rapture of the church.

He appears to be accurate in arguing that those who do not make the strictest contrast may hold to dispensationalism (a moderate or measured form as he calls it) and come to a view of the Rapture other than pretribulational. His argument shows that there is a certain independence between one's views on the relationship of Israel and the church and the Rapture. Not all dispensationalists must come to a pretribulational Rapture position.

Having said that, it still appears that dispensationalism best accords with a pretribulational Rapture. This means that we should not observe a laissez-faire approach to the relationship between dispensationalism and a position on the Rapture. It seems to me that the pretribulation Rapture is most dependent on two premises.[11] The first is that the church is a distinct body from Israel and saints of other ages. That is not to deny that there are similarities among all the saints but to recognize that the church is not identical with any of them. The second is that there is a future period of unprecedented judgment—divine wrath. This period has a variety of purposes, but none of them is related to the church in biblical revelation. Therefore, it should not surprise us that the church is removed before this period begins. If these premises are true, then dispensationalism best harmonizes with pretribulationism.

THE INCOMPATIBILITY OF PREMILLENIALISM AND A POSTTRIBULATIONAL RAPTURE

The argument of this section is directed at those who are both premillennialists and posttribulationists. The problem does not arise for amillennialists, since the difficulty is related to an earthly reign of Christ and those who enter the millennial kingdom. The argument seeks to demonstrate that the two views—premillennialism and post-tribulationism—are incompatible. That is, there are conditions in Scripture that the combination of these two views *cannot* meet.

Premillenial posttribulationism requires an interval between the Rapture of the church and the Second Coming of Christ so that there can be saved persons who enter the Millennium in nonglorified, physical bodies. Because of the importance of this argument, let us consider it in some detail.

First, we must recognize the necessity of saints with nonglori-fied bodies. Scripture teaches that in the Millennium evil will be curbed and righteousness will flourish. However, sin will still exist (e.g., there are sacrifices—Isa. 19:21; Ezek. 43:13–27), and a rebel-lion will close the reign of Christ on this earth (Rev. 20:7–10). More-over, there will be sickness and death (Isa. 65:20). Houses will be built, and vineyards will be planted (Isa. 65:21–22). None of these things—particularly committing sin—are usually thought of as a part of the glorified state.

How does this cause difficulties for a premillennial posttribula-tional eschatology? The problem centers on the fact that in this view the Rapture and the Second Coming are simply parts of a single, complex event. Believers will be glorified as they are caught up to meet the Lord in the air, and they will immediately return to this earth with Christ to set up His kingdom to rule and reign with Him. *All* the righteous will be gloried at Christ's coming either through translation or resurrection (1 Cor. 15:51–52; 1 Thes. 4:13–18). *All* the righteous will enter the kingdom in glorified bodies.

According to pretribulationists and midtribulationists, *all* the wicked will be excluded or prevented from entering the kingdom or millennial age, including the wicked among the Gentiles at the sheep and goat judgment (Matt. 25:31–46) and among the Jews when the Messiah causes them to pass under the rod (Ezek. 20:37). The prob-lem for the posttribulationist can be stated in two ways. First, where do the sheep come from in the sheep and goat judgment if all the redeemed have been raptured? Who are the sheep? Second, if all who enter the kingdom are both righteous and glorified, and there are no wicked, how can they sin in the Millennium? Clearly there is a need for some nonglorified saints. Only then will it be possible for some to sin during the Millennium, culminating in rebellion against God at the end of the Millennium.[12]

Not all premillennial posttribulationists have seen this double-sided problem, but some have, suggesting a variety of solutions. One of the most common solutions is to identify the righteous (sheep) with Jews who believe in Jesus as their Messiah as He returns to the earth after the Rapture. They will be saved and will enter the kingdom in nonglorified bodies (Zech. 12:10–13:1; Rom. 11:26). Gundry has offered a variation on this proposal. He thinks that the 144,000 may comprise the Jewish remnant who will be physically preserved through the Tribulation.[13] They will not receive the mark of the beast and will be saved at Messiah's return. This group will include both men and women, and they will replenish the millennial earth. He holds this in spite of the fact that Revelation 14:4 says that they have not defiled themselves with women, that is, they are celibate. Gundry thinks that this is a reference to spiritual, not sexual, celibacy. This is a way of saying that they have not been seduced by Satan and the Antichrist.[14]

This appears to be an inadequate answer. First, there is good evidence that the repentance *precedes* the return of Christ (Hos. 5:15–6:3). The sight of the Messiah is the cause of intense mourning over the years of rejection (Zech. 12:11–14). The return of Christ is signaled by Israel's acceptance of their Messiah rather than being the occasion for the acceptance of salvation.[15] The second aspect of the problem is that there are numerous passages that teach that Gentiles will populate the millennial earth in nonglorified bodies (e.g., Isa. 19:18–25; 60:1–3; Zech. 14:16–21). Gundry's suggested solution would permit only Jews into the kingdom in physical bodies and does not explain the presence of nonglorified, saved Gentiles in the Millennium.

A second suggestion, made by William E. Bell, that deals with both aspects of the problem is to deny that all the wicked die at Christ's return to this earth.[16] To have all the righteous raptured and all the wicked slaughtered would result in a dramatic depopulation of the earth. This, it is said, is not required by Scripture. In Bell's view, all that Scripture teaches is that the *actively rebellious* unbelievers will be destroyed in fulfillment of Revelation 19:15–18 and Jeremiah 25:31. Thus, many, even the majority, will be slain but not *all*.[17]

Bell is right when he says that not all the wicked will be destroyed at Christ's return. However, the *complete elimination* of the wicked from entrance into the kingdom is not simply the result of those who die at Christ's return but also the separation of the wicked from the righteous in the judgments mentioned above (Ezek. 20:37

and Matt. 25:31–46). So whereas it is true that not all the wicked will be slain at the return of Christ, those who survive will be separated in the judgments and prevented from entering the kingdom.

A third approach to the problem is just to affirm that the wicked will enter into the kingdom as required by the number of passages that teach that the wicked live in the kingdom (e.g., Isa. 66:15–20; Zech. 14:16–19; Rev 20:7–9). However, this is no solution at all. No premillennialist disagrees that evil will exist in the Millennium. But the existence of evil does not demand that wicked people enter the millennial age. If there are passages that teach that they will not enter the kingdom, then to say that the wicked do enter is to contradict Scripture. What passages teach that the wicked will enter?[18]

By far the most common solution offered to this problem is to argue that there are two resurrections but only one general (postmillennial) judgment. This approach posits a premillennial resurrection of all the righteous, but only one judgment including both righteous and wicked postmillennially. All the righteous will enter the kingdom and enjoy its blessings. But not all wicked will be eliminated. Many will die in the judgments that precede the Second Coming, but not all will be destroyed. In this view, the judgment of the sheep and goats in Matthew 25:31–46 occurs *after* the Millennium, not *before.* Thus, there will be unrighteous individuals, though a greatly reduced number, who enter the kingdom. This is Gundry's view.[19]

The key question for this view is whether the judgment in Matthew 25 can be harmonized with, and is identical to, the one in Revelation 20. Despite differences, such as the presence of good and evil persons in Matthew and only wicked in Revelation, they are harmonizable according to Gundry. Gundry argues that the rewards and punishments, eternal life and everlasting punishment, better precede the eternal state than the millennial kingdom.[20]

Though some of Gundry's arguments are weightier than others, it is noteworthy that he does not deal with the setting of the judgment scene: "But when the Son of Man comes in His glory, and all the angels with Him, then He will sit on His glorious throne. And all the nations will be gathered before Him" (Matt. 25:31–32a). This seems to describe events occurring at the time of Christ's return in Matthew 24:30 *after* the Tribulation.

There still remains the question as to why, at this time, the reward is eternal life and the penalty everlasting punishment (Matt. 25:46). I have argued elsewhere that the rewards of eternal life and eternal punishment do not constitute a good reason for identifying the judgment in Matthew with the one in Revelation.[21] First, Matthew

25:31 seems to set this judgment at the time of Christ's second advent before the Millennium. Just as there are phases in eternal judgment, so there will be phases in eternal life of which the Millennium is but one. The idea of phases in eternal life is demonstrated by Jesus telling His disciples that they already had eternal life as He spoke (John 3:36).

Second, Isaiah 24:21–22 teaches that there is a period of confinement before final consignment to hell. Luke 16:19–31 teaches that between death and resurrection the wicked are punished. It is a time of torment and justifiably called eternal punishment, although it is the first phase.

Third, since the millennial kingdom is the first phase of the eternal kingdom (1 Cor. 15:21–28), eternal life is not an inappropriate name for the reward of the righteous.

Finally, even if the reward and punishment could be shown to refer to the final or eternal state, that would not prove the posttribulational position. It is true in prophetic literature that two events may be foreshortened or telescoped. Thus, while they might appear to be temporally successive, in reality they are separated by many years (e.g., in Isa. 61:1–2 both advents of our Lord are mentioned, though separated by at least two thousand years; Dan. 12:1–2 and John 5:29 describe two resurrections, which are to be separated by a thousand years). Thus, Matthew 25:31 could be separated from Matthew 24:30 by a thousand years.

Douglas Moo also has struggled with the question of nonresurrected believers in the Millennium.[22] He begins by saying that this argument is the most difficult for his position to handle. The difficulty is related not just to the argument itself, but also to the fact that the evidence is both sparse and complex.[23] He then goes on to offer a number of suggestions. First, he says that the presence of evil, natural processes, and ultimately rebellion against God are problems for all forms of premillennialism in that these conditions seem to be more appropriate during this present age rather than in a Millennium. However, he acknowledges that the need for people in natural bodies is a special problem for the posttribulationist.[24]

Second, Moo thinks that there is not a lot of evidence for saints with natural bodies and the existence of evil. But he says that these conditions are taught in Scripture, and therefore the problem cannot be avoided by a posttribulational premillennialist.[25]

Third, Moo thinks that there are two suggestions that serve as possible solutions to this problem. The first is that it is entirely possible that some unbelievers will enter the kingdom in nonglorified

ISSUES IN DISPENSATIONALISM

bodies. He bases this on the fact that though some texts teach the universality of judgment on unbelievers at Christ's return they do not clearly specify that this is at the beginning of the Millennium. Moreover, he suggests that the universality of judgment may involve the telescoping of events that are premillennial and postmillennial. This, he thinks, is the reason that Matthew 25:31ff. implies that the judgment of the elect will be premillennial while the rewards and punishment of Matthew 25:46 seem to point to a postmillennial judgment. "Thus passages that describe a universal judgment along with Christ's return have as their purpose to specify the ultimately universal effects of Christ's victory; they do not require that all are judged *at the same time.*"[26] And Revelation 19 does not require that all the wicked will be destroyed at the return of Christ, so there will be unbelievers to enter the kingdom.[27] The second suggestion is that the millennial saints who have natural bodies are Jews who turn to Christ at his coming.[28]

Let us evaluate Moo's proposal, discussing issues in the opposite order from the one he set out. First, the question of whether the conversion of Jews at the time of Messiah's return precedes or coincides with His coming, and thus they do not participate in the Rapture, is of minor significance. The reason is that, even if true, it would only account for Jews in natural bodies in the Millennium, not Gentiles. At best, for Moo, this is an inference that is necessary to validate his system and is not taught explicitly in any text.

Second, the key issue involves Matthew 25:31–46 and the telescoping of events in prophetic literature. Obviously there is no problem with the general point since in this chapter we have seen examples of prophetic telescoping. The question is whether Matthew 25 is a case of telescoping. Although Moo does not say much about how a premillennial and postmillennial judgment might be blended in a single text, there are at least three ways. The universality of judgment might take place twice, once premillennially for those in the Tribulation and again for every one else postmillennially. Or the universality of the judgment might be a reference to the combined events before and after the Millennium. Or, again, the universality of judgment might be understood as a premillennial judgment of the righteous and a postmillennial judgment of the wicked.

Regardless of which one of these approaches to telescoping one takes, it fails to solve the problem. If two universal judgments, one premillennial and one postmillennial, are telescoped into one verse, this has not relieved the problem of having nonresurrected believers in the kingdom if all believers are resurrected at a posttribulation Rapture. It would simply mean the universal exclusion of the wicked from the kingdom at the beginning of the Millennium and from eternal blessedness at the end. In fairness to Moo, it is unlikely that this is what he means.

It is more likely that Moo thinks that the universality of judgment is either the result of *both* the premillennial and postmillennial judgments or that the righteous are universally judged premillennially and the wicked postmillennially. This may be why he cites the Daniel 12:1–2 and John 5:29 as examples of telescoping.

It is possible to conceive of the telescoping in a variety of ways; however, it is difficult to see how that will avoid the problem at hand. If Matthew 25 is speaking of a postmillennial judgment, then it appears that Jesus' answer at this point has little to do with the rest of the Olivet Discourse (acknowledged as premillennial) and specifically the question Jesus was asked (Matt. 24:3).

There are numerous passages that teach that the wicked do not enter the kingdom and that those who do enter the millennial age have been converted. The following passages teach either directly or indirectly that the wicked do not enter the kingdom. The rebels in Israel will be rooted out before the establishment of the kingdom (Ezek. 20:37–38). In Matthew it is only to the sheep that Jesus says, "Come, you who are blessed of My Father, inherit the kingdom" (Matt. 25:34). He never says to the wicked premillennially or postmillennially, "Enter My kingdom." Rather, his words are, "Depart from Me" (Matt. 25:41). Moreover, the Scriptures testify that only those who have been converted will enter the kingdom (Isa. 56:6–8; 60:3–5; 61:8–9; Jer. 3:17; 16:19–21; 31:33–34; Amos 9:12; Obad. 17–21; Zech. 13:9).

In the posttribulation position, the godly Gentiles would all just have been raptured and given resurrected bodies at the Second Advent. To escape the incompatibility between posttribulationism and premillennialism, nonresurrected Gentiles have to enter the kingdom. It would appear that the overwhelming witness of Scripture opposes the idea of wicked Gentiles entering the kingdom.

THE OLIVET DISCOURSE AND THE RAPTURE

A third important theological consideration is the Olivet Discourse and its relation to the Rapture. It is our Lord's longest prophetic discourse, and it comes as He looks forward to the Cross. The discourse is included in each of the synoptic gospels: Matthew 24–25; Mark 13; Luke 21:5–36. There are three issues that require attention. First, are the disciples representatives of the believing remnant in Israel or the church? Second, was the time of the fulfillment of the discourse at the fall of Jerusalem in A.D. 70 or is it eschatological? Third, is the Rapture considered in the Olivet Discourse? Although we will consider these three questions separately for ease and clarity of discussion, it will become clear that they are interrelated.

Whom Do the Disciples Represent?

One of the questions that must be answered is, Do the disciples represent the believing remnant in Israel or do they represent the foundation of the church? Gundry gives one of the most complete discussions of this issue.

He points out that the disciples are a transition group belonging both to the believing remnant in Israel and to the church. Simply to deny the possibility that they might represent the church because the discourse is in the synoptic gospels is an inadequate response. Jesus gave instructions to the church (Matt. 16:18 and 18:15–18). He promised the Holy Spirit (John 14:26). The teaching of the apostles was first given to them by Christ Himself (Acts 2:42; cf. Matt. 28:20). The longest account of the Olivet Discourse is in Matthew, which is the particularly Jewish gospel. However, it is the only gospel where there is a direct reference to the church, and the discourse is also found in the two non-Jewish gospels of Mark and Luke.[29]

Though the discourse has a decidedly Jewish imprint on it, Gundry cautions against deciding that its teaching is not for the church. He thinks that the key element is to be found in the fact that the nation of Israel has passed out of divine favor by Matthew 24–25 because of their rejection of Jesus as their Messiah. On Palm Sunday Jesus rode into the city of Jerusalem to the hosannas of the pilgrims from Galilee. The leaders of the nation, however, rejected Him. By Tuesday they challenged Jesus' authority, and He responded with three parables of judgment. This marked their final rejection of Him and His setting aside of the nation. The second parable ends with "the kingdom of God will be taken away from you, and be given to a nation producing the fruit of it" (Matt. 21:43). By Matthew 23:37–39 He gave His sorrowful farewell to the nation itself. Thus, it is best, Gundry thinks, to see contextually that Jesus was turning from the Jews and preparing the disciples for His death and His outline for the future.[30]

Gundry thinks that the Jewish elements in the discourse can be met if those Jews are ethnic, not religious Jews. That is, they are nationally related to the nation of Israel, but they were religiously a part of the church. Thus, the descriptions and instruction with a Jewish character were given to *Jewish* Christians of the future. Even the Sabbath regulations in the Olivet Discourse have a plausíble explanation. Jesus is not telling these Jewish Christians to follow them, but He simply recognized that if their flight came on the Sabbath in a Jewish society that practiced the Sabbath regulations, there would be reduced service to travelers.[31]

Gundry feels that support for the contention that the disciples represent the church can also be found outside the Olivet Discourse. Previous to receiving the discourse, they had been given instruction on church discipline (Matt. 18:15–18). Two days after this discourse, they received the Upper Room Discourse and participated in the institution of the Lord's Supper, a rite given to the church. Some weeks later they were baptized in the Holy Spirit and formed the nucleus of the first church in Jerusalem. They are the foundation of the church (Eph. 2:20), and so on.[32]

We can agree with much of what Gundry says. He is right in seeing that the disciples were a transitional group, at one time representing Israel and at another time the church. He is correct in reminding us that the gospels are not devoid of teaching for the church, even the gospel written to the Jews—Matthew. We can agree that the Olivet Discourse comes at a time when the leaders of Israel had officially rejected Jesus as the Jewish Messiah, and Jesus was then preparing for the Cross and the establishment of the church, which included both Jew and Gentile. However, that is not the end of the matter. At least as good a case can be made for the disciples being representatives of the remnant in Israel in the Olivet Discourse.

First, if the disciples stand at one time for the remnant in Israel and another for the church, it is not unreasonable for them to have dual interests. When the leaders of the Jews rejected Jesus, we would expect Jesus to begin to give instructions to the disciples in preparation for the church's founding (e.g., Matt. 18:15–18; the Upper Room Discourse, John 14). However, it should not surprise us that they would also be interested in what had become of the Jews, and in particular the promises given to them in the Old Testament. This is supported by the question of the disciples to Jesus at His ascension about restoring the kingdom to Israel (Acts 1:6).[33]

Therefore, Jesus gave the Olivet Discourse with all its Jewish elements to answer the question about fulfillment of Old Testament prophecies for the Jews. This seems to be supported by its connection with Matthew 23 and Jesus' pronouncement of doom on Israel, and the disciples' question provoked by His statement about the destruction of the Temple (Matt. 24:3).

Gleason L. Archer offers a different reason from Gundry that the disciples must be representatives of the church rather than of converted Israel. He says that denying that they represent the church is to deny one of the most basic principles of evangelical hermeneutics, the perspicuity, or clarity, of Scripture. He thinks that the disciples, though Jews, are true representatives of the Christian church since Jewish believers wrote all but one of the books of the New Testament; for the first five years of the church there was scarcely a non-Jew; and all the other exhortations and warnings were for them personally and were fulfilled in their subsequent careers. If this is so, it would mean that the only exception is the Olivet Discourse. In that case Jesus would be saying, "Look for these signs, but you will never see them." If His remarks were really addressed to a future nonexistent group of people, then what Jesus said in the Olivet Discourse comes down to this: "I am giving *you* signs to look for, but I really do not mean *you* but a generation hundreds, even thousands of years, future. Though I am telling you to look for them, you really are not to look for them, because you will not survive long enough to see them." Archer concludes: "This kind of interpretation adds up to a serious violation of the perspicuity of Scripture."[34]

One finds this kind of objection most perplexing. First, God alone knows the time of the fulfillment of prophecies that predict the future. We now can see that the fulfillment has not yet come, but it could have. If we apply this principle to all predictions or promises in the Bible, then the perspicuity of Scripture is violated repeatedly. Regardless of one's eschatology, virtually all Bible-believing Christians would agree that we are commanded to look for Christ's return. But that too has not occurred. This generation or one in the future will see it. Does saying something to one generation of believers that will be fulfilled by a later group of believers violate the clarity of Scripture? I think not. Similarly, neither does what has been said about the Olivet Discourse (i.e., Jesus' answer to the disciples' question about the fulfillment of Old Testament prophecies for the Jews), although it might be wrong to understand its teaching that way.

Douglas Moo also thinks that the disciples represent the church in the Olivet Discourse. His arguments are different from those already cited. First, he argues that in most contexts in the Gospels the disciples stand for Christians of all ages. If this were not the case, then it is difficult to understand why he would take Jesus' teaching as instruction for us. Therefore, there must be a clear reason in the context for narrowing the audience from that of all Christians. If such is the case, he contends this is lacking in the Olivet Discourse. As a matter of fact, he sets out a number of similarities between this discourse and 1 Thessalonians 4:13–18 and 2 Thessalonians 2:1–12. Second, the use of the term *elect* for those on the earth at the time of the fulfillment shows that the discourse is directed to the church. Third, the nature of the exhortations addressed to the disciples at the end of the discourse confirms that it is directed to the church. These exhortations parallel admonitions given in Luke 12:39–48 and 19:11–27, where the disciples clearly stand for the church.[35]

Each of Moo's points is open to question. First, do the disciples invariably stand for the church in the Gospels? The answer is surely yes, if the church includes all believers of all times. However, if the church begins on the Day of Pentecost, then that claim is not so clear. On the other hand, if the disciples do not, does that not call into question their use of Jesus' teaching for the church? Not at all. Such a claim overlooks the distinction between those *addressed* and those to whom the teaching may be *applied.* The teachings of Jesus may be addressed to a believing remnant in Israel but have application to believers of all ages, the church age included. There are indications discussed above—the Jewish elements in the discourse—requiring that those addressed be Jews. Moreover, the parallels that Moo cites between the Olivet Discourse and the Thessalonian epistles may be explained in two different ways. Moo's position is that the same event is discussed in the Olivet Discourse and 2 Thessalonians. My position is that though the events are different they have similarities. This also is my position on the parallels between the Olivet Discourse and 1 Thessalonians 4:13–18.[36]

Does the Term *Elect*
Invariably Refer to the Church?

It probably does if that term is used only of the church in Scripture. But that is not the case. At the very least there are elect angels. For a dispensationalist there are elect in Israel as well as in the church. However, might one not argue that the overwhelming use of the term is in reference to the church in the New Testament and therefore we should need a very good reason for deciding that it is different here? Such an argument has a good deal of initial appeal, but in the end I think it is wrong. What one needs to ask is, Whom would the hearers of Jesus (in this case the disciples) have identified with this term? Based on the context, it probably would have been the believing remnant in Israel.

Finally, do not the similarities between exhortations found in the Gospels and elsewhere in the New Testament demonstrate that the disciples represent the church? Let us assume uncritically that this is true, although in other places in the Gospels they may represent the Jewish remnant. That still would not settle the case. The similarities might be accounted for because of their general character and because the relationship between the church and the Rapture parallels the relationship between the Jewish remnant and the Second Coming.

When Is the Olivet Discourse Fulfilled?

If the disciples represent the believing remnant in Israel, the time of the fulfillment of the Olivet Discourse becomes an important issue. The reason is that those who hold such a position on the disciples are divided. Some think that the fulfillment of at least a large part of the discourse transpired with the destruction of Jerusalem in A.D. 70. Others place it yet future. Some go so far as to argue that Matthew 24:29–31 and Mark 13:24–27 are not references to the coming of Christ but are rather symbolic descriptions of the destruction of Jerusalem in A.D. 70. This last position often has been called the preterist view because it sees so much of the discourse already fulfilled historically.

The following arguments for this position have been presented in a recent work by David J. Palm.[37] Palm's thesis deals primarily with the discourse in Mark, and he argues that Mark 13:5–31 has to do with the fall of Jerusalem.

First, Jesus says that generation would not pass away without all these things being fulfilled. This referred to the disciples' generation, not some future nonexistent generation.[38] Second, there is the explicit use of "you" throughout the discourse, often in the emphatic position. This identifies the addressees as the disciples.[39] Third, references found throughout verses 5–31 identify its application to first-century Judea. The system of local councils and synagogues is first-century.[40] Fourth, the warnings to the inhabitants of Judea only make sense in a first-century context, not modern Israel.[41] Fifth, there are indications that the Tribulation did not come at the end of all things but was an historical event. Why would one flee if it was the end of all things?[42] Sixth, the parable of the fig tree ceases to make sense if one partitions the text between the destruction of Jerusalem and the coming of Christ. What can be meant by "summer is near, right at hand?"[43] Finally, evidence is found in the Old Testament for a symbolic description of divine judgment.[44]

A thorough discussion of these arguments goes beyond the scope of this chapter. However, the following response to the preterist view is given from a futurist position. First, the decisive argument for Palm comes from Matthew 24:34 and Mark 13:30. The break between the historical and the eschatological must come *after*, not *before*, the passage that is usually associated with Christ's coming because the generation to whom this discourse is addressed will see the fulfillment of the things prophesied. The only way this can be true, if one takes these words in their normal sense, is that they were fulfilled in the destruction of Jerusalem.

It does seem that Palm, along with others, has put his finger on a problem if you partition each of the accounts in the Gospels into historical and eschatological. Then, it seems that the "you" has to refer to the disciples, and they have to see the fulfillment of these things. However, it is likely that the situation is different. The question of the disciples in Matthew 24:3 does contain both a historical and an eschatological element. However, it appears that only the Lucan account treats the historical element (Luke 21:20–24), and it omits the problematic verse. Both Matthew and Mark have the statement, but neither of them describes the destruction of Jerusalem in A.D. 70 (at least not directly). If Jesus' teaching only referred to eschatological events that would occur in a future seven-year period, then the use of "generation" and "you" are a reference to that future time. Note that Jesus is not answering a different question in the different synoptic gospels. He, however, does answer different parts of that question, and this explains at least some of the differences in the accounts.

Second, there are elements in what Palm sees as the historical section that must be eschatological. There is the reference to the "abomination of desolation" from Daniel in Matthew 24:15 and Mark 13:14. In Mark, a masculine participle is used after the neuter "abomination" showing that Jesus is thinking of a person—the Antichrist of 2 Thessalonians 2.[45]

Third, it is very unlikely that what is usually understood as a description of Christ's coming is in fact a symbolic representation of the destruction of Jerusalem in A.D. 70. The first reason for rejecting the symbolic interpretation is that the association of Jesus' coming with the clouds always has reference to the Second Advent in the New Testament. Second, the judgments in Matthew 24:4–28; Mark 13:1–23; and Luke 21:5–24 and the cosmic signs in Matthew 24:29–30; Mark 13:24–25; and Luke 21:25–27 bear a striking similarity to those described by the author of Revelation in chapter 6. He holds these to be future, and he is presumably writing after A.D. 70.[46]

Is the Rapture in the Olivet Discourse?

Though the Rapture could be posttribulational even if it were not in the Olivet Discourse, it would be a decisive argument for that position if it could be shown to be there and its time determined. Archer, a defender of a mid-seventieth week Rapture, thinks that the Rapture is there, though he thinks that it is hard to pick out any point in the discourse where it occurs. He suggests some possibilities. Perhaps it is in Matthew 24:14 in "then the end shall come." Maybe it is to be found in verse 27 where the word "coming" is used. However, this seems to be at the end of the Tribulation. But in the end he concludes that "the precise timing of the Rapture cannot be clearly ascertained from the text of the Olivet Discourse."[47] One cannot help but agree in part with Archer. He may be right about where the Rapture is seen in the Olivet Discourse, but there is little clear evidence for his conclusions as to when it will occur.

Gundry and Moo take essentially the same position.[48] They see the Rapture in two places in the Olivet Discourse—Matthew 24:31 and 24:40–41. The placing of the Rapture in Matthew 24:31 is particularly important in that verse 29 makes clear that what follows is "immediately after the tribulation of those days." The identification of this verse with the Rapture rests on two grounds. First, Jesus describes a "gathering" that takes place at the sound of a great trumpet, a figure found in both 1 Corinthians 15:51–52 and 1 Thessalonians 4:16–17. The verb "to gather together" (*episunago*) is used here, and its noun form (*episunagoge*) is used in 2 Thessalonians 2:1 of the Rapture. Though both the verb and noun occur only nine times in the New Testament, there is reason enough, so the argument goes, to identify the two on the verbal similarity and other parallels.[49] Second, the use of the term *elect* shows that it is the church that is in view.[50]

We already have considered the question of whether *elect* is always a reference to the church in the New Testament. Let us then examine the use of the verb "to gather together" in connection with a trumpet. The trumpet is a common eschatological symbol. It has a number of uses. There are seven trumpet judgments in the book of Revelation and trumpets that gather the elect. There is a similarity, but the use of trumpets in prophetic literature is not confined to a posttribulational Rapture. The noun and verb "gather together" are found only nine times in the New Testament, as Moo admits. Only three of the nine have eschatological significance: Matthew 24:31; its synoptic parallel, Mark 13:27; and 2 Thessalonians 2:1. The other six occurrences are of a nontheological, general character. This term is not a technical term for a posttribulational coming. The eschatological occurrences are so few that little can be said about the term.

Could not the parallels between Matthew and the Thessalonian epistles simply be semantic similarity? Though there are some similarities, the differences seem to be more numerous and more significant. Matthew 24:31 has the elect gathered by the angels, while 1 Thessalonians 4:16–17 teaches that the Lord Himself will do it. Matthew has the great trumpet call the elect from the four winds; in 1 Thessalonians it announces the descent of our Lord. Matthew makes no mention of either a resurrection or the translation of living saints; Rapture passages do, and these are important features in those passages. In Matthew, the gathering seems to be on the earth, whereas in 1 Thessalonians it is in the air. First Thessalonians omits any reference to heavenly changes; these are an important element in Matthew 24. In 1 Thessalonians an order of ascent is given; it is not clear that there is any ascent at all in Matthew 24. The dissimilarities in detail and the paucity of occurrences of "gather together" make the identification of the Rapture in Matthew 24:31 rest on the slimmest of evidence.

A second possibility for the Rapture in the Olivet Discourse is Matthew 24:40–41 and its parallel in Luke 17:34–35, where one is "taken" and one is "left." The verb "to take" is used of the Rapture in John 14:1–3. It is possible, however, that the one taken here goes to judgment, but Moo thinks that it is significant that the verb for "take" in Matthew 24:40–41 is different from the word used in verse 39.[51]

Moo gives enough reasons in his discussion of this text to question his identification. He admits that the one taken in verses 40 and 41 may go to judgment, not into the kingdom. This seems clearly to be the case from the parallel in Luke 17:34–35. Moreover, the verb "taken" is used in a variety of ways, and is not a technical term of a posttribulational return of Christ. As a matter of fact, it is quite a common word with many general uses.[52]

CONCLUSION

This chapter has not established the pretribulation Rapture of the church. That was not its purpose.[53] Rather, we have considered three issues at the interface of dispensationalism and the Rapture. I have tried to show that, though there is a certain independence between dispensationalism and a pretribulation Rapture, the former is most compatible with the latter. I have argued that there is an incompatibility between posttribulationism and premillennialism because of the need for nonglorified saints in the Millennium. And finally, I have examined the Olivet Discourse to see if it requires that the church be part of a posttribulational Rapture. My conclusions are that the disciples are not representative of the church; and, though the discourse is eschatological, there is no mention of the Rapture in it, a conclusion quite in keeping with a pretribulational Rapture.

NOTES

1. Robert H. Gundry, *The Church and the Tribulation* (Grand Rapids: Zondervan, 1973), 12–28.
2. Ibid., 12.
3. Ibid., 12–13.
4. Ibid., 14–15.
5. Ibid., 15–18.
6. Gundry, *The Church,* 19–21.
7. Ibid., 21–23.
8. Ibid., 23.
9. Ibid., 23–24.
10. Ibid.
11. For much fuller defense of this claim, see John F. Walvoord, "The Coming of Christ for His Church," *Bibliotheca Sacra* 123 (1966), 3–14.
12. John F. Walvoord, *The Rapture Question* (Findlay, Ohio: Dunham, 1957), 92–95; John F. Walvoord, *The Blessed Hope and the Tribulation* (Grand Rapids: Zondervan, 1976), 53; Allen Beechick, *The Pretribulation Rapture* (Denver: Accent, 1980), 39–57; Gleason F. Archer, "The Case for the Mid-Seventieth-Week Rapture Position," in Gleason F. Archer et al., *The Rapture: Pre-, Mid-, or Posttribulational?* (Grand Rapids: Zondervan, 1984), 120–22.
13. Gundry, *The Church,* 82.
14. Ibid.
15. For a fuller discussion of this point, see Paul D. Feinberg, "The Case for the Pretribulation Rapture Position," in *The Rapture: Pre-, Mid-, or Posttribulational?* 73.
16. William E. Bell, *A Critical Evaluation of the Pretribulation Rapture Doctrine in Christian Eschatology* (Ph.D. dissertation, New York Univ., 1967), 247–48. See also E. Michael Rusten, *A Critical Evaluation of Dispensational Interpretations of the Book of Revelation,* 2 vols. (Ann Arbor, Mich.: University Microfilms International, 1977).
17. Bell, *A Critical Evaluation of the Pretribulation Rapture,* 247–48.
18. For a fuller discussion of this matter, see Feinberg, "The Case for the Pretribulation Rapture Position," 74–76.
19. See Gundry, *The Church,* chap. 14.
20. Ibid., 166.
21. Feinberg, "The Case for the Pretribulation Rapture Position," 76–79.
22. Douglas J. Moo, "Response: Douglas J. Moo," in *The Rapture: Pre-, Mid-, or Posttribulational?* 161–65.

23. Ibid., 161.
24. Ibid.
25. Ibid., 162.
26. Ibid., 163.
27. Ibid.
28. Ibid., 163–64.
29. Gundry, *The Church*, 129–31.
30. Ibid., 131–32.
31. Ibid., 132–33.
32. Ibid., 134.
33. Gordon R. Lewis, "Biblical Evidence for Pretribulationism," *Bibliotheca Sacra* 124 (1968), 220.
34. Archer, "The Case for the Mid-Seventieth-Week Rapture Position," 123–24.
35. Douglas J. Moo, "The Case for the Posttribulational Rapture Position" in *The Rapture: Pre-, Mid- or Posttribulational?* 192–95.
36. I have argued this point in more detail in Feinberg, "The Case for the Pretribulation Rapture Position," 80–86, 229–30.
37. David J. Palm, "The Signs of His Coming: An Examination of the Olivet Discourse from a Preterist Perspective" (M.A. Thesis, Trinity Evangelical Divinity School, June, 1993).
38. Ibid., 11.
39. Ibid., 12.
40. Ibid., 12–13.
41. Ibid., 13–14.
42. Ibid., 14–15.
43. Ibid., 15–18.
44. Ibid. (see chap. 3).
45. Moo, "The Case for the Posttribulational Rapture Position," 191.
46. Ibid., 191–92.
47. Archer, "The Case for the Mid-Seventieth-Week Rapture Position," 123. For the more extended discussion of this point by Archer, see pp. 122–23.
48. Gundry, *The Church*, 134–39; and Moo, "The Case for the Posttribulational Rapture Position," 195–96.
49. Gundry, *The Church*, 135; and Moo, "The Case for the Posttribulational Rapture Position," 195.
50. Gundry, *The Church*, 135; and Moo, "The Case for the Posttribulational Rapture Position," 194.
51. Moo, "The Case for the Posttribulational Rapture Position," 196. See also Gundry, *The Church*, 137–39.
52. For fuller discussion of this point, see John F. Walvoord, "Is a Posttribulational Rapture Revealed in Matthew 24?" *Grace Theological Journal* 6 (1985), 262–66.
53. I have tried to give a case for a pretribulational Rapture in Feinberg, "The Case for the Pretribulation Rapture Position," 47–86. Even there not everything that could or should be said for the position was said.

As dispensationalists look to the future, they should be highly motivated that there are no prophesied events needing to take place before the church is caught up to meet our Lord in the air, forever to be with Him. This anticipation of the any-moment return of the Lord is supported by a four-fold argument beginning with the linguistic support. The word study by itself, however, is inconclusive until it is united with the contextual argument to formulate the doctrinal argument. With increasing force, the view of the apostles serves to confirm the view historically; and the any-moment doctrine is seen to be practically relevant as we await, with eager anticipation, its fulfillment.

12

THE IMMINENT
RETURN OF THE LORD

Earl D. Radmacher

O ur great-great-great grandchildren will not starve; they will be squeezed to death," said Professor Heinz von Foerster of the University of Illinois when he set the date for the end of the world—"Doomsday"—for Friday, November 13, 2026. This conclusion was based on the exploding world population, which the professor says is to reach infinity and overrun the earth by that time, plus or minus some five years.[1]

Von Foerster is only one of many, however, who have attempted to set dates for the consummation of the earth's history. In spite of the fact that Jesus said, "But of that day and hour no one knows, neither the angels in heaven, nor the Son, but only the Father" (Mark 13:32), there have been those throughout history who seemingly could not resist the temptation to set dates. Using the septa-millennial theory as a basis, Augustine calculated that the end of human history would be about A.D. 650.[2] When this did not materialize, others attempted to salvage the idea by resetting the clock for A.D. 1000, again for the year 1044, and then again for 1065.[3]

Another well-known date was 1843, the year set by William Miller, forerunner of the Millerites, or Adventists, in his work entitled *Evidence from Scripture and History of the Second Coming of Christ, About the Year 1843*. Again, a well-respected and effective Bible teacher of the last generation attempted to find the fulfillment of the trumpet judgments of Revelation in the events of World War II. With reference to the second trumpet he said, "The 'great mountain burning with fire' seems a clear reference to Germany, suddenly 'cast into the sea' of nations."[4]

One of the leading missionary statesmen of that same generation proclaimed that according to his calculations "the Great Tribulation, the revival of the Roman Empire, the reign of the Antichrist and the Battle of Armageddon, must take place before the year 1933."[5] How many others are there who have identified with dogmatism that the Antichrist was Mussolini or Stalin or Hitler or Khrushchev, only to be embarrassed by the lack of fulfillment?

Embarrassment, however, is the mildest of the results. Much more seriously, God's people are hurt and the integrity of God's Word is questioned. Think of the thousands of South Koreans from the Tami Mission Church who waited eagerly for the Rapture on October 28, 1992, because of the date-setting of their leaders.[6] An estimated five thousand sold their homes and deserted their jobs and families to await Jesus' return. Reportedly, several expectant mothers had abortions so as to be more easily raptured. Even more recently (1993), think of the magnitude of harm to the Branch Davidians and hundreds of others as a result of the doomsday prophecies from David Koresh's misuse of Scripture.

Equally as unjustified as date-setting for Christ's return are the numerous sermons attempting to find fulfillment of prophecy in this age. Typical of them is a popular author, conference speaker, and television personality who has stated his belief that the "paramount prophetic sign" is that Israel had to be a nation again in the land of its forefathers. This condition was fulfilled, he claims, on May 14, 1948. This pronouncement is simply representative of hundreds, perhaps thousands, of others who, although eager in their anticipation of Christ's coming, distort the Scripture and cause terrible confusion for God's people.

This situation is further confused by the fact that many of the very ones who preach such messages today also proclaim with equal force (justifiably, I believe) that there are no biblical prophecies that need to be fulfilled before the Lord Jesus Christ returns for His church. This conflicting emphasis begets the rather embarrassing plight of talking about signs of a signless event. One amillennial writer was quick to notice this inconsistency: "In no respect is the inconsistency of Dispensationalists more glaringly apparent than in their persistent efforts to discover signs of the nearness of an event which they emphatically declare to be signless."[7] (One must hasten to add that, while this seeming inconsistency may be charged to the presentation of some dispensationalists, it is by no means necessary to or inherent in dispensational theology.)

This whole situation becomes even more serious when one realizes that the embarrassment and chagrin (to say nothing of the harm) that this date-setting has occasioned could have been avoided by simply recognizing the doctrine of the imminency of the Lord's return as it is taught in God's Holy Word, the Bible. Our final court of appeal on any matter of faith is the Word of God; thus, we turn to it to gain a clearer understanding of our Lord's imminent return.

THE LINGUISTIC ARGUMENT

It seems that a logical question to ask right at the beginning is, What does the word *imminent* mean? The need for clarification at this point becomes apparent when one recognizes that theologians with contradictory eschatological opinions both claim to believe in imminency. According to Oswald Allis, "Amillennialists, who believe in a spiritual millennium which is past or nearly past, and . . . Amillennialists who do not believe in any earthly millennium at all, may approximate very closely to that of Premillennialists regarding the imminence of the coming."[8]

Further confusion reigns when one reads contradictory statements made by a writer within the confines of the same book. For example, in opposition to George Ladd's statement that "a real 'any-moment' expectation is neither Biblically nor historically sound,"[9] the amillennial writer, Ray Summers, insists that the imminent, any-moment hope is emphatically stressed in the New Testament[10] and seems to take the view that "the Lord may come at any moment, and when he does come, he will raise the dead, exercise final judgment, terminate the present world order, and introduce the eternal order."[11] Several pages later, however, when expounding passages from 2 Thessalonians, he explains that certain predicted events must first take place. He states that "the Lord's return would be preceded by other events—the falling away, the revealing of the man of sin, and the removal of the restraining one."[12] This would appear to contradict his initial emphasis of an any-moment return.

The question arises, then, Does the language of the Bible teach that the Lord may return for His church at any moment, or does it teach that the Lord's return for His church will be preceded by the fulfillment of certain predicted events, such as the revelation of the man of sin, the Great Tribulation, and so on?

Theological Terminology

Webster defines the word *imminent* as follows: "1. Threatening to occur immediately, impending;—said especially of misfortune or peril. 2. Projecting over; overhanging." He lists the word *impending* as a synonym, and under that word he gives the following definition: "Syn. Impending, imminent, threatening to occur very soon. But impending implies signs that keep one in suspense; imminent more strongly suggests the shortness of time before happening." In light of this, one must say that Ladd is more consistent with his eschatology when he uses the word *impending* than Summers is when he uses *imminent,* because both of these men believed that the Lord's return for His church would be preceded by the fulfillment of certain clearly predicted events. Neither of these words is altogether satisfactory, however, because one could conclude that "soonness" rather than "next prophesied event" is the thrust. Rather than "soon," the theological emphasis is the "next prophesied event" on God's prophetic timetable. Thus, we need to turn to the specific words of Scripture.

Biblical Terminology

The words *imminent* and *impending* are not found in Scripture. This is not unusual, however, for neither are some other commonly used theological terms. The Greek word on which the theological term is built is *engus,* which simply means "near" but is most generally translated "at hand" in the Authorized Version. Unfortunately, Scofield attempted to make the word a statement of the doctrine. He defined it: "'At hand' is never a positive affirmation that the person or thing said to be 'at hand' will immediately appear, but only that no known or predicted event must intervene."[13] In this statement Scofield has used a *possible* lexical meaning of a word as its only meaning. In other words, he has not properly differentiated between a word and a term.

In his *Methodical Bible Study,* Robert Traina presents this important distinction:

> A term is a given word as it is used in a given context. It therefore has only one meaning, whereas the same word may have several. For instance, the word 'trunk' may mean the main stem of a tree, the main body of anything, the proboscis of an elephant, or a box or chest. Though in all of these cases the same word is used, 'trunk' is one term when it signifies the main stem of a tree and another when it denotes the proboscis of an elephant.[14]

This exegetical error, which is very common among those who seek to prove their point from word studies alone, is explained by James Barr: "The error that arises when the meaning of a word (understood as the total series of relations in which it is used in the literature) is read into a particular case as its sense and implication there, may be called 'illegitimate totality transfer.'"[15]

One must be careful, therefore, how much one reads into a word. With respect to the word *engus*, when it is used in Matthew 26:45–46, for example, the thing spoken of as being "at hand" took place while the speaker was yet speaking: "'Behold, the hour is at hand, and the Son of Man is being betrayed into the hands of sinners. Rise, let us be going. See, he who betrays Me is at hand.' And while He was still speaking, behold, Judas, one of the twelve, . . . came." When the same word is used in 1 Peter 4:7, however, we see quite a different situation in which "the end of all things" is declared to be at hand. In this case we know that almost two thousand years have already intervened, and there will be many predicted events fulfilled before we witness the end of all things in this world scene. The common usage, however, seems to have the idea of nearness in some sense of the word.

James states: "Therefore, be patient, brethren, until the coming of the Lord . . . for the coming of the Lord is at hand [*engiken*]. . . . Behold, the Judge is standing at the door!" (James 5:7, 9). The perfect tense is brought out by the rendering of the NASB ("the judge is standing right at the door") and the Berkeley Version ("See, the judge has stationed Himself at the doors"). The idea seems to be that He has taken a position nearby and could enter at any moment (cf. Phil. 2:30; Mark 1:15; Luke 10:9, 11). It is only necessary for Him to open the door and make His appearance. It may happen in a few minutes (Matt. 26:45–47) or in a few thousand years (1 Peter 4:7). The latter case definitely included predicted intervening events; thus, the argument for no intervening events cannot be made strictly by word study alone, apart from the specific contexts.

What conclusions can be drawn, then, on the basis of the usage of the word *engus* in the New Testament? First, it does not necessarily mean "soon." Failure to recognize that imminency does not demand that we understand it to mean "soon" has caused much confusion. For example, Louis Berkhof attempted to show the fallacy of the belief in imminency: "To teach that Jesus regarded the second coming as immediately at hand, would be to represent Him as in error, since almost two thousand years have already elapsed since that time."[16] It should be noted, however, that while *engus* does not necessarily mean "soon," neither does it necessarily mean a long way off, as Berkhof seems to imply. His conclusion is faulty because he has made an "illegitimate totality transfer."

Second, the word *impending* is not satisfactory because it may imply that certain signs will precede the looked-for event, and this is not necessary to the word.

Third, the word *proximate* seems to fit in most of the cases that refer to eschatological subjects (i.e., the next following event). We must caution the reader, however, against formulating a doctrine simply on the basis of the meaning of a word; therefore, we would say that the linguistic argument is inconclusive, but it certainly does not militate against the any-moment idea, which understands the return of Christ to be the next predicted event.

THE DOCTRINAL ARGUMENT

When one begins to systematize the varied eschatological usages of the words related to the doctrine of the Lord's return, a problem appears, for there are those places where signs specifically precede the Lord's return and there are other places where signs are just as definitely not involved. Thus, at times it appears to be imminent and at other times it appears to be impending. The distinction may be reconciled by differentiating between the Rapture and the Second Coming.

The Second Coming Is Not Imminent

This assertion simply means that the Second Coming will be preceded by signs that are the specific fulfillment of events predicted in the Scriptures. In this respect, therefore, premillennialists can agree with the statement made by Berkhof, an amillennialist, that "several important events must occur before the return of the Lord, and therefore it cannot be called imminent."[17] Among the things that must occur he lists the calling of the Gentiles, the national conversion of Israel, the Apostasy and Great Tribulation, the coming revelation of the Antichrist, and various predicted signs and wonders.

At this point, however, a very important clarification must be made with respect to the meaning of the phrase "the return of the Lord," often referred to simply as the Second Coming. This latter term is theological, rather than scriptural, phraseology; but it certainly has its justification from such verses as Acts 1:11 and Hebrews 9:28. However, in the Greek New Testament three nouns are used of the Second Coming: *parousia, apocalupsis,* and *epiphaneia.* These words have been worked overtime by some premillennialists (both pretribulational and posttribulational) and amillennialists trying to prove their respective viewpoints.[18] We must remind ourselves again, however, that words apart from their contexts must not be used to establish doctrine. A word out of a context may have several meanings, but in a given context it only has one meaning.

Let us, therefore, look at the meanings of these words. The word *parousia* may mean "coming," "arrival," or "presence." *Apocalupsis* means "unveiling," or "revelation." *Epiphania* means "manifestation" or "appearance." It is important to note that each of these words is used in the New Testament in both a technical and a nontechnical sense. The nontechnical sense does not have any eschatological implications whatsoever (cf. Luke 2:32 for *apocalupsis;* 2 Tim. 1:10 for *epiphaneia;* and 1 Cor. 16:17 for *parousia*). Furthermore, within the eschatological references, there is not a clear-cut distinction (on the basis of the words used) as to whether they refer to the Rapture or to the Second Coming, because all three words are used for both events. Whereas most of the usages of *parousia* refer to the Rapture (cf. 1 Thess. 2:19; 4:15; 5:23), it appears quite evident that such verses as 2 Thessalonians 2:8 refer to the Second Coming. The eschatological usages of *apocalupsis* appear to be rather evenly divided. Romans 8:19; 1 Corinthians 1:7; and 1 Peter 1:7, 13 seem to refer to the Rapture, whereas 2 Thessalonians 1:7; 1 Peter 4:13; and Revelation 1:1 appear to refer to the Second Coming to the earth. Finally, we note that *epiphaneia* is used of the Second Coming in 2 Thessalonians 2:8.

The study of these usages suggests that a distinction between the Rapture (the return of Christ *for* His saints) and the Second Coming (the return of Christ *with* His saints) cannot be made on the basis of the Greek words themselves. As a matter of fact, it is possible that one may conclude that this is sufficient evidence to prove that there is no distinction between these two events; in fact, that they are not two events at all but simply two aspects of the Second Coming. This is the thinking of such men as Louis Berkhof,[19] an amillennialist, and George Ladd,[20] a posttribulational premillennialist. But before one hastens to the conclusion that all of the references are to a single event, which seems so obvious on the surface, one should probe deeper into Scripture.

First, there is no reason to conclude that the Rapture and the Second Coming must be one single event because the word *parousia* is used of both of them. This is a major flaw in the reasoning of Marvin Rosenthal, who asserts that the use of *parousia* demonstrates the fact of the Rapture's inclusion in the Second Coming. Noting that *parousia* can mean "arrival" and "presence" (which is certainly clear in Scripture), he concludes that because it is used of both the Rapture and the Second Advent the two are a single event.[21] With respect to Rosenthal's reasoning, Paul Karleen states,

> The author has committed the linguistic error of *illegitimate totality transfer,* in which meanings of a word in various occurrences and contexts are all poured into one particular occurrence. An example of this would be saying that *horn* means "a projection from an animal's head," "the end of a crescent," "a brass or other wind instrument," "a noise-making device on a vehicle," "one of the alternatives in a dilemma" and "a telephone" all at the same time and in all occurrences.[22]

It is interesting to note in Scripture that the Jews did confuse the first and second comings by failing to see an interval between them. This simply was not a matter of revelation in the Hebrew Scriptures. A vivid example of this is seen in the use of Isaiah 61:1–2 by Christ (Luke 4:16–22). This is precisely why Christ gave the revelation of Matthew 13 to explain the character of the time between the first and second comings. Even after these explanations, the disciples still did not completely understand (see Luke 19:11 and Acts 1:6). This problem of the early disciples may be similar to the contemporary problem of failing to distinguish events that God has distinguished.

In the second place, when the contexts of the Greek words are studied, a number of distinctions between the Rapture and the Second Coming become very apparent. John F. Walvoord has listed a number of these distinctions in his book, *The Rapture Question,*[23] but one of the most obvious distinctions is that which is the theme of this paper. Passages demanding imminency would refer to the Rapture, whereas passages demanding signs would refer to Christ's Second Coming. Failure to recognize this distinction and trying to see the Rapture and the Second Coming as a single event has forced certain writers into the dilemma of having a second coming that is imminent in some passages and not imminent in other passages.[24] Surely the Spirit of God cannot be accused of contradicting Himself.

Oswald Allis, an amillennialist, finds a way out of the predicament when he says, "Whether this coming to earth will follow the coming into the air immediately *or after an interval of time* may be regarded as uncertain" (italics mine).[25] By injecting this interval of time he seems to admit that the events are not synonymous. Recognizing the problems, he continues: "If these events are all practically contemporaneous, or if the intervals between them, whether short or long, are of relatively minor importance, the language used in the New Testament to describe them, the confusing use of such words as coming and appearing, is sufficiently accounted for." Now, if the interval between these events is of relatively minor importance as to its length, why should it pose a problem to these men to see at least a seven-year interval, namely, Daniel's seventieth week, beginning with the covenant between the world-ruler, the Antichrist, and the nation of Israel guaranteeing them peace? Also, if Allis is right, then Ladd is wrong when he states, "The distinction between the Rapture of the Church and the Revelation of Christ is an inference which is nowhere asserted by the Word of God. . . . Any division of Christ's coming into two parts is an unproved inference."[26]

Finally, it should be noted with respect to the Greek words used that it is not necessary to understand them as *categorizing* words but rather as *characterizing* words. It will only lead to confusion to try to make a distinction between the Rapture and the Second Advent on the basis of the words alone; rather, they should be seen in their respective contexts as words that characterize both of the events. Thus, we would agree with Ladd's statement that "the Vocabulary used of the Lord's return lends no support for the idea of two comings of Christ or of two aspects of His coming," but we take exception to his subsequent statement that the vocabulary "substantiates the view that the return of Christ will be a single, indivisible glorious event."[27] The vocabulary is not categorizing (cf. *parousia* used of both comings), but it is characterizing. When one investigates all of the contexts of these words in the New Testament, however, it appears that two specific events are in view, namely, the coming of Christ in the air *for* His saints and the coming of Christ *with* His saints to the earth. In the latter case there will be specific signs such as are outlined in Matthew 24 and 2 Thessalonians 2.

The Rapture Is Imminent

It is essential that one understand the distinction between the Rapture and the Second Advent before it is possible to understand imminence. All of the arguments for a pretribulation Rapture of the church could be injected at this point to sustain this distinction; however, it is not the purpose of this paper to defend the pretribulational viewpoint but simply to show that it is essential to a proper understanding of imminency.

When one investigates the passages of Scripture dealing with the Rapture, there are no signs given that must be fulfilled. At this point a word should be said concerning the inconsistency of those who believe in the imminency of the Rapture and yet insist on preaching on the "signs of the times." Certainly Spirit-controlled believers ought to be able to discern the spiritual climate of the last days as they come upon us, but let us beware of the dangerous, though sometimes fascinating, art of finding specific fulfillments of prophecy in these days. Spectacular attempts at date-setting may bring vast crowds to the services, but they can lead only to confusion. We should not be looking for prophetic signs of the times when we are not in the time of prophetic signs.

The doctrine of imminency has not only been confused by the misinterpretations of some who hold to it, but also by the misunderstandings of those in opposition to it. As a case in point, Ladd reasons erroneously when he analyzes the pretribulational viewpoint:

> According to this system, the Rapture occurs at the beginning of the seventieth week predicted in Daniel 9:27. . . . If this is a correct interpretation of the prophetic future, *the Rapture of the Church is not the next event upon the prophetic calendar;* it is rather the return of Israel to her land. The Rapture of the Church is then preceded by a sign, the 'Sign of the fig tree,' the sign of Israel.[28]

Now, if Ladd's premise is correct, we must accept the conclusion. But does the Rapture occur at the beginning of the seventieth week of Daniel? When reading Daniel 9:27, one finds that the week begins when the Antichrist establishes a covenant of peace with Israel. Even Ladd evidences this understanding of the position: "The last seven years begin when Antichrist—who is not yet recognized as such—makes a covenant with Israel, now restored in Palestine as a nation."[29] Thus, the rapture of the church has no part in the seventieth week. The Rapture takes place prior to the revelation of the Antichrist.

The posttribulationists have suggested other hindrances, however, to the coming of the Lord at any moment: (1) the predicted experience of the church (persecution [John 15:20; 16:1–3], greater works [14:12]); (2) the witness to all nations (Acts 1:4–8); (3) the predictions concerning the persecution of Paul (9:16, 23) and the death of Peter (John 21:18, 19); (4) the prophecy of the destruction of Jerusalem preceding the Second Coming (Luke 21:20–24); and (5) the implication of an extended period of time before the King's return (19:11–26).

Several avenues of refutation of these objections should be noted. These have been handled in brief by Leon J. Wood in *Is The*

Rapture Next?[30] By way of general response, it may be seen upon investigation that most of these objections would apply only to imminency in the first century. If the hindrance no longer existed after the first century, one could say that they are not hindrances to the acceptance of the doctrine of imminency in this day. To be more specific, however, we must ask the question, Were these present-day objections hindrances to belief in imminency on the part of the early church? Under the historical argument (to be discussed later) we will find that the answer is no. But why? Several factors may serve as an answer to this.

In the first place, it seems apparent that there could be no doctrine of imminent Rapture until the church was brought into existence at Pentecost. Christ could not come for His church before it had been founded. Second, there would be very little understanding of the doctrine of imminency until the "waiting" and "hoping" passages of Scripture had been written. By the time of the writing of the New Testament the aforementioned hindrances no longer existed. Third, under the pretribulational interpretation, time is allowed for events to be fulfilled after the translation of the church, such as the specific signs given in the Olivet Discourse. Thus, we maintain that there are no intervening events that militate against the imminent return of the Lord to rapture the church.

THE HISTORICAL ARGUMENT

One question that needs to be asked is, What did the early disciples expect? Did they believe that the Lord may return for His church at any moment? C. K. Barrett comments on John 21:22: "The possibility is contemplated, though (as John hastens to point out) not definitely affirmed, that the beloved disciple might live until the return of Christ. . . . Undoubtedly the earliest Christian belief was that the *'parousia'* would take place before the first generation of Christians had disappeared."[31]

A study of the early church Fathers reveals a strong belief in the imminency of the Lord's return. According to Pentecost, "Eschatology of the early church may not be altogether clear on all points for that subject was not the subject of serious consideration, yet the evidence is clear that they believed in the imminent return of Christ."[32] Likewise, Payne says, "The ante-Nicene fathers . . . were committed to the concept of the imminence of the Lord's return."[33]

But we are not so interested in general evaluations as we are in the specific beliefs and teachings of the apostles who wrote, under inspiration, the infallible Word of God. For example, it is clear that Paul believed that the Lord might come in his own lifetime: "Behold, I tell you a mystery: We shall not all sleep, but we shall all be changed—in a moment, in the twinkling of an eye, at the last trumpet. For the trumpet will sound, and the dead will be raised incorruptible, and we shall be changed" (1 Cor. 15:51–52). Here the apostle is distinguishing between the two groups to be found at the Lord's return, the dead and the living. Significantly, he expects to be among the living who shall be changed. Paul, then, had an any-moment hope. There may be delay, but there would be no necessary prophesied event before the coming of Christ for His church. Lenski comments:

> The simple fact is that Paul did not know when Christ would return. He was in the exact position in which we are. All that he knew, and all that we know, is that Christ may come at any time. So Paul spoke in his time exactly as we speak in ours, namely in two ways: Christ may come immediately; or he may delay a long while.[34]

Commenting on the same passage, Robertson and Plummer confirm that "the first person plural does not necessarily imply that St. Paul felt confident of living till the Second Advent; but it does imply expectation of doing so in company with most of those whom he is addressing. Those who die before the advent are regarded as exceptions."[35]

This expectation is even more strongly expressed in 1 Thessalonians 4:15: "For this we say to you by the word of the Lord, that we who are alive and remain until the coming of the Lord will by no means precede those who are asleep." The Greek construction makes very clear and emphatic here that Paul is not talking simply about those who are alive at the *parousia* but about those who survive until the *parousia*. He thus betrays the expectation that he and his contemporary Christians will remain alive until Christ comes.

As a matter of fact, this expectancy of the Lord's imminent return characterized the apostle Paul to the very last days of his life. H. A. A. Kennedy has listed evidence of this in his work, *The Theology of the Epistles*.[36] Another splendid summary of this theme is given by Hogg and Vine.[37] However, at the same time as he expressed this expectancy, the apostle was able to keep a balanced perspective and realization that he might meet the Lord any time by way of death. "Longing for the Parousia of Christ, which is certain to come, yet not afraid of death, which may possibly come first, is, then, the characteristic attitude of each generation of Christians."[38]

This understanding of Paul's eager anticipation of the imminent return of the Lord seems to throw light on two rather difficult passages. One of these is Philippians 3:11: "if, by any means, I may attain to the resurrection from the dead." Literally translated, the last words read, "the out-resurrection out of the dead." There are a number of possible suggestions for the meaning of the resurrection here: the general resurrection, the first resurrection, the spiritual resurrection, the attainment of rewards at the judgment seat, a partial Rapture, and the rapture of the church. A combination of Rapture and consequent reward at the Judgment Seat of Christ is strongly supported by several factors.

First, the context is strongly in its favor. We have already seen that in the broad context of Pauline epistles a recurring emphasis is placed on the Rapture. An even stronger Pauline emphasis is the consequent reward for believers who have endured faithfully (Rom. 8:17; 14:10–12; 1 Cor. 3:8–15; 9:24–27; 2 Cor. 5:10; Col. 3:23–25; 2 Tim. 2:11–13; 4:7–8). In the narrower context of Philippians, we see the same emphasis. Several verses (1:6, 10; 3:20–21; 4:5) all lay stress on the eschatological day of Christ and the imminent appearing of Christ, whom we are to be eagerly and momentarily expecting. In the immediate context of Philippians 3:11 Paul has discussed justification (v. 9) and sanctification (v. 10). We agree, therefore, with the conclusion of S. Lewis Johnson: "It is certainly fitting that his thought move into the future, because glorification is the natural consummation of the life of grace."[39] This is further confirmed by the future look in verses 20 and 21. Thus, Paul is speaking of something to attain while still living, namely, his translation and consequent reward at the Rapture.

A second factor in favor of the Rapture here is the doubt and uncertainty expressed in the verse. The particles *ei pos* ("if by any means") are used in only three other places (Rom. 1:10; 11:14; Acts 27:12), and in each occurrence doubt is expressed. This uncertainty is further confirmed by the use of the subjunctive mode of the verb *katantao* ("I may attain"). The indicative mode is the mode of certainty, whereas the subjunctive expresses contingency and uncertainty. A. T. Robertson says, "It is the mood of doubt, of hesitation, of proposal, of prohibition, of anticipation, of expectation, of brooding hope, of imperious will."[40]

This evident uncertainty makes it inconceivable, then, that Paul is speaking of the first resurrection, for his previous words in 1 Corinthians 15:1–34 evidence anything but doubt. Nor can it refer to the spiritual resurrection, for Paul states in many other passages that all believers do partake of the resurrection life of Christ (Rom. 6:3–11; Eph. 2:5, 6; Col. 3:1). Again the partial Rapture view is untenable because of its "works" foundation and the fact that the Body of Christ will not be split up at the Rapture. Rather, "we [not some] shall be changed" (1 Cor. 15:52). The only solution that fits the doubt and uncertainty of the passage is that of the Rapture. Simply stated, Paul is uncertain, though full of expectancy, as to whether or not he will remain alive (cf. 1 Thess. 4:15) until the Rapture. Johnson cogently summarizes: "Paul's doubt is not concerning the fact of his resurrection but concerning the circumstances of it."[41]

A final argument in favor of the Rapture view is the unusual word *exanastasis* ("out-resurrection"). This is its only occurrence in the New Testament, although the similar word *anastasis* ("resurrection") occurs forty-one times. Forty of these times it refers to the physical resurrection. Now, the fact that *anastasis* is used in verse 10 and *exanastasis* in verse 11 evidently singles out the latter as having some special significance. Interestingly enough Hippocrates and Polybius use the word in the sense of a rising up into the air.[42] This certainly fits the idea of the Rapture, and it does account for the change of words.

It is our conclusion, then, that the eschatology of the context, the uncertainty with expectancy of the text, and the *hapax legomenon* (i.e., the only occurrence in the New Testament) *exanastasis* all together give strong support to the idea that it was Paul's eager anticipation that the Rapture might take place at any moment and that he might, therefore, remain alive until the Rapture and thus be translated.

A final Pauline passage that takes on new meaning when one understands the apostle's belief in the imminency of Christ's return is 2 Corinthians 5:1–10:

> [1]For we know that if our earthly house, this tent, is destroyed, we have a building from God, a house not made with hands, eternal in the heavens. [2]For in this we groan, earnestly desiring to be clothed with our habitation which is from heaven, [3]if indeed, having been clothed, we shall not be found naked. [4]For we who are in *this* tent groan, being burdened, not because we want to be unclothed, but further clothed, that mortality may be swallowed up by life. [5]Now He who has prepared us for this very thing is God, who also has given us the Spirit as a guarantee. [6]Therefore, we are always confident, knowing that while we are at home in the body we are absent from the Lord. [7]For we walk by faith, not by sight. [8]We are confident, yes, well pleased rather to be absent from the body

and to be present with the Lord. ⁹Therefore we make it our aim, whether present or absent, to be well pleasing to Him. ¹⁰For we must all appear before the judgment seat of Christ, that each one may receive the things done in the body, according to what he has done, whether good or bad.

A close examination here reveals that the chapter division is not well made. The "for" of verse 1 gives the reason for Paul's hope in the previous chapter (4). Paul reminds the believers that they need not be unduly concerned about the dissolution of this body of humiliation because there is a new body awaiting them that is eternal in the heavens. He then goes on to express his strong desire and anticipation that he shall receive this new body before death. Notice the figure in his statement, "earnestly desiring to be clothed with our habitation which is from heaven." The eternal garment is to be drawn over the temporal one, as one garment is drawn over another, and is to take its place. The dead receive their spiritual bodies through resurrection, but the living through transfiguration (1 Cor. 15:38, 51), and it is the living who are described here. This is further substantiated by verse 3, which views death before the Rapture as an unclothed or "naked" state.

Then in verse 4 Paul expresses his strong desire that his earthly body may be clothed upon with his heavenly body before the earthly one is taken away so that there may be no interval of separation between soul and body. The following context points up, however, that Paul is perfectly willing to rest his confidence in the Lord's timing, looking forward to his acceptance by the Lord and the receiving of the Lord's evaluation of his ministry and life at the Bema (Judgment Seat) of Christ. Every indication is that he expects that this may occur at any time, and there certainly is no indicator that he expects the revelation of the Man of Sin or the Great Tribulation to occur before that time.

The uncertainty of the time of the Lord's appearing is also taught by the apostle John by the use of the subjunctive mode in 1 John 2:28. The "when" in this verse is from *ean* ("if") used with the subjunctive mode, which is the mode of uncertainty or probability. Thus, it is better translated, "And now, little born ones, be abiding in him, in order that whenever he may be made manifest, we may have instant freedom of speech and not be made to shrink away from him in shame at his personal presence."[43] The uncertainty does not concern the fact of the Lord's coming (cf. 2:28) but the time of that coming. Robertson sees this as "a clear reference to the second coming of Christ which may be at any time."[44]

Perhaps these words of imminency, "Whenever he may be made manifest," echo the "If I will that he remain till I come" of the Lord's enigmatical saying about the apostle (John 21:22). Referring to these words of Jesus, Findlay concludes,

> The possibility of His coming within the Apostolic era and while St. John remained in the flesh, was bound to be entertained: and the prolongation of the Apostle's life to the verge of human age might well encourage the hope of an early advent—delayed indeed but to be expected before the veteran Apostle's departure, and now therefore, possibly quite imminent.[45]

Again, the apostle James certainly entertained the eager expectancy of the imminent return of the Lord as he sought to encourage those who were suffering persecution:

> Therefore, be patient, brethren, until the coming of the Lord. See how the farmer waits for the precious fruit of the earth, waiting patiently for it until it receives the early and latter rain. You also be patient. Establish your hearts, for the coming of the Lord is at hand. Do not grumble against one another, brethren, lest you be condemned. Behold, the Judge is standing at the door! (James 5:7-9)

There are two words in this context that stress the imminency of the Lord's return. The first is *engiken,* which the Authorized version translates "draweth nigh." This translation makes it seem to be a present tense. In actuality, however, it is a perfect tense that emphasizes not continuing action but completed action. Instead of "draweth nigh" or even "at hand" (NKJV), it is better translated "has drawn near." The process is completed. At any moment we may be caught up into the presence of our Lord.

This teaching is further demonstrated by the figure of speech, "the Judge is standing at the door." Once again, this is a perfect tense of the verb *histemi* and is better translated "has taken a stand." The Lord is at the door. At any moment He may open the door and receive us. One could hardly think of a more fitting illustration of the imminent return of the Lord. There seems to be ample evidence, then, that the earliest followers of our Lord eagerly anticipated the any-moment return of the Lord, and the inspired exhortations they have left for us give us every reason to have the same hope. It is of particular significance that the late J. Barton Payne, a confirmed posttribulationist, could not avoid the conclusion that "belief in the imminency of the return of Jesus was the uniform hope of the early church."[46]

THE PRACTICAL ARGUMENT

A final question, then, needs to be answered: What are the exhortations given to the church, the Body of Christ? While this is one of the strongest arguments for imminency, it is also an area of great confusion both in the defense and in the opposition. Careful thinking is demanded here.

The Church Is Not to Watch for Signs

Some writers have attempted to make a case against imminency on the basis of the exhortations to watch. After examining the passages that include an exhortation to watch, Ladd concludes that "all of these exhortations have reference to the glorious appearing of the Son of Man at the end of the Tribulation."[47] The obvious conclusion, then, is that the exhortations would be pointless unless the church were present on the earth at the end of the Tribulation.

The conclusion comes, however, from a failure to observe that in every case, except one, where "watch" is used in an eschatological passage, *the addressee is Israel.* (The exception is 1 Thessalonians 5:6, and it will be dealt with presently.) Those living in the Tribulation are first exhorted to watch for certain signs and then, after the signs, to watch for the return of Christ to establish His kingdom. The pattern of exhortation seems to be, "When ye shall see these things, then look for the Son of Man" (cf. Matt. 24:15; Mark 13:29; Luke 21:31).

Of the five words translated "watch" in the Authorized version, only two (*gregoreo, agrupeno*) have reference to the Second Coming and neither is ever used in connection with the Rapture. At this point a word of explanation is needed with reference to 1 Thessalonians 5:6. The previous context (4:13–18) dealt with the Rapture. The immediate context (5:1–11) deals with the things preceding the Second Coming. The first is related to the Day of Christ and the second to the Day of the Lord.

Whereas many have had a difficult time explaining the relationship between these two passages, the pretribulationist has an adequate explanation. If the terrible judgment of the Day of the Lord is to begin shortly, or immediately, after the Rapture, then it is possible to explain 5:1–11 logically as pertaining to our conduct in light of the future program. This is a very acceptable motivation. The fact that Christians are to be delivered from the prophesied day of wrath ought to be a compelling motive to live lives characterized by vigilance and sobriety. Peter uses this same motivational principle in 1 Peter 4:7 and 2 Peter 3:10–12.

The immediate occasion of the exhortation of 1 Thessalonians 5:1–11 was undoubtedly a question from the Thessalonians regarding the *time* of the coming of the Day of the Lord (cf. vv. 1–3). They were anxious that the Lord might come soon, while they were yet living, because they thought that only the living would enjoy the full blessedness of Christ's *parousia*. Paul does not give them any further instructions regarding the time, except to remind them of what they already knew—the uncertainty of the time of its arrival. The day is to come suddenly, as the birth pang to the woman with child, and unexpectedly, as the thief in the night, so that none of the inhabitants of the earth in that day shall by any means escape it. In contrast to the time of terrific warfare before the Second Coming (cf. Matt. 24:15–28), there will be an atmosphere of peace and security just before the coming of the Day of the Lord.

The other teaching of this passage is the certainty that the believers will not be here when it comes (1 Thess. 5:4–11). Paul establishes this with an array of reasons, stating it both negatively and positively, so that there should be no doubt left in their minds. In the first place, the Day of the Lord is a day of judgment and darkness, and the believers do not belong to the realm of darkness (v. 4a). In the second place, positively stated, the Day of the Lord shall not "overtake" them (v. 4b). Third, not only are they in the realm of the light, but they are characterized by the nature of the light, by the very nature of Christ Himself (v. 5). Furthermore, in the sovereign purpose of God they have not been appointed to wrath but to full and complete deliverance (v. 9). Finally, the ground of assurance for all this rests in the instrument of their deliverance, the Lord Jesus Christ, who died for them so that, regardless of their degree of spiritual attainment when He comes, they shall live together with Him forever (v. 10).

Because of these marvelous manifestations of God's grace, surely those who have nothing to do with the darkness will exercise continual watchfulness (*gregoreo*, "to be mentally alert") and self-control (vv. 6–8). At the same time they are to be comforting one another with these words, and each one is to be building others up in this temple of the Body of Christ (v. 11). Thus, in 4:13–18, Paul assured them that both the living and the dead will be gone before the Day of the Lord arrives.

The Church Is to Look for the Savior

Passages such as 1 Corinthians 1:7; Titus 2:13; and Philippians 3:20 are applicable at this point. The believer is pictured as eagerly waiting and earnestly expecting the Savior. Watching for signs is entirely foreign to these passages. It never occurs. Not even once. Furthermore, not only is the believer to look for the any-moment return of the Lord, but he is to direct his life in the light of it (cf. Rom. 13:11–14; James 5:7–8; 1 John 3:1–3). If, on the other hand, there are specific prophesied signs, in reality we would not be looking for the Savior at any moment but instead should be watching for the revelation of the man of sin, the Great Tribulation, etc. There would be at least a seven-year preparation period.

Oswald Allis takes issue with this so-called "psychological argument" that assumes, he says, "that men cannot expect and watch for the coming of Christ and be stimulated and safeguarded by the thought of it unless they can believe that it may take place 'at any moment.'" He claims that "intensity of affection disregards time and distance."[48] Whatever else may be said by way of answer, one thing is certain: the Bible does use the imminent return of the Lord as a motivation for holy living (cf. Rom. 13:11–14: 1 John 3:1–3; James 5:7–9). If this is improper, then we would have to bring the writers of Scripture in question.

Furthermore, Allis's argument is contrary to human experience, for hope is realistic in proportion to its imminency; otherwise, why does Paul appeal to the "nearer" argument (Rom. 13:11–12)?

Apparently, then, our Savior receives greater glory as a result of the any-moment expectancy on the part of His children. Facing this problem realistically, if there were not the tendency toward carelessness or unconcern when an event is far removed, there would be little purpose for the exhortations. But, whatever the differences of opinion may be, is it not a very beautiful, practical fact that for almost two thousand years believers from every generation have lived in the constant expectation that the Lord Jesus Christ may come at any moment, and yet His failure to come did not discourage succeeding generations from having the same hope? Instead the intensity of the hope seems to grow as the years pass for they know that His assured coming is closer than before.

CONCLUSION

In conclusion, then, on the basis of the linguistic, doctrinal, historical, and practical arguments, the Scriptures give abundant support for the any-moment return of the Lord to rapture the church. The church is never given any prophesied sign for which it is to watch, but it is to wait expectantly with eager anticipation for the return of Christ at any moment.

NOTES

1. "Window on the World," *Eternity* (January 1961).
2. Oswald T. Allis, *Prophecy and the Church* (Philadelphia: Presby. & Ref., 1945), 3.
3. John F. Walvoord, *The Millennial Kingdom* (Findlay, Ohio: Dunham, 1959), 19–20.
4. Norman B. Harrison, *The End: Re-Thinking the Revelation* (Minneapolis: Harrison, 1941), 218.
5. Oswald J. Smith, *Is The Antichrist At Hand?* (Toronto: Tabernacle, 1926), 19.
6. "Miscalculated Rapture: October 28, 1992," *WEF-Theological News* 23, no. 4 (Oct.-Dec. 1992), 1.
7. Allis, *Prophecy,* 174.
8. Ibid., 167–68.
9. George Eldon Ladd, *The Blessed Hope* (Grand Rapids: Eerdmans, 1956), 154.
10. Ray Summers, *The Life Beyond* (Nashville: Broadman, 1959), 124–29.
11. Ibid., 128.
12. Ibid., 130.
13. C. I. Scofield, *The Scofield Reference Bible* (New York: Oxford Univ., 1967), 998.
14. Robert Traina, *Methodical Bible Study* (New York: Ganis & Harris, 1952), 34.
15. James Barr, *The Semantics of Biblical Language* (Glasgow: Oxford Univ., 1961), 218.
16. Louis Berkhof, *Systematic Theology* (Grand Rapids: Eerdmans, 1953), 697.
17. Ibid., 696.
18. See J. F. Strombeck, *First the Rapture* (Moline, Ill.: Strombeck Foundation, 1950); Ladd, *The Blessed Hope;* Allis, *Prophecy;* Robert H. Gundry, *The Church and the Tribulation* (Grand Rapids: Zondervan, 1973); Marvin Rosenthal, *The Pre-Wrath Rapture of the Church* (Nashville: Nelson, 1990).
19. Berkhof, *Systematic Theology,* 695–96.
20. Ladd, *The Blessed Hope,* 69.
21. Rosenthal, *The Pre-Wrath Rapture,* 215–30.
22. Paul S. Karleen, *The Pre-Wrath Rapture of the Church: Is it Biblical?* (Langhorne, Pa.: B F Press, 1991), 83.
23. John F. Walvoord, *The Rapture Question* (Findlay, Ohio: Dunham, 1957), 198–99.
24. Ray Summers, *Worthy Is the Lamb; An Interpretation of the Revelation* (Nashville: Broadman, 1951), 123–30.
25. Allis, *Prophecy,* 187.
26. Ladd, *The Blessed Hope,* 69.
27. Ibid., 70.
28. Ibid., 153–54.
29. Ibid., 153.
30. Leon J. Wood, *Is the Rapture Next?* (Grand Rapids: Zondervan, 1956), 35–40.
31. C. K. Barrett, *The Gospel According to St. John* (London: S.P.C.K, 1960), 488.
32. J. Dwight Pentecost, *Things to Come* (Grand Rapids: Zondervan, 1958), 201.
33. J. Barton Payne, *The Imminent Appearing of Christ* (Grand Rapids: Eerdmans, 1962), 13.

34. R. C. H. Lenski, *The Interpretation of St. Paul's First and Second Epistle to the Corinthians* (Columbus, Ohio: Wartburg, 1937), 737.

35. Archibald Robertson and Alfred Plummer, *A Critical and Exegetical Commentary on the First Epistle of St. Paul to the Corinthians* (Edinburgh: T. & T. Clark, 1914), 376.

36. H. A. A. Kennedy, *The Theology of the Epistles* (London: Gerald Duckworth, 1919), 108–11, 245–48.

37. C. F. Hogg and W. E. Vine, *The Epistles to the Thessalonians* (Fincastle, Va.: Bible Study Classics, 1914), 138–40.

38. Ibid., 138.

39. S. Lewis Johnson, "The Out-Resurrection from the Dead," *Bibliotheca Sacra* 110 (April 1953), 140.

40. A. T. Robertson, *A Grammar of the Greek New Testament in the Light of Historical Research* (Nashville: Broadman, 1934), 928.

41. Johnson, "The Out-Resurrection from the Dead," 144.

42. Joseph Henry Thayer, *A Greek-English Lexicon of the New Testament* (Cambridge, Mass.: 1889), 221.

43. Kenneth Wuest, *An Expanded Translation of the New Testament* (Grand Rapids: Eerdmans, 1956), III:139.

44. A. T. Robertson, *Word Pictures in the New Testament* (Nashville: Broadman, 1933), VI:219.

45. George G. Findlay, *Fellowship in the Life Eternal* (Grand Rapids: Eerdmans, 1955), 232.

46. Payne, *The Imminent Appearing of Christ,* p. 102. Payne further states, "It must therefore be concluded that the denial of the imminence of the Lord's coming on the part of post-tribulationists who have reacted against dispensationalism is not legitimate. There have been, it is true, extremists throughout the course of church history who have interpreted imminence to mean that the Lord's advent must be soon, or even at some set date; but no such impropriety rests upon imminence when it is understood in its basic definition of 'ready to befall or overtake one,' that is, that Christ's coming could be at any time. There are, indeed, a number of verses that have been, and are, used uncritically to substantiate this doctrine and that do not constitute valid proof. But, at the same time, the preceding section has validated a considerable group of passages that do demonstrate its legitimacy. In fact, no natural reading of Scripture would produce any other conclusion."

47. Ladd, *The Blessed Hope,* 112. See also Gundry, *The Church and the Tribulation,* 29–43.

48. Allis, *Prophecy,* 169.

INDEX OF
SELECTED SCRIPTURES

Moody Press, a ministry of the Moody Bible Institute,
is designed for education, evangelization, and edification.
If we may assist you in knowing more about Christ
and the Christian life, please write us without obligation:
Moody Press, c/o MLM, Chicago, Illinois 60610.